Jeremy Bentham on Police

Jeremy Bentham on Police

*The unknown story and
what it means for criminology*

Edited by

Scott Jacques and Philip Schofield

UCLPRESS

First published in 2021 by
UCL Press
University College London
Gower Street
London WC1E 6BT

Available to download free: www.uclpress.co.uk

ISBN: 978-1-78735-647-4 (Hbk)
ISBN: 978-1-78735-641-2 (Pbk)
ISBN: 978-1-78735-617-7 (PDF)
DOI: https://doi.org/10.14324/111.9781787356177

*To the sagacious and learned
Reverend Doctor John Langborn*

Contents

Notes on contributors

Scott Jacques is Director of Criminology Open and Professor of Criminal Justice and Criminology at Georgia State University. His areas of interest are deterrence, opportunity prevention, offender decision-making, qualitative and mixed methods. His prior books are *Grey Area: Regulating Amsterdam's Coffeeshops* (UCL Press 2019) and, co-authored with Richard Wright, *Code of the Suburb: Inside the World of Young Middle-Class Drug Dealers* (University of Chicago Press 2015). He serves as Director of CrimRxiv and is editor of two journals, the *International Criminal Justice Review* and *The Journal of Qualitative Criminal Justice and Criminology*. You can learn more about him at https://scottjacques.us.

Philip Schofield is Director of the Bentham Project, Faculty of Laws, University College London (UCL), and General Editor of the new authoritative edition of *The Collected Works of Jeremy Bentham*, in which he has edited or co-edited a dozen volumes. He is the author of *Utility and Democracy: The Political Thought of Jeremy Bentham* (Oxford University Press 2006) and *Bentham: A Guide for the Perplexed* (Continuum 2009), as well as numerous articles on Bentham and the history of utilitarianism.

Anthony A. Braga is the Elmer V. H. and Eileen M. Brooks Distinguished Professor in the School of Criminology and Criminal Justice and the Director of the Center on Crime and Community Resilience at Northeastern University. Dr Braga's research involves collaborating with criminal justice, social service and community-based organizations to address illegal access to firearms, reduce gang and group-involved violence, and control crime hotspots. He has collaborated with the Las Vegas Metropolitan Police Department, New York City Police Department and Boston Police Department on the implementation and evaluation of their body-worn camera programmes. Braga is a Fellow of the American Society of Criminology (ASC) and also received the 2014 Joan McCord Award (recognizing his commitment to randomized experiments) from the Academy of Experimental Criminology as well as the ASC Division of Policing's Distinguished Scholar Award (2019) and ASC Division of Experimental Criminology's Outstanding Experimental Field Trial Award (2019).

Ronald Clarke is the Associate Director of the Center for Problem-Oriented Policing, a virtual institute (www.popcenter.org), and he has been Visiting Professor at UCL since 2001. In 2015, he was awarded the Stockholm Prize in Criminology. Before moving to the United States in 1984, he was employed for 15 years in the British government's criminological research department, the Home Office Research and Planning Unit, of which he became the Director in 1982. While at the Home Office, he jointly developed the rational choice perspective on crime with Derek Cornish and led the team that originated situational crime prevention. He is now considered to be the world's leading authority on that approach. Dr Clarke is author or joint author of more than 300 books, monographs and papers, including *Problem-Oriented Policing: Successful Case Studies* (Routledge 2020), *Outsmarting the Terrorists* (Praeger 2006) and *Become a Problem Solving Crime Analyst* (US Department of Justice 2005). His current research focuses on wildlife crimes.

David J. Cox is Reader in Criminal Justice History at the University of Wolverhampton. Specializing in early modern policing and the Victorian convict prison system, he has authored/co-authored numerous books, including *'A Certain Share of Low Cunning': A History of the Bow Street Runners 1792–1839* (Routledge 2012) and *Crime in England, 1688–1815* (Routledge 2014), and has recently co-edited (with J. McDaniel and K. Stonard) *The Development of Transnational Policing: Past, Present and Future* (Routledge 2020).

Stephen Douglas is a doctoral student in the School of Criminology and Criminal Justice at Northeastern University. His research interests include examining the link between crime and place and the evaluation of legal responses to place-based crime problems. Originally from Northern Ireland, Stephen earned his undergraduate degree at the University of Ulster and served as a police officer in Aberdeenshire, Scotland, prior to enrolling in the doctoral programme at Northeastern.

Stephen Engelmann is Associate Professor of Political Science at the University of Illinois at Chicago. He is the author of *Imagining Interest in Political Thought* (Duke 2003) and editor of *Selected Writings: Jeremy Bentham* (Yale 2011). His teaching and research interests are in the history of political thought, utilitarianism, biopolitics and political economy, and he is currently working on a book on economic rationality for Polity.

G. Geltner is a social historian of pre-industrial Europe at Monash University. He has written extensively on different forms of social, environmental and religious deviance, as well as on the history of incarceration and corporal punishment. His projects and publications, many of which are available in open access form, can be viewed at www.guygeltner.net.

Joel F. Harrington is Centennial Professor of History at Vanderbilt University. He has published seven books and many articles on pre-modern Germany, including *Dangerous Mystic: Meister Eckhart's Path to the God Within* (Penguin Press 2018), which was honoured in 2020 with a Literature Award from the American Academy of Arts and Letters, and *The Faithful Executioner: Life and Death, Honor and Shame in the Turbulent Sixteenth Century* (Farrar, Straus & Giroux 2013), which has been translated into 13 languages and was named one of the Best Books of 2013 by *The Telegraph* and *History Today*. He has been awarded fellowships from – among others – the John Simon Guggenheim Foundation, the Fulbright-Hays Program, the National Endowment for the Humanities, the German Academic Exchange Service (DAAD) and the American Philosophical Society.

Jonathan Jacobs is Professor of Philosophy at John Jay College of Criminal Justice and is on the Doctoral Faculty of Philosophy at CUNY Graduate Center. He has written widely on criminal sanction and the relation between the political order, civil society and the moral psychology of punishment. He also writes on Adam Smith and on medieval philosophy. His most recent book is *The Liberal State and Criminal Sanction* (Oxford University Press 2020).

Paul Knepper is Professor of Justice Studies in the Department of Justice Studies at San José State University and Visiting Professor of Criminology in the School of Criminal Sciences, University of Lausanne.

Formerly, he was Professor of Criminology in the School of Law at the University of Sheffield. He is the author of *Writing the History of Crime* (Bloomsbury 2016) and co-editor of *The Oxford Handbook of the History of Crime and Criminal Justice* (OUP 2016).

Gloria Laycock has a BSc and PhD in psychology from UCL. She established and headed the Police Research Group in the UK Home Office and was founding Director of the UCL Jill Dando Institute. She has carried out research and development in prisons, policing and crime prevention and acted as a consultant and trainer around the world. She is Professor of Crime Science at UCL and was awarded an OBE in 2008 for services to crime policy.

Gary T. Marx is Professor Emeritus at MIT. As well as having articles in all the usual and some unusual places, he is the author of *Protest and Prejudice* (Harper and Row 1967); *Undercover: Police Surveillance in America* (University of California Press 1988); *Undercover: Police Surveillance in Comparative Perspective* (with C. Fijnaut; Kluwer Academic Publishers 1995) and, most recently, *Windows into the Soul: Surveillance and Society in an Age of High Technology* (University of Chicago Press 2016). Additional information can be found at www. garymarx.net.

Daniel S. Nagin is Teresa and H. John Heinz III University Professor of Public Policy and Statistics at the Heinz College, Carnegie Mellon University. He is an elected Fellow of the American Society of Criminology, the American Association for the Advancement of Science and the American Academy of Political and Social Science, and the recipient of the American Society of Criminology's Edwin H. Sutherland Award in 2006, the Stockholm Prize in Criminology in 2014, Carnegie Mellon University's Alumni Distinguished Achievement Award in 2016 and the National Academy of Science Award for Scientific Reviewing in 2017.

Graeme R. Newman is Distinguished Professor Emeritus at the University at Albany, New York. He has written many books and major articles on the history, philosophy and practices of punishment, international criminal justice, cybercrime, terrorism, migration and crime, community policing and crime prevention. He has taught hundreds of doctoral students and co-written or edited books and articles with many of his former students. He currently writes novels under the pen name of Colin Heston.

Pat O'Malley is Distinguished Honorary Professor of Sociology at the Australian National University and Adjunct Research Professor in Sociology at Carleton University in Canada. Previously he was Professorial Research Fellow in Law at the University of Sydney. Recent relevant publications include '"Smart" Crime Prevention? Digitization and Racialized Crime Control in a Smart City', *Theoretical Criminology* (2021), and (with G. J. D. Smith) 'Driving Politics: Data-Driven Crime Prevention and Resistance', *British Journal of Criminology* (2017).

Eric L. Piza is an Associate Professor at John Jay College of Criminal Justice, City University of New York. Prior to entering academia, he was the GIS Specialist of the Newark, NJ Police Department, responsible for the agency's crime analysis and programme evaluation activities. Dr Piza's research focuses on the spatial analysis of crime, crime control technology and the integration of academic research and police practice. He received his PhD from Rutgers University.

Michael Quinn completed his PhD on equality in contemporary theories of justice at LSE in 1988. He has edited four volumes in *The Collected Works of Jeremy Bentham* and co-edited a fifth, with a sixth in press and two more available in preliminary pre-publication versions from UCL Discovery, the university's digital repository. Between 2004 and 2019 he was Senior Research Fellow at the Bentham Project, UCL, and is currently a visiting Research Fellow at Philipps University of Marburg/Justus Liebig University Giessen.

Kim Rossmo holds the University Chair in Criminology and is the Director of the Center for Geospatial Intelligence and Investigation in the School of Criminal Justice and Criminology at Texas State University. He has published in the areas of environmental criminology, the geography of crime and criminal investigations. Dr Rossmo was formerly the Director of Research for the Police Foundation, a management consultant for the ATF, and a Detective Inspector with the Vancouver Police Department.

Lucia Summers is an Associate Professor and the Associate Director of the Center for Geospatial Intelligence and Investigation in the School of Criminal Justice and Criminology at Texas State University. Her research focuses on offender decision-making, situational crime prevention and the spatio-temporal patterns of crime. Before joining Texas State University, Dr Summers spent nine years working as a researcher at the UCL Jill Dando Institute of Crime Science in London, where she also completed her PhD.

Dean Wilson is Professor of Criminology and Head of the Department of Sociology in the School of Law, Politics and Sociology at the University of Sussex. He is a criminologist and historian with research interests in the history of policing, technology and surveillance. Professor Wilson is also Treasurer of the international Surveillance Studies Network and co-author (with Jude McCulloch) of *Pre-crime: Pre-emption, Precaution and the Future* (Routledge 2015).

Acknowledgements

We thank the authors for their contributions and patience; UCL Press for supporting the work coming out of the Bentham Project; and SAGE for granting us permission to include the following works, first published in *International Criminal Justice Review* in 2021: Ronald V. Clarke's 'Regulating Crime and the International Crime Drop'; Daniel S. Nagin's 'Utilitarianism and Policing in the United States'; Michael Quinn's 'Bentham on Preventive Police: The *Calendar of Delinquency* in Evaluation of Policy, and the *Police Gazette* in Manipulation of Opinion'; Kim Rossmo and Lucia Summer's 'Bentham and the Philosophical Nature of Preventive Policing'. All rights to these specific articles remain with the copyright holder. The editors are especially grateful to Dr Chris Riley for compiling the index.

Part I
Chapters

1

The Story of *Jeremy Bentham on Police*: Bridging the Bentham Project to Criminology

Scott Jacques

This book is born from correspondence that began in 2017. By then, I was a huge fan of Jeremy Bentham (1748–1832).[1] He is best known for the hedonistic calculus and for the surveillance architecture known as the panopticon. He advocated radical positions that have become the norm, such as the view that admittance to government office should be based on merit, not social class, race or sex. His famous sayings include the maxim that the goal of government should be the greatest happiness for the greatest number, and that all inequality is a source of evil. Among the many terms he coined are 'international', 'maximize', 'minimize' and 'sexual desire'.

Perhaps like you, I first read about Bentham in articles and books that describe him as a co-parent of 'classical criminology', which emphasizes rational choice and, by extension, deterrence.[2] As a PhD student, I began citing his work. I got to know him better by purchasing *An Introduction to the Principles of Morals and Legislation*. It is a difficult read, but I was drawn to Bentham's theoretical approach: highly conceptual, systematized, general and comprehensive.

In my relationship with Bentham, a watershed moment was meeting him in 2007. I was in London, attending the British Society of Criminology Conference. My adviser, Richard Wright, wanted us to stop by University College London (UCL) to see the 'Auto-Icon'.[3] Basically, it is Bentham's decapitated skeleton stuffed inside a full set of clothes with accessories (shoes, hat and cane), sat on a chair in a wooden cabinet that has a glass wall so he can be seen. It sounded cool, in a macabre kind of way.

The Auto-Icon has since moved to a new spot and into an all-glass cabinet, but it was then in UCL's landmark domed building. We passed under UCL's gate on Gower Street, into the courtyard, up a few stairs on the building's right side, and through the door. Before us, maybe 20 metres away, sat Bentham. We got a close look, read the surrounding placards, grabbed some leaflets,[4] laughed, talked, took pictures, purchased some postcards featuring his wax head and left. Coming face to face with the Auto-Icon transformed it from an oddity to a moving experience. I remember thinking, 'Wow, that's Jeremy Bentham'. It piqued my interest. I slowly but surely became more and more interested in Bentham; not only in his ideas and writings, but also his life and personality.[5]

The Bentham Project

Back to 2017. That spring, I began corresponding with Philip Schofield. He is Director of the Bentham Project and General Editor of *The Collected Works of Jeremy Bentham*. In the next chapter, Schofield describes and explains the Bentham Project and that edition, including their past, present and future. Therefore, I will not say too much about those things in this chapter.

Yet I do want to go on the record about something that I hope will spur you to investigate further: scientific methods give us findings, but it is theorists who give us ideas. No theorist is more important to criminology than Bentham. And like the man himself, the Bentham Project is vastly underappreciated by criminologists; too few of us know what Bentham wrote, what the project does, and how both can be used to improve our understanding of lawmaking, lawbreaking, and how we react to those.[6] Whether you already see, or come to see, Bentham as a protagonist or antagonist, he deserves a leading role in criminology's ever-unfolding story. And the only way to properly engage with Bentham is to know and use the Bentham Project.

I would like to make another point: scholarship produces findings and ideas, but it is scholarly communication that spreads them. The potential for scholarly insights to have an impact is a function of how well they are disseminated. This sentiment is seen in how authors try to increase their readership by making their work open access (or by feeding into 'prestige' publishing). What the Bentham Project does is increase Bentham's readership by transforming words in archive boxes into published volumes.

This book's purpose is to amplify the voice and impact of the Bentham Project and thus Bentham, especially with respect to his writings on the police. The present chapter describes and explains how the book achieves this. Also, reflecting the importance of scholarly communication, this chapter describes and explains what was involved in making the book. Given the book's purpose, what decision points did I face, what choices did I make, and why?

Returning to the autumn of 2017, Schofield and I were exploring ways to fund a project on the panopticon. To prepare, I was perusing Transcribe Bentham. It is the Bentham Project's crowdsourcing technology for transcribing Bentham's manuscripts – literally, his handwriting on paper – into digital text suitable for analysis and organizing into volumes of the Project edition.[7] (In the next chapter, Schofield also details Transcribe Bentham.)

On Transcribe Bentham (n.d.(a)) is a webpage to 'Select a Manuscript'. Therein is a section on 'Subject matter', explaining that 'Bentham wrote on an enormous range of subjects, ranging from religion to colonization, from sexual morality to political economy. Here are a list of some of the topics contained in the manuscripts uploaded to the Transcription Desk' (Transcribe Bentham n.d.(b)). I scrolled through the list of subjects, seeing the usual suspects of criminological interest: capital punishment, convict transportation, crime and punishment, law, moral philosophy, New South Wales, panopticon, penal code and torture. I also saw something that caught my surprise. I recall asking myself, 'Bentham wrote about "preventive police"?'

Bentham on police

I knew what Bentham had to say about crime and criminal justice, or so I thought. He wrote about how to make law, prosecute offences and punish offenders, all of which reflected his theory of why people commit crimes and his emphasis on prevention. In relation to our contemporary criminal justice process, however, there was a missing link: police. They connect the law to prosecution and, in turn, to punishment. I knew the notion of 'police' was a relatively new concept; they arrived much later in England than in France, and their role was responding to crime, not preventing it (Williams 2014). I figured that Bentham did not write about the police because they were not of particular importance in his era, or he was too busy writing about other things.

From browsing the Transcribe Bentham website, I found out that I was wrong. Bentham had, in fact, written about the police; and, as we could expect of him, he emphasized their role in preventing crime. But that is all I knew. I emailed Schofield for further details. He informed me that 'Michael Quinn [Senior Research Fellow at UCL] has virtually completed the editing of Bentham's police writings – they are going to form Volume III of the Economic Writings'.[8] I replied, 'I'm glad the police writings came up. Otherwise, I wouldn't realize to keep an eye out for Volume III of the Economic Writings. Are you ok with me asking Michael about the possibility of writing a synopsis or analysis of the police writings for my journal, *International Criminal Justice Review* [*ICJR*]?'[9]

Quinn on Bentham on police

ICJR is a journal on which I serve as Editor-in-Chief. In that capacity, I am on the lookout for unpublished work of global importance. Bentham's ideas on the police struck me as exactly that. I figured criminologists would profit from Quinn writing a paper about those ideas: their content, historical context, motivation and effect. So, with Schofield's blessing, I emailed Quinn. I requested he 'consider writing a synopsis or analysis of the police writings for my journal. All criminologists learn about him [Bentham], but I'm guessing very few know he wrote about the police. Thus, when I heard of your progress, it struck me that criminologists could benefit, and would appreciate, you telling us about those writings in an article.'[10]

Quinn responded favourably, agreeing in principle to write the paper. From the very start of our correspondence, I learned about Bentham on police:

> The police writings of 1798–9 are unusual in the Bentham corpus in that he was, in a sense, writing to order. Having met Patrick Colquhoun when the latter wrote to offer his support in connection with the panopticon prison scheme, and having received Colquhoun's endorsement of the scheme in his evidence to the Finance Committee of the House of Commons in 1798, he offered his assistance in drafting two Bills, the first dealing with the policing of the river Thames, and the second containing a proposal to licence many occupations liable to be practised by receivers of stolen goods, under the supervision of a central board of police. It would be entirely fair to say that the central provisions

of both Bills were the product of Colquhoun rather than Bentham, and that if you are familiar with Colquhoun's police writings you won't find many surprises in the text. However, it is also true that in several areas, most notably in relation to two proposed publications of the Board, the 'Police Gazette' and the 'Calendar of Delinquency', Bentham moves well beyond Colquhoun, contrary to the impression given by commentators such as Neocleous.

It turned out that Quinn had already written something similar to what I had requested. He attached it to his reply email, described its background and content, explained how it meshed with what I had suggested and, as academics tend to do, expressed concerns about the timeline:

> Having no background in criminology, I've been hesitant to offer any contributions to journals in that discipline, so your invitation is most welcome. I think the idea of an article along the lines you suggest sounds very attractive, and in principle I'd be very happy (and very flattered) to offer such an article. Given the unremitting time pressure we operate under, what would be helpful for me would be an idea of time-scales which might work for you. Last year, at the International Society of Utilitarian Studies, I presented the paper which I have attached, which begins with Bentham's use of the expression 'police', and then focuses more closely on the Gazette and Calendar, before ending with some reflections on the tensions (or contradictions) between the Bentham as the self-conscious manipulator of public opinion which emerges in the police writings, and the radical democrat Bentham who emerged a decade later. The paper meets some of the objects outlined in your message, but its focus, especially in its latter sections, doesn't match the intended brief. Could I ask you to cast an eye over it, and let me know how far it stands from the target?[11]

I looked at Quinn's paper and liked what I saw. With criminologists in mind, I requested 'adding some citations to connect it with contemporary criminology (reviewers and I would help here), and a little more description of the Bentham Project'.[12] I asked Quinn to confirm that it had not been previously published, and, if not, confirmed my interest in seeing it submitted to *ICJR* for consideration for publication. He responded in kind: 'I'll have a go at broadening the first section of the paper and cutting down the final two sections a little, with a view to sending you a revised version by the end of March. Let me know if that sounds acceptable, and thanks again for the encouragement.'[13] I found his proposal more than acceptable, so we were on our way.

Quinn's submission arrived shortly after spring's arrival in 2018. I sent it out for blind review, promising Quinn that I would be in touch. By the end of April, I had my two reviews in hand. Based on these and my read of the paper, I conditionally accepted it for publication in *ICJR*. Before going into print, I wanted him to address issues that the reviewers and I thought would make the paper better. I also asked Quinn to seek out and address feedback from Schofield and Tim Causer (another member of the Bentham Project), if he had not already done so. *ICJR* published that paper as 'OnlineFirst' in early 2019 and then in 2021 as part of a special issue devoted to it (Quinn, 2021). More or less the same paper is published in this volume, following Schofield's chapter. The most importance difference between the version in *ICJR* and this book is that the latter is open access (i.e. free). I explain why and how that came to be after the next section.

Tying into the next section, you should note that Quinn's chapter differs in tone from other parts of the book. This is to be expected, for a couple of reasons. As explained below, I gave commentators a lot of leeway to write as they please. This nudged them, apparently, towards writing in an informal yet engaging tone. Quinn's chapter is more 'academic', which it should be. It is a detailed, thorough, lengthy engagement with, and portrayal of, Bentham on police. It takes time and effort to read and understand Quinn, as it does Bentham. It is appropriate that of all the book's parts, the tone of Quinn's writing is closest to that of Bentham.

Criminologists on Bentham on police

My thinking was that by publishing Quinn's paper, Bentham's ideas on the police would be more likely to impact criminology. By 'impact', I do not simply mean cited and downloaded. Rather, I mean change criminologists' approach to research, education and practice. That impact hinges on getting Quinn's paper and, in turn, Bentham's ideas into criminologists' hands (or on their screens), thinking about their applicability and putting them to use.

How could I accomplish those goals? The best way, I decided, was to invite top criminologists to write a comment for publication alongside Quinn's paper. As an editor, asking people for their participation is risky; it does not always have utility. By that, I mean the benefits may not outweigh the costs in terms of time, effort and social capital. People inevitably decline your offer, if they bother to reply. Others agree, but never follow through, or only after missing deadlines. On top of managing other people, you have to contend with your own shortcomings, delays, broken promises, and the associated stress and embarrassment. For those very reasons, I promised myself I would never edit a volume like this one, but here we are. Why?

Bentham's newly edited writings on the police are well worth criminologists' time, attention and thought. Quinn's paper is a stepping stone to Bentham's *Writings on Political Economy, Volume III: Preventive Police* (Bentham 2018). To make the leap shorter still, I asked prominent criminologists to write something about Bentham's ideas on policing. The solicitation email read like this, or close to it:

> I would be grateful, as would readers, to see your perspective included in *Bentham on Police*. Whereas Quinn's paper describes Bentham's ideas on police, the comments will show how those ideas connect to criminology and crime/control in the real world, past and present. By 'comment', to be clear, I'm imagining short papers (e.g. about 1,000 words, though more is welcome) in which authors give their impression about how Bentham's ideas on policing are similar to or different from current theories, concepts, findings, moral dilemmas, data sources or practical issues, for example. You'd be free to write about whatever interests you the most, so long as Quinn's paper is used as a springboard, at least a little. If you write a comment, I hope it'll reflect your personal interests, perspectives and so on. Hopefully, the writing will be more fun than work.[14]

We, as a field, are fortunate that so many esteemed scholars agreed to write a comment. It is an eclectic crowd of great prominence, present and future. The list of names speaks for itself. So, too, do the titles of their contributions. In a spot in an introductory chapter like this, or at its end, it may be expected that I will describe each comment. Truth is, I always skip that section in a book (monograph or edited volume), and so it would be hypocritical for me to write such words. What I do want to make clear is that the comments have no topical organization. They are listed alphabetically by the (first) author's last name. You are encouraged to read them in any order, for any reason, before or after those of Schofield and Quinn. Again, the goal is to get criminologists thinking (more) about Bentham and thereby shape our approach to research, education and practice.

Freeing Bentham on police

ICJR's biggest problem is that a paywall blocks its content. Legally, the only way to directly access the 'versions of record'[15] is to purchase articles individually,[16] have subscription access via your institution, or be a member in the ACJS[17] International Section. Paywalled access is the norm for criminology journals (see Criminology Open 2020). There are several reasons why knowledge is locked up that way, and I needn't lengthen this chapter by covering them (but see Suber 2012; Willinsky 2006). What is important to know is that paywalls reduce the impact of publications (see Hitchcock 2013), in addition to causing other problems. The opposite is achieved by making publications open access: 'digital, online, free of charge, and free of most copyright and licensing restrictions' (Suber 2012, 4).

I started to worry about the implications of putting a price on Quinn's paper and the comments. It was in opposition to my goal: to help Bentham's ideas on the police make an impact on criminology. I decided that Quinn's paper and the comments had to be open access. To make that happen, first I reached out to *ICJR*'s publisher, Sage. I should say that among publishers in its class, Sage is the friendliest to open access. I thought it plausible, therefore, that it would grant my request to make an exception for those works by making them open access. Unfortunately, Sage declined, citing the concern that subscribing institutions do not like paying for material that is made free to everyone.

UCL Press

With that news, I had a new publisher in mind: UCL Press, the UK's first fully open access press (UCL Press n.d.(a)). It is the perfect place to publish thoughts on Bentham. He is the spiritual father of the university (Bentham Project n.d.(f)); the Bentham Project is part of UCL; and, in 2020, UCL Press and the Bentham Project entered into a transformative agreement to publish future volumes of the project edition. Moreover, I had a working relationship with this press, which was in the midst of publishing my second book (Jacques 2019).

At UCL Press, my main point of contact is Chris Penfold, a commissioning editor. In late 2018, I emailed him with a pitch for the volume.

I described its origin, where things stood with *ICJR* and Sage, and what contents (e.g. Quinn's paper) were in hand or promised, before proclaiming the volume 'will be part of the canon for policing students and scholars. Anyone interested in crime and control should be interested [in the volume], as it touches on history, statistics, surveillance, discrimination and much more.'[18]

At that point, I had not brought the idea of moving to the authors. I figured it was best not to bother them if Penfold proved to be un-interested. I explained to him: 'If you're in favour of a formal proposal and believe the ultimate decision will be "publish", I'd run the idea by the authors to get their approval. Then I'd submit a proposal.' Penfold responded positively to the pitch and requested a full proposal, but he also presented two problems. The first was copyright, which I over-optimistically replied to him as 'definitely not a problem' (more about this in the next subsection). The second problem was funding. For UCL Press to waive its BPC (book-processing charge), I needed to recruit a co-editor based at UCL (see UCL Press n.d.(b)). I asked Schofield to come on board, given his leadership of the Bentham Project, his expansive editorial experience and expertise, and the fact that I had corresponded with him frequently. Again, thankfully, he agreed, solving the funding problem.

With Schofield onboard, a week later we submitted a formal proposal to UCL Press. Penfold shot us back some requested changes, which took time to address. Mostly, we had to grow the list of commentators, and get abstracts for each comment. Almost to the day two months later, we returned a revised proposal for consideration by the press. Here is how we summarized the book, followed by its main aims and scope:

> Bentham's ideas on punishment are famous. But secret is his adventure into policing. *Jeremy Bentham on Police*[19] investigates this untold story and what it means for criminology. The story, in short, is Bentham helped Patrick Colquhoun draft Bills to regularize the new Thames Police Office and establish a Central Board of Police. Though Colquhoun is the 'author of the system', Bentham shaped it with his utilitarian philosophy. His ideas shed light on the twin role of licensing in providing the finance required for police expansion, and generating information for use in deterring, detecting and apprehending criminals. (The full story is told in Quinn's chapter.)
>
> ...

Every criminology student is taught about Bentham. Every academic has to contend with him, as an advocate or opponent.[20] This discourse concerns his ideas about punishment, namely with respect to legislation and the panopticon. Yet, students and academics are ignorant of Bentham's ideas on police. Hitherto, they have been practically unknowable. Now, thanks to UCL's Bentham Project, these ideas are public. With contributions from the world's foremost Benthamists and criminologists, this volume tells the untold story of Bentham's adventure into police; the process that went into publishing his police writings; and their relevance to the past, present and future of criminology.

Copyright conflict

Before and after the resubmission, I worked to resolve the copyright problem. Once I had veered toward open access, my intention was to publish the contents only with UCL Press, not also in *ICJR*. No one had signed a contract with Sage, so their works were still legally theirs to publish elsewhere. I emailed the authors who had agreed to publish something in *ICJR* (more authors joined later), explaining my intention and asking for their blessing to change course. Here is part of my email:

> Instead of having the contents appear as a paywall-protected special issue in *ICJR*, they could form an [open access] OA edited volume. A plus of an edited volume is the contents stay better connected as a single object (e-book or bound copy), compared to different links on a webpage and across a website. The perfect publisher is UCL Press; https://www.ucl.ac.uk/ucl-press. It is widely regarded as the premier OA university press. It is not-for-profit. Aesthetically, its books look as good, or better, than books produced by other presses. From personal experience, I know its staff are excellent in every way. Icing on the cake is Bentham's strong connection to UCL … [T]he proposed change is better in every way. Your comment will be more accessible. It will be better publicized (Sage won't publicize it at all). It will be part of a single object (see above). And it will help grow an outstanding university press. Note that I would not profit from the change. Any proceeds go back to UCL Press so they can grow. A final note is that if we go this route, my co-editor will be Philip (mentioned above). So, are you ok with me formally pitching the contents to UCL Press? Hesitant? Adamant no? It is perfectly all right if you

are not in favour of my proposal. I realize, and apologize, that I am suggesting a different outlet. I only do so because I think the benefits outweigh the costs, not only for contributors but also potential readers.

Almost all contributors agreed to the change, and seemingly quite liked it. A couple of authors, though, expressed the understandable viewpoint that it is more rewarding to have one's work published in a journal than an edited volume. This is true in some places, as you may know.[21] It would be unfair to those authors to promise them one thing (publication in a journal) and then go another route (publication in a book) without their consent.

So, I had to publish their papers in *ICJR*. I could have given up on the UCL Press route, but that was a non-starter to me; such was my conviction that the ideas had to be open access. I paved a middle road. In *ICJR*, I would publish Quinn's chapter along with some comments; in the UCL Press volume, I would republish those works along with new chapters (by Schofield and me) and many more comments. The question, then, was how to do so without violating copyright? The easiest way was the most expensive: Purchase, from Sage, the right to republish the works originally published in *ICJR*. The cost was $500 per paper, which I would owe out of my own pocket. It was possible for me to pay that amount, but obviously far from ideal.

A better option, and the one that ultimately proved successful, was to spend some of my social capital to obtain gratis permission from Sage. I emailed my former contact at Sage, Sarah Shinkle, on the last day of January 2019. She ushered along my 'ask' to the Rights Coordinator at Sage. After a few months and emails, I happily received permission to reuse the Quinn article and three comments: those by Ronald V. Clarke, Daniel S. Nagin, and Kim Rossmo with Lucia Summers. Everything else in this volume is published for the first time.

From the past to the future

In early May 2019, Penfold sent us two reviews of our proposal. We addressed the referees' concerns in a revised proposal. Penfold discussed them with the UCL Press Executive Board in June 2019, and the decision was made to offer a contract. It took longer than expected to get this book into its final form. It always does, in my experience. Certainly, a global pandemic was counterproductive. Now, to be seen is how you and others use the book; whether it will shape criminology – research, teaching and practice, be it specific to the police or other aspects of crime and control.

Moving forward, we ask you to be careful not to overstate Bentham's contribution. Useful information on Bentham's predecessors and the history of the police is found in the comments by Cox, Geltner and Harrington. This book is less about the history of the police than it is about Bentham's ideas on the police and Benthamite themes in criminology. That is especially apparent in the comments. Recall that in soliciting them, I told prospective authors: 'You'd be free to write about whatever interests you the most … If you write a comment, I hope it'll reflect your personal interests, perspectives and so on.'

By design, I wanted the comments to reflect how criminologists *actually* use Bentham.[22] The norm is to treat Bentham as a mascot or, more flatteringly, as a totem: 'The species that designates the clan collectively is called its *totem*' (Durkheim 2001, 88). Bentham is the 'species' for the 'clan' of criminologists who focus on the rationality of and opportunity for crime and control. He is used as such by scholars of legislated and administered punishment, including their effect on (potential) offenders.

To date, Bentham is not a totem of police scholars. That should change with this volume. At a minimum, when criminologists write and talk about preventive police, they should tip their cap to Bentham and the project in his name. Better yet will be to read, study and put his words to use, enabling the history of ideas on the police to have their proper place in the future.

This volume makes that 'call to action' easier to meet. Useful background information is found in the chapters by Schofield and Quinn, which are followed, eventually, by comments that provide fresh insights into how Bentham's ideas on the police relate to criminology and crime/control. Between the chapters and comments is arguably the book's most important part, not mentioned until now: extracts from Bentham's *Writings on Political Economy, Volume III: Preventive Police*. It will be published in its entirety at a later date, also with UCL Press. As a whole, however, the volume is intimidating. To ease the pain, the extracts zoom in on the parts most important to criminology, while illustrating its main themes. It serves as an introduction to Bentham's ideas on the police, in his own words.

Notes

1   The best place to start learning about Bentham is the Bentham Project (n.d.(a)) website: https://www.ucl.ac.uk/bentham-project/.
2   The other co-parent is Cesare Beccaria.
3   For more information on the Auto-Icon, see Bentham Project (n.d.(b)).
4   You can view the leaflets at Bentham Project (n.d.(c)).
5   For more information on his life and personality, see Bentham Project (n.d.(d)).
6   This bit paraphrases Sutherland's (1942) definition of criminology.
7   For more information, see Transcribe Bentham (n.d.(a)) and Bentham Project (n.d.(e)).
8   Taken from Philip Schofield's personal correspondence with Scott Jacques (13 November 2017).
9   Taken from Scott Jacques's personal correspondence with Philip Schofield (15 November 2017).
10 Taken from Scott Jacques's personal correspondence with Michael Quinn (15 November 2017.
11 Taken from Michael Quinn's personal correspondence with Scott Jacques (19 November 2017).
12 Taken from Scott Jacques's personal correspondence with Michael Quinn (19 November 2017).
13 Taken from Michael Quinn's personal correspondence with Scott Jacques (26 November 2017).
14 The wording in my email changed from person to person, either based on how well I knew them or from seeing how I could improve the solicitation.
15 It is legal and free to access postprints of *ICJR*'s articles.
16 On 2 July 2020, the cost was $37.50.
17 ACJS stands for the Academy of Criminal Justice Sciences.
18 Taken from Scott Jacques's personal correspondence with Chris Penfold (20 November 2018).
19 Originally, the title had 'policing', not 'police', but we changed this to address Referee 2's concerns, described in the last section. In this quote, I changed the title to its final form to avoid confusing readers. Also, in the following quote, the last use of 'police' was originally 'policing'.
20 In hindsight, this should read 'should have to contend with him'. The original statement is an overstatement, though, in a perfect world (to me), it would not be such.
21 A different issue is whether it should be more rewarding to publish in a journal than an edited volume. For a counterargument to the norm of evaluating works based on their place of publication, see the San Francisco Declaration on Research Assessment (n.d.).
22 I would have loved to see each commentator dig deep into Bentham's ideas on the police. Yet it is very difficult to get people to do what you want, and even harder to get academics to do so. Requiring a particular level of engagement from commentators would be beneficial, but I deemed it to be outweighed by the risk: fewer people would have agreed to write a comment; of those who agreed, fewer would have wound up submitting something; and of those who did, few would have actually followed the instructions. Those are serious risks for an editor, but not the principle reason for giving commentators a large amount of leeway in what to write.

References

Bentham, Jeremy. 2018. *Writings on Political Economy, Volume III: Preventive Police*, edited by Michael Quinn. Pre-publication version. Online. http://discovery.ucl.ac.uk/10055084/ (accessed 23 April 2021).
Bentham Project. n.d.(a). 'Home'. Online. https://www.ucl.ac.uk/bentham-project/ (accessed 11 November 2020).

Bentham Project. n.d.(b). 'Auto-Icon'. Online. https://web.archive.org/web/20201020144230/https://www.ucl.ac.uk/bentham-project/who-was-jeremy-bentham/auto-icon (accessed 20 October 2020).

Bentham Project. n.d.(c). 'Leaflets on Bentham's Life and Work'. Online. https://web.archive.org/web/20201020144621/https://www.ucl.ac.uk/bentham-project/publications/leaflets-benthams-life-and-work (accessed 20 October 2020).

Bentham Project. n.d.(d). 'Who Was Jeremy Bentham?'. Online. https://web.archive.org/web/20200902010330/https://www.ucl.ac.uk/bentham-project/who-was-jeremy-bentham (accessed 20 October 2020).

Bentham Project. n.d.(e). 'Transcribe Bentham'. Online. https://web.archive.org/web/20200805085129/https://www.ucl.ac.uk/bentham-project/transcribe-bentham (accessed 20 October 2020).

Bentham Project. n.d.(f). 'Bentham and UCL'. Online. https://web.archive.org/web/20201020165505/https://www.ucl.ac.uk/bentham-project/who-was-jeremy-bentham/bentham-and-ucl (accessed 20 October 2020).

Criminology Open. 2020. 'List of criminology journals'. Online. https://doi.org/10.21428/b7013076.5dcdaeb1 (accessed 28 April 2021).

Durkheim, Emile. 2001. *The Elementary Forms of Religious Life*. New York: Oxford University Press.

Hitchcock, Steve. 2013. 'The Effect of Open Access and Downloads ("Hits") on Citation Impact: A Bibliography of Studies'. *The Open Citation Project*. Online. https://web.archive.org/web/20210324135106/http://opcit.eprints.org/oacitation-biblio.html (accessed 14 May 2021).

Jacques, Scott. 2019. *Grey Area: Regulating Amsterdam's Coffeeshops*. London: UCL Press.

Quinn, M. (2021). 'Bentham on Preventive Police: *The Calendar of Delinquency* in Evaluation of Policy and the Police Gazette in Manipulation of Opinion'. *International Criminal Justice Review* 31: 229–56.

San Francisco Declaration on Research Assessment. n.d. 'Read'. Online. http://web.archive.org/web/20210126053908/https://sfdora.org/read (accessed 1 February 2021).

Suber, Peter. 2012. *Open Access*. Cambridge: MIT Press.

Sutherland, Edwin H. 1942. *Principles of Criminology*. Chicago and Philadelphia: J. B. Lippincott Company.

Transcribe Bentham. n.d.(a). 'Welcome to the Transcription Desk'. Online. https://web.archive.org/web/20201020145307/http://transcribe-bentham.ucl.ac.uk/td/Transcribe_Bentham (accessed 20 October 2020).

Transcribe Bentham. n.d.(b). 'Manuscripts'. Online. https://web.archive.org/web/20200929062551/http://transcribe-bentham.ucl.ac.uk/td/Manuscripts (accessed 20 October 2020).

UCL Press. n.d.(a). 'Who We Are'. Online. https://web.archive.org/web/20201020165322/https://www.uclpress.co.uk/pages/who-we-are (accessed 20 October 2020).

UCL Press. n.d.(b). 'Financing Your Book'. Online. https://web.archive.org/web/20201021001200/https://www.uclpress.co.uk/pages/financing-your-book#waiver (accessed 20 October 2020).

Williams, Chris. 2014. *Police Control Systems in Britain, 1775–1975: From Parish Constable to National Computer*. Manchester: Manchester University Press.

Willinsky, John. 2006. *The Access Principle: The Case for Open Access to Research and Scholarship*. Cambridge, MA: MIT Press.

2
Jeremy Bentham, the Bentham Project and *The Collected Works of Jeremy Bentham*

Philip Schofield

The Bentham Project was established in 1959 in order to produce the authoritative edition of *The Collected Works of Jeremy Bentham*. Bentham (1748–1832), the English philosopher and reformer, is important both for his historical influence and his continuing relevance. In ethics, he is generally recognized as the founder of classical utilitarianism, one of the most influential moral theories of the past two hundred years (see, e.g., Wolff 2018, 125–33). In jurisprudence, Hart (1983, 146–7) noted that 'since [Bentham's] death in 1832 much argument and counter-argument about the nature of law, about the relation between law and morality, and about the forms of legal reasoning appropriate to legal adjudication have circled round ideas to be found in Bentham's works', and went on to identify Bentham as the founder of the modern doctrine of legal positivism (see also Hart 1982). Twining (1984, 43) stated that Bentham's critique of the French Declaration of Rights of 1789 (see Bentham 2002, 317–401) 'should be treated as one of the classic texts for the linguistic analysis of such fundamental legal and political concepts as rights, obligations, and liberty', and noted that Bentham produced 'what is still by far the most comprehensive general theory of evidence ever produced' (see also Twining 1975 and 1985). Honderich (2006, 74–111) identified Bentham as a major exponent of the deterrence theory of punishment, with its stress on proportionality, compensation and reformation, rather than revenge and retribution. In politics, at the outbreak of the French Revolution in 1789, Bentham (2002, 67–78, 246–9) produced the earliest utilitarian defence of political equality (even advocating women's suffrage before the publication of Mary Wollstonecraft's celebrated *A Vindication of the Rights of Woman* in 1792). Later, in *Constitutional Code*, he produced a sophisticated

and detailed blueprint for representative democracy within a repub-
lican state (Bentham 1983; see also Rosen 1983). Bentham's *Political
Tactics* (1999) was the first systematic treatise on the organization of
a political assembly. Foucault (1977) gave a central place to Bentham's
panopticon prison scheme when describing the modern liberal state.[1]
Hence, the interdisciplinary field of surveillance studies begins with
Bentham (see Horne and Maly 2014). He put forward a scheme to
promote peace between nations, advocating an international court of
arbitration and a proportional reduction of armed forces (Bentham
1843, ii, 535–60). Indeed, the term 'international' was invented by him
(1970, 296n). Examples of Bentham's significance could be multiplied.

   Having said that, Bentham is often portrayed as a villain. Posner
(1976, 599–600), for instance, claimed that Bentham's 'assault on
traditional language … prefigured the totalitarian assault on language
by Newspeak, Hitler, and the Soviet press', while his recommendations
for '[c]ompulsory self-incrimination, torture, anonymous informers,
abolition of the attorney-client privilege and of the jury, and depre-
cation of rights' constituted 'parts of Bentham's legacy to totalitarian
regimes'. Millgram (2017, 14–21) referred to 'the low intellectual
quality of Bentham's thought and writing', characterized his work as
'philosophically uninteresting, intellectually flat, endlessly repetitive
crankiness', and suggested that his deductive method of reasoning
led to 'revolutionary movements [in Nazi Germany and Maoist China,
for instance] perversely inflicting widespread suffering and mass
murder on the populations in their power in the name of humanitarian
ideals'. Whether one is in general sympathetic or antipathetic towards
Bentham, it is difficult (despite Millgram) to deny that his thought
is formidably challenging across a whole range of topics and that it
therefore remains relevant. As Foucault (1994, ii, 594) commented:
'Bentham is more important for our society than Kant and Hegel.'

The need for an authoritative Bentham edition

Prior to the establishment of the Bentham Project, the problem for
anyone who wished to engage with Bentham was that there was
no adequate edition of Bentham's writings. The problem has still
only partially been solved, since the Bentham Project is less than
halfway through its work. During his lifetime, Bentham published
nearly 50 works of varying lengths, but this represented only a
fraction of his writings, for there exists an extraordinarily large

collection of unpublished material. UCL Library contains around 60,000 folios (amounting to around 80,000 pages) of Bentham's manuscripts. The British Library contains a further 12,500 folios (amounting to around 15,000 pages). Since Bentham destroyed the manuscripts of the works that he published himself, the folios in the Bentham Papers represent works that have never been published or were published by editors, either during his lifetime or since. In his will, Bentham appointed John Bowring (1792–1872), merchant, later radical Member of Parliament (MP) and diplomat, as his literary executor, with instructions to produce a new edition of his works. Bowring farmed out the work to a variety of editors, leading to the publication of an 11-volume edition of *The Works of Jeremy Bentham* at Edinburgh between 1838 and 1843 and reissued as a complete set in 1843. In 1849 Bowring deposited Bentham's manuscripts in UCL Library.

As for the material in the British Library, the bulk of it consists of Bentham family papers, made up in the main of correspondence, which came into the possession of Bentham's nephew George Bentham (1800–1884), the botanist, who bequeathed them to his fellow botanist Sir Joseph Dalton Hooker (1827–1911), who in turn sold them to the British Museum (the British Library was subsequently separated from the British Museum in 1973). The British Library also possess a collection of around 1,500 folios in the Grote Papers. These papers had been bequeathed by Bentham to Harriet Grote (1792–1878), whose husband George Grote (1794–1871), the historian of Greece, had drawn on them for *Analysis of the Influence of Natural Religion on the Temporal Happiness of Mankind* (somewhat dubiously treated in much of the literature as a Bentham work), which he had published anonymously in 1822.

The Bowring edition is poorly edited and incomplete. Bowring decided, for instance, to exclude Bentham's writings on religion, on the grounds that they would upset too many of the potential readers (Bowring 1877, 339). As the nineteenth-century readers of the Bowring edition seem to have been few and far between, he perhaps had little need to worry. One major exception was Leslie Stephen (1832–1904), whose account of Bentham in *The English Utilitarians* was based almost exclusively on the Bowring edition (Stephen 1900), which in turn illustrates the point that the manuscripts themselves were neglected until 1892, when they were put into a rough order by UCL Library (Taylor Milne, comp., 1962). They were then drawn upon by the French scholar Élie Halévy (1870–1937) for his classic study *La formation du radicalisme philosophique*, which appeared in 1901. This work presumably generated interest in Bentham's papers, since, around the time of the Bentham centenary celebrations of 1932, it had come to be accepted by the authorities at UCL that the Bowring edition was totally inadequate for the needs of modern scholarship and that a new edition should be prepared. A Bentham Manuscripts Committee was established and attracted a distinguished membership, including Friedrich Hayek (1899–1992), Charles Kay Ogden (1889–1957) and Piero Sraffa (1898–1983). Hayek (1932) advised the committee to publish a new, complete edition of Bentham's works – that is an edition based both on unpublished manuscripts and published works – and to divide it into appropriate subject matters, such as constitutional law, penal law and economics. A series of desultory efforts were made to raise the funds and to begin the editorial work. Little progress had been made when the Second World War intervened. UCL was badly bombed, but since the Bentham Papers had been sent for safekeeping to the National Library of Wales at Aberystwyth, they survived intact.[2]

The establishment of the Bentham Project

It was not until the late 1950s that serious thought was once again given to Bentham's manuscripts, when the Bentham Committee was established as a National Committee of UCL in order to oversee a new authoritative edition of *The Collected Works of Jeremy Bentham*,[3] which was very much based on the outline – whether consciously or not, I do not know – proposed by Hayek. The Bentham Committee held its first meeting on 19 October 1959. It appointed J. H. Burns as the first General Editor in 1961, followed in 1978 by J. R. Dinwiddy and in 1983 by Frederick Rosen, with whom I shared the role from 1995 until his retirement in 2003, since when I have been sole General Editor. The Bentham Committee continues to meet, though it now has a supervisory role rather than attempts to raise any funds, a task that it has devolved to the General Editor. Editorial work is undertaken by the Bentham Project, which, having at first been attached to UCL's Department of History, is now an academic unit in the Faculty of Laws. The first two volumes were Volumes I and II of the *Correspondence* in 1968. In the 'General Preface', which appeared at the beginning of the first volume of the *Correspondence*, the Bentham Committee estimated that the edition would run to 38 volumes. A basic division in the edition was made between Bentham's correspondence and his works. The initial focus was placed on the correspondence, on the grounds that 'understanding of [Bentham's] life and personality has at times been distorted by lack of access to the essential biographical data contained in his letters' (Bentham, 1968, p. vi). The Bentham Committee took the sensible decision to publish letters both *to* and *from* Bentham. There is, moreover, no doubt that, given the limited resources, the correspondence was the correct place to begin, since it not only incorporates material of historical interest but sheds light on the formal works that Bentham was engaged in writing, in terms of their provenance, history of composition and subsequent dissemination, and as such may be regarded as the 'backbone' of the edition as a whole. In turn, as more of Bentham's works are edited, we are better able to understand the views and concerns expressed in the correspondence.

In total, 12 volumes of Bentham's *Correspondence*, reproducing Bentham's letters through to the end of June 1828, have appeared. The first volume begins with three letters between Bentham's father and mother, before reproducing Bentham's earliest surviving letter, written to his grandmother when he was aged three. The twelfth volume ends with letter 3,419, dated 23 June 1828, when Bentham was aged 80. One more volume, containing a further 400 letters, will take the *Correspondence* through to Bentham's death. A final, fourteenth volume will contain indexes and around 100 'missing' letters – that is, letters discovered since the relevant volume was published. The first five volumes of the *Correspondence* have recently been reissued, with corrections (especially to the letters written in French), by UCL Press as an open-access publication.

The remainder of the volumes belong to the works. They are based either on original manuscripts or on texts printed by Bentham himself, or on a combination of both. Twenty-two volumes of works have thus far been published in the edition, making a grand total of 34,[4] with the 35th due for publication in 2021 and a dozen more at various stages of preparation (though work is not currently progressing on most of these). I expect that the edition, if it is ever completed, will run to more than 80 volumes.

The construction of the text

The Bentham Project has developed a set of editorial techniques to produce coherent texts from Bentham's disorganized manuscripts. The initial stage in our editorial process is to identify all of the manuscripts relevant to the text in question and then to transcribe them.[5] Given Bentham's difficult handwriting, the complexity of his syntax, and his sparse and inconsistent use of punctuation, this is a painstaking task that requires a significant investment in terms of time and expertise. Once a readable text for each sheet of manuscript has been produced, we decide upon the most appropriate ordering of the material. As he composed a text, Bentham might write several drafts of the same section or chapter, add new sections, divide existing sections, and discard other sections. Each sequence of manuscript has, therefore, to be located in its proper place in the history of the composition of the text: in other words, we need to understand the way in which Bentham, at any given time, envisaged how the text would appear. Having done this, we are in a position to assess how a printed version of the text should be structured and which parts of the manuscript material should be incorporated into that structure. The draft text is entered into the 'Bentham Template' (a specially formatted Microsoft Word document), which provides an attractive layout for our editorial work, enabling us, in the case of the works, to mark-up headings, text, marginalia, Bentham's footnotes and sub-footnotes, and editorial notes; and in the case of the correspondence, such features as salutations, valedictions and addresses, and to see at a single glance how each element relates to the others.

Once the text has been established, the next major task is annotation. As well as providing textual notes, we attempt to explain all of the allusions, whether historical or literary, that occur in the text, by referring to Bentham's own sources or sources available to him. The annotation, which is written to elucidate the text and not to provide a commentary upon it, is vital if the texts are to be properly appreciated by contemporary and future readers. Once the text has been annotated, the editorial introduction is written. The editorial introduction is again not intended as a commentary on the text – that will come with the secondary literature that the volume will generate. Instead, it describes the 'history of the work' (the context in which it was written, Bentham's motives in writing it, the reception it encountered and so forth) and the sources on which it is based; it explains the editorial methods used in the presentation of the text, indicates which materials have been included in the volume and guides scholars to related material that has been excluded. The volumes are completed with comprehensive subject and name indexes.

The Bentham Project has always recognized that to survive, never mind to prosper, it has to meet the highest scholarly standards in its textual editing and employ innovative techniques and strategies in order to contain costs and maintain productivity. In 1985 the Project acquired its first computers and began to transcribe manuscripts directly onto disk. By 2010 the Project had transcribed around 20,000 folios. It is worth noting that many transcripts – perhaps as many as a half – for any particular work have not been, nor ever will be, published in a traditional print volume, since they contain discarded drafts, copies, notes, marginal summaries and miscellanea. We cannot know, of course, whether this material will be published until we know what it says; it helps us to understand Bentham's composition of the work, and is often of interest to scholars and students in terms of tracing the detailed development of Bentham's ideas. These transcripts, created in various proprietary formats (Scientex, WordPerfect and MS Word), constitute our 'legacy transcripts'. Yet at the rate we were going between 1985 and 2010, it would have taken another 50 or 60 years to produce a complete transcript of the Bentham Papers.

Transcribe Bentham, the Project's prize-winning scholarly crowdsourcing initiative, was conceived as a potential solution to this problem (Transcribe Bentham 2020a). Transcribe Bentham would not have been possible without the Bentham Papers Database (2020). Funded by the UK's Arts and Humanities Research Board's Resource Enhancement Scheme, the database was compiled between 2003 and 2006 by Deborah McVea (now Colville). Created as a finding aid for editors and researchers working on the UCL Bentham Papers, the database catalogue records up to 15 fields of metadata, including dates, headings and titles, for each of the 60,000 folios in the UCL Bentham Papers. The success of the database was based on the fact that Bentham Project editors had an intimate knowledge of the material they were dealing with, built up over decades, and had a definite purpose in mind – that is, to make the editorial process not only faster (and hence cheaper), but more accurate. It was not a free-floating enterprise, but located at the centre of a humanities project whose relevance and importance was widely recognized.

The database, as well as proving to be a resource for Bentham editors and scholars, also provides the metadata for Transcribe Bentham. The Transcribe Bentham programme was initially funded by the Arts and Humanities Research Council's Digital Equipment and Database Enhancement for Impact Scheme. This was a 'one-off' call, with a maximum duration of one year and specifically intended to build on projects that had initially been funded by the Resource Enhancement Scheme. The programme began in April 2010 and the

Transcribe Bentham transcription desk (Transcribe Bentham 2020b), created in partnership with the University of London Computer Centre (but since 2018 hosted by UCL's Information Systems Division), was launched to the public in September 2010. Volunteers are presented with high-quality images of Bentham manuscripts that have not been transcribed, together with a free text transcription box. They are asked to transcribe the manuscripts and add the relevant mark-up to produce documents encoded in Text Encoding Initiative (TEI)-compliant XML.

The distinguishing feature of Transcribe Bentham as a crowd-sourcing project is that volunteers do not perform repetitive, easily done tasks, such as correcting Optical Character Recognition (OCR)-generated text or transcribing material that is generally formulaic, or at least reasonably straightforward to decipher and understand.[6] Transcribing the difficult handwriting, idiosyncratic style, and dense and challenging ideas of an important philosopher, as well as adding XML mark-up to the resulting transcripts, is a demanding and complex task that requires a high degree of commitment and concentration. Once the volunteer has completed and submitted their transcript, a researcher at the Bentham Project (the Transcribe Bentham Editor) checks it for textual accuracy and encoding consistency. The key questions are whether any appreciable improvements are likely to be made through further crowdsourcing and whether it forms a viable basis for editorial work. If approved, the transcript is 'locked' to prevent further editing, with the formatted and rendered transcript remaining available for viewing and searching. Locked transcripts are converted into TEI-compliant XML files and stored on a shared drive until they are uploaded to UCL's digital repository. Our quality-control regime ensures that locked transcripts are a reliable guide to the content of the original manuscript. The transcripts contributed by volunteers have already formed the starting point for published volumes in *The Collected Works of Jeremy Bentham*, with volunteers acknowledged in the Prefaces to the relevant volumes.[7]

In 2012–14 the Bentham Project secured funding from the Andrew W. Mellon Foundation in order to improve the transcription tool and to investigate the potential economic benefits of crowd-sourcing. The new iteration of Transcribe Bentham was known as the Consolidated Bentham Papers Repository (CBPR) – TB Mark II, for short – and was a collaborative exercise that brought together UCL, the British Library and the University of London Computer Centre. Improvements were made to the transcription interface and, with some further investment from UCL, the digitization of the whole of the Bentham Papers in both the UCL Library and British Library collections was completed in May 2018. The digital images are progressively being made available for crowdsourcing, completed transcripts and images are being added to UCL's digital repository (UCL Library Services 2020), and the back file of almost 20,000 legacy transcripts – a corpus of approximately 10 million words – has been converted to basic TEI XML.

The purpose of the CBPR was not only to create a resource that would benefit Bentham scholarship and provide a template for other crowdsourcing activities, but also to make an assessment as to whether scholarly crowdsourcing made economic sense. We attempted to determine whether crowdsourced transcription of historical documents could result in cost avoidance in terms of time and money, without compromising quality. Transcribe Bentham demonstrated that the crowdsourcing of complex manuscript material in a scholarly arts and humanities context was viable, that the transcripts produced were of a high enough quality to be stored for public access in a digital repository, and that they could be utilized as part of an academic editorial project. We addressed two major concerns about crowdsourced transcription. First, would the time and money required to develop and deliver a platform, to recruit and manage volunteers, and to check that crowd-sourced submissions were of the required standard, mean that it was more expensive than simply employing experts to do the job? Second, would the work of volunteers be of a high enough standard to form the basis for further editorial and other scholarly work?

Without going into details, the main conclusion of our analysis was that, were volunteers to complete the transcription of the remainder of the Bentham papers, the overall cost avoidance to the Bentham Project would be £880,000 and that the task might be completed within a decade or so, rather than within five or six decades.[8] There were other advantages that we were unable to put a price upon. If no images had been created, for instance, the manuscripts and transcripts would have remained accessible only to those able to visit UCL and the British Library. The increased accessibility has in turn given further stimulus to Bentham scholarship through engagement with the manuscripts. Since the software for the transcription desk has been released on an open-source basis, other organizations that adopt it for their own purposes will avoid costs of around £100,000 in software development, and also costs in terms of staff time to develop the concept. The efficiencies involved in Transcribe Bentham have the potential to allow those organizations that wish to adopt and adapt its methodology to avoid significant start-up costs.

The third phase of Transcribe Bentham has arguably been even more exciting. The Bentham Project has been involved in developing an online platform that is producing a revolution in research in the arts and humanities that involves archival material. The Bentham Project has been a partner in two research programmes that have led to the application of Handwritten Text Recognition (HTR) software to historical documents: first, the tranScriptorium (2020) programme;[9] and second, the Recognition and Enrichment of Archival Documents (READ) (2020) programme with its Transkribus platform.[10] The vast majority of the many millions of pages of handwritten documents that form the basis of a great deal of research in the humanities remain inaccessible, except to the individual scholar who has the time and resources to visit the archive where the material is deposited and the palaeographic skills required to survey and read it. The creation of an automated process that will allow such material to be machine-read is having a transformative effect on scholarship and research.

The vision behind HTR is that, beginning with digital images of handwritten documents, the software application will generate a typewritten transcript that not only reproduces the words themselves but also their layout on the page. A second element is Key Word Spotting, whereby the software will find, according to the degree of confidence specified by the researcher, any word or phrase in handwritten documents that have not been transcribed. Working in collaboration with computer scientists at the Technical University of Valencia, we have applied the technology to the entirety of the Bentham Papers, and it is proving to be a tremendously useful resource. I have used it, for instance, to find passages on particular subjects of which I had previously been unaware, to answer queries about whether or where Bentham used a particular phrase, and to identify particular manuscripts for which the Bentham Project had transcripts dating back to the early 1980s but which did not record their precise location.[11]

The Bentham Project was asked to be involved in the tranScriptorium and READ programmes because of our crowdsourcing experience, with a view to developing and testing a crowdsourcing platform that would incorporate HTR. Though that particular aspect of the programme was not developed within READ, we still have ambitions to take it forward. Nevertheless, the importance of the Transkribus platform for research in the arts and humanities was recognized when it received, in September 2020, one of five European Union Horizon 2020 Impact Awards, in competition with 220 entries from across all disciplines.

The printed critical edition in the digital age

Transcribe Bentham has succeeded because it is part of a wider scholarly enterprise – the production of *The Collected Works of Jeremy Bentham* – and because there is demand for its content, which is of outstanding historical and philosophical importance. Traditional scholarship and the Digital Humanities have been combined in a mutually beneficial way. Digital Humanities, or rather the digital revolution more generally, nevertheless poses significant challenges to traditional scholarship – indeed, if it does not threaten its very existence, it is forcing it to present its findings in a different way.

The pressing issue for me in my role as General Editor of *The Collected Works of Jeremy Bentham* is, given the expense of production, whether there is any future for the traditional scholarly edition of the works of major philosophers, presented in a series of printed volumes. If the printed edited text were to be abandoned, what would replace it? At one extreme, one might provide unedited and unannotated online transcriptions of manuscripts, while at the other extreme one might provide a fully edited online authoritative text. The former alternative would not, in my opinion, be conducive to high-quality academic research, but would be a retrograde step in comparison with traditional scholarship, and so we need to find a way to combine the best elements of both.

I will illustrate the value of traditional scholarship from the perspective of the Bentham edition. A researcher begins with a series of Bentham manuscripts. The first problem the researcher encounters is reading the words on the page. The second problem is reconstructing sentences, assuming the researcher has been able to read the words. The third problem is ordering the pages in appropriate sequences. The fourth problem is reconstructing the sequences so that they form a coherent work. The fifth problem is understanding the content without annotation. I defy anyone to take an average Bentham manuscript, read it, and immediately understand it fully. Each of the stages I have described adds interpretative value to the physical mass of ink and paper that the researcher begins with, and it is only when the researcher gets to the edited text, with expert annotation, that he or she is provided with a sound basis for philosophical and historical investigation. There is no substitute for the scholarly edition.

As a quick example, take the following short letter:

Q.S.P. 13 Jany 1820

Dear Aspasia

Come to the embrace of poor old Great-Grand-papa on Sunday. If your husband behaves well, bid him attend you.
Amongst you—for it went by Bingham you ought to have a receipt for *Curry*. If you have it, bring it with you.

Persons unfamiliar with Bentham's handwriting would probably struggle to read more than a few words of this letter, given that it was written when Bentham was more than 70 years old, his eyes were poor and his handwriting was a scrawl. Since the letter has no signature, you would, however, either need to be familiar with Bentham's handwriting, or need to know that he lived at Queen's Square Place (Q.S.P.), in order to identify the penner. But assuming that you have managed to read it (perhaps aided by HTR), what assumptions would you be led to make? That it was written to his great-granddaughter Aspasia, and that he was thinking about having a spicy Indian-style dinner? There are some problems with these assumptions. First, Bentham had no children and so could not have had any great-grandchildren. Second, he had no one in his acquaintance called Aspasia. Third, was Bentham likely to order a curry? The addressee of the letter (we have a detached page containing her name and address) was Sarah Austin (1793–1867), who had recently married John Austin (1790–1859), later the first Professor of Jurisprudence at the University of London. Bentham was affectionately comparing her to the consort of Pericles and playfully reminding her of their difference in age. One also needs to realize (which very few commentators have done) that Bentham had a keen sense of humour. As for the curry, we may need to do more research to establish whether there was an Indian takeaway in Westminster in 1820, but the reference is presumably to an edition of John Curry's *An Historical and Critical Review of the Civil Wars in Ireland*, which had been first published at Dublin in 1775 but republished as late as 1810. The work had been sent to Bentham by Thomas Nolan, an Irish barrister, in November 1819. The 'Bingham' referred to was Peregrine Bingham (1788–1864), another lawyer associated with Bentham and his circle.

Even if you are convinced that the scholarly edition is necessary for the highest-quality research, you might ask whether it needs to be a print edition. Would it not be better, in terms of cost effectiveness and dissemination, to make texts available online? There is still the need to present the text in an attractive format, which means, in effect, as a series of pages. The printed Bentham volumes need to be typeset, and with a work typically consisting of body text, tables of various sorts, Bentham's footnotes and sub-footnotes, and editorial footnotes, typesetting is a specialist undertaking requiring a high level of skill and sensitivity towards the material. In the case of the Bentham edition, the initial copy-editing and subsequent typesetting is paid for by the publisher, which also pays for the marketing and the printing and binding of the book. The reader who pays for the book is in effect paying the costs of the copy-editing, typesetting, production and marketing (and the publisher's profit).

Were the Bentham Project to make the text freely available online in the form of a properly typeset volume, it would increase our costs because we would have to fund the typesetting. Moreover, we would lose out on one of the great advantages of the book, namely its physical permanency, both in terms of the fact that it sits securely on one's shelf and that it will not become unreadable because of technological change. The printed page also fixes the location of the content and thereby allows for stable referencing. Having said that, making corrections to a printed book is far more cumbersome than updating a computer file.

Open access and funding

Since the early 1980s, the Bentham edition has been published by Oxford University Press (OUP), but in July 2020 I signed an agreement to transfer the publication of future volumes to UCL Press. While OUP has produced an attractive cloth-bound volume for the initial print run, the quality of its subsequent print-on-demand volume has been inferior – the covers are variable, the binding is glued instead of stitched, and the print itself is less sharp. Moreover, while the cloth-bound volume sells for around £85, the print-on-demand volumes cost up to £285 each. OUP has also refused to issue any volumes in paperback, except for *An Introduction to the Principles of Morals and Legislation*, and even that is priced at £72. I came increasingly to think that this situation was unacceptable – after all, the purpose of the Bentham Project is to make Bentham's writings available, and not to discourage scholars from using them through an extortionate pricing regime. It was, moreover, becoming increasingly untenable due to the requirement of funding bodies that the results of the research conducted under their grants be made freely available. The Bentham Project has met this condition through the somewhat unsatisfactory method of making pre-publication versions of texts freely available online (as in the case of *Political Economy, Volume III*, 2018).

By moving to UCL Press we will be fully compliant with the most stringent requirements for open-access publishing. Future volumes will be available to purchase in both hardback and paperback versions at relatively modest prices, while they will be freely accessible online and as downloadable PDFs. I am confident that UCL Press will have the capacity to typeset volumes to the standard traditionally associated with the *Collected Works*, since the Press has already produced revised and attractive reissues of the first five volumes of Bentham's *Correspondence* (originally published by the Athlone Press, and not by OUP, with the Bentham Committee retaining copyright) and has typeset a complex sample from another recent volume.

All 34 volumes published so far in the edition appear on OUP's Oxford Scholarly Editions Online platform, and if OUP is so inclined, it will be able to add the new volumes to this platform. Given the healthy download figures generally for UCL Press, and in particular for the *Correspondence* volumes and the pre-publication versions of texts that we have made available online, I anticipate that this development will produce a much increased readership for our volumes and accelerate the growing interest in Bentham that is being stimulated by the appearance of volumes in the *Collected Works*.

Whatever the future holds in terms of publishing may cease to be relevant anyway. The Bentham Project relies almost exclusively on the ability of the General Editor to raise external grants, and there is no guarantee that I will continue to have the success I have hitherto enjoyed in this respect. In fact, one funder has told me not to apply again since its officers have come to the conclusion that enough support has already been given to the Bentham edition. Every three or four years we face a funding crisis, and I have to undertake the unpleasant task of either making experienced and valued staff redundant or threatening them with redundancy. Three major grants came to an end in 2019 and, as I write, for the first time since I joined the Bentham Project in 1984, we hold no external grants, apart from a small annual grant that we receive as an accredited British Academy Research Project. This means that the British Academy recognizes the importance of our work, the quality of our scholarship and the professionalism of our management.

The major problem faced by the Bentham Project, and by other long-term projects in the United Kingdom, is that no mechanism exists to give them relatively secure, long-term support. The way in which funding operates in the United Kingdom is to award relatively short-term grants to random projects that will never have the lasting importance for academic research that projects such as the Bentham edition will have. Other countries do things differently. It is not hard to imagine that if Bentham had been an American or a German, a permanent institute would have been established to edit his writings and to further the study of his ideas. As things stand at present, the Bentham Project is almost totally reliant for its existence on the generosity of UCL's Faculty of Laws. I am grateful that the Project is in an environment where colleagues actually seem pleased to host it.

The Bentham Project was established as a central UCL initiative, and so there is a case for saying that UCL centrally should do much more to help the Project. The Bentham Project operates on a shoestring, in barely adequate accommodation, and without any direct central financial support from the institution that established it. When I explain the situation to scholars from elsewhere, they find it astonishing, especially given Bentham's inherent importance and, moreover, his importance as the intellectual inspiration for UCL. It has been suggested more than once in the past that UCL should hand over the Bentham manuscripts to an institution that is prepared to invest serious resources in the production of the edition.

Notes

1 For a detailed history of Bentham's attempts to build the panopticon prison in London, see Semple (1993).
2 For a more detailed account of the early attempts to edit Bentham's manuscripts, see Schofield (2009a).
3 The Bentham Committee has been chaired successively by the judge Lionel Leonard Cohen, the economist Lionel Robbins, H. L. A. Hart, W. L. Twining and Jonathan Wolff.
4 The first eight volumes in the edition (five of correspondence and three of works) were published by the Athlone Press; the remainder have been published by the Clarendon Press.
5 One of the difficulties faced by Bentham editors has been the lack of transcripts for the whole of the Bentham Papers. Had funding been available, the best way to have gone about preparing the new edition would have been to produce in the first instance such a complete transcription. This would have made it much easier to identify and consider all of the manuscripts relevant to a particular work, and the connections between different works, and to make properly informed choices about the structure of the edition in general and of individual volumes in particular. See Schofield (2019b).

6   For more detail on Transcribe Bentham's volunteers, see Causer and Wallace (2012).
7   See, for instance, the acknowledgement of volunteers in the editorial introductions to Bentham (2018a) and, subsequently, Bentham (2018b, as linked to in Causer 2018).
8   For a full discussion see Causer et al. (2018).
9   tranScriptorium received funding from the European Union's Seventh Framework Programme for research, technological development and demonstration, under grant agreement no. 600707.
10 READ received funding from the European Union's Horizon 2020 research and innovation programme under grant agreement no. 674943. At the time of writing, the Transkribus platform can be freely downloaded from https://transkribus.eu/Transkribus/.
11 At the time of writing, the tool is freely available at http://prhlt-carabela.prhlt.upv.es/bentham/.

References

Bentham, Jeremy. 1843. *The Works of Jeremy Bentham*, edited by J. Bowring. 11 vols. Edinburgh: William Tait.

Bentham, Jeremy. 1968. *The Correspondence of Jeremy Bentham, Volume I: 1752–76*, edited by T. L. S. Sprigge. London: Athlone Press.

Bentham, Jeremy. 1970. *An Introduction to the Principles of Morals and Legislation*, edited by J. H. Burns and H. L. A. Hart. London: Athlone Press.

Bentham, Jeremy. 1983. *Constitutional Code, Volume I*, edited by F. Rosen and J. H. Burns. Oxford: Clarendon Press.

Bentham, Jeremy. 1999. *Political Tactics*, edited by M. James, C. Blamires and C. Pease-Watkin. Oxford: Clarendon Press.

Bentham, Jeremy. 2002. *Rights, Representation, and Reform: Nonsense upon Stilts and Other Writings on the French Revolution*, edited by P. Schofield, C. Pease-Watkin and C. Blamires. Oxford: Clarendon Press.

Bentham, Jeremy. 2018a. *Writings on Political Economy, Volume III: Preventive Police*, edited by Michael Quinn. Pre-publication version. Online. http://discovery.ucl.ac.uk/10055084/ (accessed 23 April 2021).

Bentham, Jeremy. 2018b. *Writings on Australia*, edited by T. Causer and P. Schofield. Pre-publication version. Online. https://blogs.ucl.ac.uk/bentham-project/2018/09/05/benthams-writings-on-australia-pre-publication-versions-now-online/ (accessed 28 April 2021).

Bentham Papers Database. 2020. 'Introduction'. Online. http://web.archive.org/web/20201110173604/http://www.benthampapers.ucl.ac.uk/ (accessed 11 November 2020).

Bowring, Lewis. 1877. *Autobiographical Recollections of Sir John Bowring*. London: Henry S. King and Co.

Causer, Tim. 2018. 'Bentham's "Writings on Australia" – Pre-publication Texts Now Online'. Online. https://blogs.ucl.ac.uk/bentham-project/2018/09/05/benthams-writings-on-australia-pre-publication-versions-now-online/ (accessed 10 November 2020).

Causer, Tim, Kris Grint, Anna-Maria Sichani and Melissa Terras. 2018. '"Making Such Bargain": Transcribe Bentham and the Quality and Cost-Effectiveness of Crowdsourced Transcription', *Digital Scholarship in the Humanities* 3: 467–87.

Causer, Tim and Valerie Wallace. 2012. 'Building a Volunteer Community: Results and Findings from Transcribe Bentham'. *Digital Humanities Quarterly* 6. Online. http://www.digitalhumanities.org/dhq/vol/6/2/000125/000125.html (accessed 20 April 2021).

Foucault, Michel. 1977. *Discipline and Punish: The Birth of the Prison*, translated by A. Sheridan. New York: Vintage.

Foucault, Michel. 1994. *Dits et écrits, 1954–1988*, edited by Daniel Defert, François Ewald and Jacques Lagrange. 4 vols. Paris: Gallimard.

Hart, H. L. A. 1982. *Essays on Bentham: Jurisprudence and Political Theory*. Oxford: Oxford University Press.

Hart, H. L. A. 1983. *Essays in Jurisprudence and Philosophy*. Oxford: Oxford University Press.

Hayek, Friedrich, to Allen Mawer, Provost of UCL. 20 July 1932. University College London Record Office, 2/1.

Honderich, Ted. 2006. *Punishment: The Supposed Justifications Revisited*. London: Pluto Press.

Horne, Emily and Tim Maly. 2014. *The Inspection House: An Impertinent Guide to Modern Surveillance*. Toronto: Coach House Press.

Millgram, E. 2017. 'Mill's Epiphanies'. In *A Companion to Mill*, edited by Christopher Macleod and Dale E. Miller, 12–29. London: Wiley.

Posner, Richard A. 1976. 'Blackstone and Bentham', *Journal of Law and Economics* 19: 569–606.

Recognition and Enrichment of Archival Documents (READ). 2020. 'Home'. Online. http://web.archive.org/web/20201110174358/https://readcoop.eu/ (accessed 10 November 2020).

Rosen, Frederick. 1983. *Jeremy Bentham and Representative Democracy: A Study of the Constitutional Code*. Oxford: Clarendon Press.

Schofield, Philip. 2009a. 'Werner Stark and Jeremy Bentham's Economic Writings', *History of European Ideas* 35: 475–94.

Schofield, Philip. 2009b. *Bentham: A Guide for the Perplexed*. London: Continuum.

Semple, Janet. 1993. *Bentham's Prison: A Study of the Panopticon Penitentiary*. Oxford: Clarendon Press.

Stephen, Leslie. 1900. *The English Utilitarians*. 3 vols. London: Duckworth and Co.

Taylor Milne, Alexander (compiler). 1962. *Catalogue of the Manuscripts of Jeremy Bentham in the Library of University College, London*. 2nd ed. London: Athlone Press.

Transcribe Bentham. 2020a. 'Welcome to Transcribe Bentham!'. Online. http://web.archive.org/web/20201110173026/https://blogs.ucl.ac.uk/transcribe-bentham/ (accessed 10 November 2020).

Transcribe Bentham. 2020b. 'Welcome to the Transcription Desk'. Online. https://web.archive.org/web/20201020145307/http://transcribe-bentham.ucl.ac.uk/td/Transcribe_Bentham (accessed 20 October 2020).

tranScriptorium 2020. 'Home'. Online. http://web.archive.org/web/20201110173904/http://transcriptorium.eu/ (accessed 10 November 2020).

Twining, William L. 1975. 'The Contemporary Significance of Bentham's Anarchical Fallacies', *Archiv für Rechts- und Sozialphilosophie* 41: 325–56.

Twining, William L. 1984. 'Why Bentham?', *The Bentham Newsletter* 8: 34–49.

Twining, William L. 1985. *Theories of Evidence: Bentham and Wigmore*. Redwood City, CA: Stanford University Press.

UCL Library Services. 2020. 'Bentham Manuscripts'. Online. http://web.archive.org/web/20201110174631/https://www.ucl.ac.uk/library/digital-collections/collections/bentham (accessed 10 November 2020).

Wolff, Jonathan. 2018. *An Introduction to Moral Philosophy*. New York: W. W. Norton.

3

Bentham on Preventive Police: The *Calendar of Delinquency* in Evaluation of Policy, and the *Police Gazette* in Manipulation of Opinion

Michael Quinn

This chapter originated in a generous offer from the editors, and in a desire to advertise the existence of, and provide some introduction to, a practically unknown and previously unpublished set of writings by Jeremy Bentham, the English philosopher, theorist and aspirant reformer of law and legal procedure, and would-be governor of a panopticon prison, while highlighting those elements presented below as Bentham's specific and original contributions to a project usually identified as the practically exclusive production of Patrick Colquhoun. The Bentham Project's raison-d'être is the production of a critical edition of Bentham's works. In a writing career extending over six decades, Bentham wrote every day, and published only a small fraction of his extraordinary output. Most of Bentham's surviving papers, some 60,000 foolscap sheets, reside in the care of Special Collections at University College London Library, while another 12,000 folios are held in the British Library. Within a few years of his death in 1832, an 11-volume edition of Bentham's works was produced (Bentham 1843), which suffers from many weaknesses in terms of both selection (for instance, Bentham's critical writings on religion and sexual morality, even those that had previously been published, were entirely excluded) and of organization and editing (Schofield 2009, 24–35). The goal of the Project in relation to works that Bentham did not publish, or which he published only in 'Outline' or 'Abstract' form, is to reconstitute them, insofar as possible, in accordance with

Bentham's own stated intentions, and above all to avoid repeating the errors of the earlier edition in splicing together, into something resembling a readable text, sequences that share similar ostensible themes, but which, drafted at different periods and for different purposes, simply do not belong together.[1] Thanks to the generosity of the Leverhulme Trust, the project has been able to continue the task of editing Bentham's writings on political economy, and *Preventive Police* (Bentham 2018) will be the third volume in this sub-series to be published.[2] The volume contains 11 works written in 1798–9, of which the central pair, a 'Thames Police Bill' and a 'Bill for the establishment of a Board of Police', provide the rationale for the division of the volume into two parts.[3] In relation to the volume, some 900 sheets of manuscript were surveyed, transcribed,[4] put into sequences with the assistance of Bentham's surviving plans and brouillons, and the resulting text annotated.

The *Preventive Police* volume is unusual in Bentham's corpus in that Bentham was, in a sense, writing to order. The outlines of the proposals for reform both in the policing of the River Thames and by the establishment of a Board of Police to administer a licensing system for dealers in second-hand goods, originated with Patrick Colquhoun, and find expression in Colquhoun's *Treatise on the Police of the Metropolis* (1797, 27–8, 66–7, 346–8, 359–68, 426–7).[5] Bentham met Colquhoun in December 1796, and the latter became an enthusiastic supporter of Bentham's panopticon prison scheme. In 1798 their interests coincided when both men gave evidence to the Select Committee on Finance, whose twenty-eighth report, 'Police, including Convict Establishments', printed over the summer of 1798, endorsed both Colquhoun's general plan for the reform of police and Bentham's panopticon (Lambert 1975, 31–2). Colquhoun, who warmly endorsed the panopticon in his evidence to the Finance Committee, sought Bentham's assistance as, effectively, a parliamentary draftsman, and over the next 12 months Bentham drafted two Bills, together with a series of explanatory and justificatory comments on them.

Colquhoun himself has been identified as a pivotal figure in the shift between a notion of police as a broad governmental responsibility for moral regulation and oversight, and a recognizably modern notion of police as an apolitical service focused on the prevention and investigation of crimes (Dodsworth 2007; 2008; Neocleous 2000). In the summer of 1799, Colquhoun believed that he had the strong support of William Pitt's administration, and that both the Bills Bentham had drafted would soon become law. In the event, his confidence turned out to be groundless. For reasons that remain unclear, in the second half of 1799 a decision was taken to limit that support to endorsement of a truncated version of one of the bills, so that the Thames Police Act of 1800 (39 & 40 Geo. III, c. 87) was the only legislative enactment of any part of Colquhoun's plan.

In that Bentham consistently recognized Colquhoun as 'the author of the system' (Bentham 2018, 63, 96n, 98 {UC cl. 139, 656, 736}), it might appear that his police writings offer little of interest to scholars of police or of Bentham, since the substance, if not the words, are not his but Colquhoun's. Some assessment of the nature and extent of Bentham's role, with particular emphasis on the *Police Gazette* and the *Calendar of Delinquency*, is attempted below (see 'The police writings: Colquhoun or Bentham?'). Yet what seems evident is that in his 'Notes to the Police Bill' and 'Elucidations relative to the Police Revenue Bill', liberated on the one hand from the constraints of Parliamentary 'surplusage' and on the other from the directing hand of Colquhoun, Bentham provided some striking examples of his utilitarian reasoning in action in the drafting and justification of public policy.

Police, policy and indirect legislation

English attitudes to police in the eighteenth century were coloured by both suspicion of alien terminology and fears over the importation of continental oppression (Dodsworth 2007; 2008; Radzinowicz 1948–86, iii, 1–8). The origins of the word 'police', and the concept, in translation of Aristotle's *Politics*, made the European under-standing capacious enough to encompass all of the actions of the state that had a domestic or internal focus: at its broadest, police was everything states did to maintain the internal order and well-being of the commonwealth (Neocleous 2000, 720–3). In this broad continental sense, and not unreasonably, the English word 'policy' has been suggested as a more appropriate equivalent.[6] Bentham's lifetime witnessed a revolution in this definition of police, and the development of a modern understanding of police as, first, a profes-sionalized, expert and non-political institution, and, second, an institution whose responsibilities were limited more narrowly to the prevention and investigation of crimes.

The earlier continental idea of police was not entirely rejected in British discourse. The concept appears, without negative comment, in the work of several British writers in the third quarter of the eighteenth century, including Jonas Hanway (1775),[7] Adam Smith (1978)[8] and William Blackstone. For Blackstone:

> By the public police and oeconomy I mean the due regulation and domestic order of the kingdom: whereby the individuals of the state, like the members of a well governed family, are bound to conform their general behaviour to the rules of propriety, good neighbourhood and good manners; and to be decent, industrious, and inoffensive in their respective stations. (1765–9, iv, 162)

The central core of Blackstone's police was thus the maintenance of order. He went on to argue, in discussion of recognisances (that is, forfeitable securities deposited with courts for future good behaviour), that, where feasible, 'preventive justice is … preferable in all respects to punishing justice' (1765–9, iv, 248).[9]

Colquhoun consistently highlighted the importance of preventing crimes. However, as Neocleous notes (2000, 712), he in fact deployed both old and new senses of police in his definition:

> POLICE in this Country may be considered as a *new Science*, the properties of which consist not in the Judicial Powers which lead to *Punishment*, and which belong to Magistrates alone; but in the PREVENTION AND DETECTION OF CRIMES, and in those other Functions which relate to INTERNAL REGULATIONS for the well ordering and comfort of Civil Society. (Colquhoun 1800, unpaginated preface)

Police and prevention in Bentham's writings

For the most part, Bentham mentions police only in passing in his early jurisprudential writings, where he too stresses prevention, describing police as 'the power which occupies itself in preventing mischief' (1970a, 198n).[10] Bentham divides the functions of police into prevention of mischief by natural calamity and mischief by internal enemies – that is, criminals. In relation to the latter, he distinguishes between 'preventive police' and justice:

> As to mischief from internal adversaries, the expedients employed for averting it may be distinguished into such as may be applied *before* the discovery of any mischievous design in particular, and

such as can not be employed but in consequence of the discovery of some such design: the former of these are commonly referred to a branch which may be styled the *preventive* branch of the *police*: the latter to that of justice. (1970a, 198)

In a long note, Bentham argues that although it will often be difficult to distinguish between the functions of justice and those of the police, his suggested distinction appears to be the only plausible line of separation (1970a, 198n). This distinction was partly temporal – police refers to things done to combat mischief before the authorities become aware of specific mischievous designs; justice to things done in awareness of such designs – and partly a matter of a significant variation in focus. Thus measures of justice concern only the specific type or types of offence in relation to which judgement is demanded, and apply exclusively to the particular individual manifestations thereof in question; measures of police might easily concern the former, but never the latter. In one sense, this seems a long way from a modern definition, in which the police spend most of their time investigating specific instances of criminality, but in another sense it anticipates Colquhoun's distinction between the punishment of crime, which is the preserve of the magistracy, and its prevention, which is the business of police. Although Bentham frankly admits that the idea of police 'seems to be too multifarious to be susceptible of any single definition', two inferences might be drawn as to his understanding of the concept. First, police is essentially preventive. Second, police includes action against calamity as well as against crime.

In both parts of its field of action, police was to be distinguished from other regulatory systems that might be, and often were, confused with it, by its negative or prophylactic focus on preventing evil as opposed to producing positive good: 'Other functions, commonly referred to the head of police, may be referred either to that power which occupies itself in promoting in a positive way the increase of national felicity, or that which employs itself in the management of the public wealth' (1970a, 199n). In discussing offences under the former head, Bentham lists breaches of a series of trusts that the agents of the state might undertake, whose objects range from the promotion of knowledge to ensuring (whether by providing directly or by regulating private provision is unclear) good education, to the care of those suffering from physical diseases and of the insane, to the care of the poor, the provision of compensation to victims of mischief and, finally, 'the *hedonarchic* trust', or that of presiding over pleasures (1970a, 262n). Bentham does not expand on 'these examples of the principal establishments which should or might be put on foot' for making positive increases in national felicity (1970a, 262n), but they appear to remove many of the responsibilities ascribed to police by the continental understanding. In relation to offences against the public wealth, Bentham lists non-payment of monies owing to the state, such as forfeitures and taxes, and a further series of breaches of public trusts involving peculation or mismanagement of public funds (1970a, 262n). Insofar as the management of public monies might plausibly be seen as part of the maintenance of good order, this classification removes a further set of responsibilities from the European notion of police.

Further light is shed on the distinction between the prevention of evil and the promotion of good by turning to Bentham's essay on 'Indirect Legislation', written in 1782. He opens his text thus:

> The end of government, wherever it is what it ought to be, is to provide for the happiness of the governed. Happiness is provided for partly by combating mischief, partly by promoting good. The former way is that in which there is most to be done by government, and in which the necessity of its interference is least contestible. (Bentham, UC lxxxvii. 2)

After listing the possible sources of mischief, and limiting the focus of the essay to expedients for the prevention of delinquency and misrule (that is, breaches of the trust that constitutes the rationale of government or, in other words, misconduct on the part of the sovereign or her agents), Bentham continues:

> A word or two concerning that branch of government of which the principal destination is to promote good. Opposite as are the ideas annext to the *words* good and evil, this is not equally the case with the *propositions* in which those terms occurr. To avert evil is one way of promoting good; nor will any good which is introduced be acknowledged to be of any value, except in as far as it stands clear of evil. The things themselves being thus intimately blended, the prevention of evil, I mean, and the production of good, it will not be wondered at if the case should be the same with regard to the operations which are planned with a view to the giving birth to such effects.[11]

After introducing political economy, Bentham makes the comment that 'the promotion of positive good' by government is to be assigned to that branch of political economy (the other being the provision of revenue for the exercise of the functions of the state) 'which consists in the promoting the encrease of the national wealth and the national population'. Political economy is thus distinguished from indirect legislation on the one hand, and from police on the other. Further, remember Bentham's list of public trusts for increasing national felicity in *An Introduction to the Principles of Morals and Legislation*: unless promoting the increase of population and wealth could be brought under the rubric of caring for the diseased and the poor and presiding over pleasures respectively, the sphere of the provision of positive good as understood in 'Indirect Legislation' is rather more limited than it is in the former work.[12]

Given the centrality of prevention to Bentham's notion of police, one might expect the latter concept to feature centrally in 'Indirect Legislation', which he summarized as 'the several ways of preventing misdeeds otherwise than by (force of) punishment immediately applied to the very act which is obnoxious' (1971, 127). Like almost all of Bentham's works, 'Indirect Legislation' was written from the perspective of the legislator (in modern parlance, the government, or public policy) whose raison d'être was to 'provide for the happiness of the governed'. From this perspective, as Hume notes, 'indirect legislation was focused ... on the techniques of government, the means of establishing social control' (1981, 96). In the essay, Bentham notes, echoing Blackstone's judgement: 'It is evident enough with regard to any offence whatsoever that any expedients by which the progress of it can be checked without the expence of punishment are better than any which consist in punishment' (Bentham, UC lxxxvii. 13).[13] However, police is very far from being the explicit focus of the essay. The single chapter in which police receives more than a passing mention discusses the amelioration of the political sanction – that is, state-inflicted punishment. Bentham deals first with accessory offences,[14] and then lists 25 'crime-preventing' expedients, ranging from street lighting, to registers of travellers, provision of identifying marks for all subjects of the state, regulation of the sale of poisons, establishment of standard weights and measures, publication of accounts and giving publicity to 'proceedings of state' (Bentham, UC lxxxvii. 35–8). Despite this lack of centrality, Hume is surely correct in judging that Bentham's development of 'Indirect Legislation' 'accounted for and legitimized preventive police as an activity of government', and in reading large swathes of the essay as 'a sort of manual of preventive police' (1981, 77, 97).

We cannot be certain of the reasons why police, which might easily have been adopted as the main subject of 'Indirect Legislation', cuts so marginal a figure in the work. Perhaps one part of the answer lies in the fact that the ostensible subjects of 'Indirect Legislation' – delinquency and misrule – extended to only half of the sphere of police, since Bentham had explicitly excluded from discussion any consideration of the prevention of calamity. Another part may lie in a reluctance to make systematic use of an idea to which he knew that an English audience was liable to react negatively. Finally, while the explanation cannot simply lie in his ignorance of the concept – it is clear from his earlier discussion that he knew more or less what he understood by it – his admission that the concept was too multifarious to be easily definable might also explain his reluctance to make it the centre of his analysis.

In the mid-1780s, Bentham drafted considerable material in French for a projected work, 'Project of a complete body of laws',[15] much of which was used as source material by his Genevan editor and disciple Étienne Dumont for his recension *Traités de législation civile et pénale* (Bentham 1802), while this work was itself later translated and incorporated in various volumes of the Bowring edition of Bentham's works (Bentham 1843). In analysis of the 'Form' of the law, included in that edition as 'A General View of a Complete Code of Laws', Bentham undertook a further brief discussion of police, which is defined as 'a general system of precaution, either for the *prevention of crimes* or of *calamities*' (1843, iii, 155–210, at 169). Bentham's original draft of this discussion survives,[16] and perhaps provides further evidence concerning his hesitation about the term, since he notes that 'Police is one of the vaguest of appellatives: there are few more so, or more intractable: one finds materials from which to nail it down [in import] neither in etymology nor even in usage. Nonetheless, it is necessary to use it still, since however bad a language might be, it is not up to one individual to correct it.'[17] (Bentham, UC lxii. 20) In the final years of his life, Bentham did make provision in his *Constitutional Code* for a 'Preventive Services Minister', whose functions consisted in 'the prevention of delinquency and calamity' (1983, 171), but the intended chapter detailing those functions remained unpublished in Bentham's lifetime, and the version included in the Bowring edition of his works focuses almost exclusively on calamity rather than delinquency (Bentham 1843, ix, 439–41).

In 1798, the idea of police (in both the broad and narrow senses of the word, but with heavy emphasis on the latter) formed the organizing core of Colquhoun's proposals for the establishment of a 'Board of Police'. Just as police appears peripheral to the text of 'Indirect Legislation', indirect legislation makes almost no explicit appearance in Bentham's writings on preventive police.[18] Bentham's Police Bill would have established a Central Board of Police in London, charged with achieving the primary object of the Bill as set forth by Bentham in 'Elucidations relative to the Police Revenue Bill', namely 'subjecting to controul and regulation the conduct of the persons whom it subjects to the obligation of taking out a licence' (Bentham 2018, 89 {UC cl. 727}). In 1794, Colquhoun had proposed that 12 classes of traders known to contain many receivers of stolen goods should be licensed, in order to assist in 'relieving Government of the Expences of a Vigilant … system of Police' (Bentham, UC cxlix. 15–16).[19] In *Treatise on the Police of the Metropolis*, Colquhoun listed 19 classes that should be obliged to register with local magistrates, adding to his earlier list publicans, watch-makers, gold and silversmiths, dealers in furniture and in building materials, stable-keepers and horse-slaughterers (1797, 366–7n).[20] In Colquhoun's evidence to the Finance Committee, he provided two similar lists, the second of which, excepting its omission of one class, coincided exactly with that of 1794 (Lambert 1975, 45–8).[21] Colquhoun had thus repeatedly identified the ease of traffic in stolen goods as an obvious failing on the part of the criminal law, which was traceable partly to not making receipt of such goods a discrete offence, partly to failure to identify, define and prohibit other accessory offences, partly to incompetent drafting, and partly to failure to establish anything like an inventory of dealers in second-hand goods (1797, 10–17, 176–91, 423–4). Bentham played no part in this analysis, which had appeared in print before he made Colquhoun's acquaintance. For his own part, in 'Indirect Legislation' he had discussed accessory offences at length (Bentham, UC lxxxvii. 172–7), and praised the discretionary licensing of public houses (Bentham, UC lxxxvii. 66, 93), which his Bill adopted as its model.

Bentham also agreed with Colquhoun that the drafters of previous statute law were culpable for effectively encouraging offences. As he noted in 1799, in discussion of 'Coin Police': 'The mischiefs that prevail in this department ought not to be imputed to the individual, who is whatever the law makes him or suffers him to be, but to legislation.' (Bentham 2018, 145 {UC cl. 174}). He was thus ready to accept the principle of Colquhoun's analysis enthusiastically, and invested time and effort in suggesting amendments to Colquhoun's list of classes to be licensed, and in reflecting on how best to prioritize their regulation to maximize the prospects of success:[22] as he put it in 'Elucidations relative to the Police Revenue Bill': 'The classes in question are more or less suspected of containing individuals whose dealings are at present not only eventually auxiliary, but wilfully conducive [and] accessory to depredation or other enormities; and the preventing them from being so in future is the object with a view to which the controul is thus proposed to be applied.' (Bentham 2018, 89 {UC cl. 727}).

Both the Thames Police Bill and the Police Bill attempted, in obstructing the trade in stolen goods, to address all three of what Bentham had identified in 'Indirect Legislation' as the necessary conditions for voluntary action, namely power, knowledge and inclination (Bentham, UC lxxxvii. 4, 7–8). Thus, the power of receivers of stolen goods was to be reduced, and their inclination simultaneously modified, by the new obligations to acquire the licence (accompanied by the creation of the new offence of dealing without a licence) (Bentham 2018, 150–5, 183–4 {UC cl. 182–92, 245} (i.e. 'Police Bill' §§ 1, 32)), to keep accounts of receipts and sales, inspectable by the officers of the Board (Bentham 2018, 177–9, 186 {UC cl. 233, 249} (i.e. 'Police Bill' §§ 27, 35)), and to submit to search of premises (Bentham 2018, 184–5 {UC cl. 246–8} (i.e. 'Police Bill' §§ 33–4)). The third condition for voluntary action, knowledge, to the wide dissemination of which Bentham devoted much space in 'Indirect Legislation' (Bentham, UC lxxxvii. 154–71), was central to what Bentham identified in 'Elucidations relative to the Police Revenue Bill' as the secondary object of the Bill, the 'obtaining information' (Bentham 2018, 89 {UC cl. 727}). Thus, the exposure of licensed dealers to observation, not only by police surveyors but by the public, made successful fraud on their part more difficult. Knowledge of offences (and thereby the ability to locate, detain and punish offenders) would be vastly increased by the *Police Gazette* (Bentham 2018, 194–6 {UC cl. 266–7} (i.e. 'Police Bill' §45)). In terms of using increases in public knowledge to reduce offences, reducing temptations to offend by increasing the difficulty of offending, and providing organized invigilation or surveillance, the Police Bill appears to be no less than a systematic exercise in indirect legislation.

Neocleous argues that the modern understanding of police as limited to the control and investigation of crime marks a typically liberal attempt to postulate civil society as an autonomous and spontaneously self-governing sphere that is independent of the state, demonstrating 'liberalism's inability to grasp the nature of state power' (1998, 427). The development of a modern concept of police as an institution for combating disorder in the shape of criminality is presented as proceeding in parallel with the development of classical political economy and its assertion of the 'natural' order of market exchange. For Neocleous, the different treatments given to police by Smith in his unpublished 'Lectures on Jurisprudence' on the one hand (where police refers to a wide-ranging responsibility of government that encompasses, among other things, the best arrangements for generating prosperity), and in *Wealth of Nations* on the other (where it refers exclusively to erroneous and restrictive mercantilist interferences with natural liberty), illustrate the two related developments, and offer a striking example of the change in the meaning of the concept. Under the old understanding, 'because the task of police was the maintenance of order in all its aspects', no meaningful distinction was to be made between 'government' and 'police', since 'the condition of the order which was to be maintained by the police was the order of the state' (Neocleous 1998, 432). Under the new understanding, civil society was understood to be self-policing, or rather as subject to the natural policing of the market, which was identified as 'the operating principle behind civil society. This *depoliticized* the state of prosperity' (1998, 444).

For Neocleous, the consequence of divorcing state from civil society was that the 'concerns of police and the concerns of political economy are torn apart, the science of wealth seemingly cut off from the science of police' (1998, 445). This might be true of Adam Smith, but as Neocleous himself notes elsewhere (2000, 717), it is not true of Colquhoun (and nor, we might add, of Bentham). It might seem surprising, then, that Bentham's political economy does seem to fit Neocleous's characterization of the liberal political economy that emerges from the cleft opened up between state and civil society in Smith's writing, and the corresponding reduction of the sphere of state competence: 'the tasks of the sovereign body are narrowed down to internal and external security and of providing the sort of public works and institutions which it is not in the interest of individuals to supply' (Neocleous 1998, 443). And compare both Bentham's general advice to government in 'Method of an Institute of Political Economy' on its role in directly increasing wealth, that is 'Be quiet' (Bentham, UC xvii. 211, 26 June 1801; Bentham 1952–4, iii, 333), and his recognition that the maintenance of security was the key to the increase of wealth:

> The *application* of the matter of wealth to its several purposes, in the character of an instrument of general *security*, is evidently of anterior and superior importance to the *encrease* of it. But this

class of operations belongs to other heads: to legislation and administration in general—to the establishment of laws distributive and laws penal, and the institution, collation, and exercise, of powers military, fiscal, judicial, and of the police. (Bentham, UC xvii. 322, 11 March 1804)

And further:

> With few exceptions, and those not very considerable ones, the attainment [of] the maximum of enjoyment will be most effectually secured by leaving each individual to pursue the attainment of his own particular maximum of enjoyment in proportion as he is in possession of the means. Inclination in this respect will not be wanting on the part of any one. (Bentham, UC xvii. 218, 22 August 1801; Bentham 1952–4, iii, 337)

For Neocleous, the shrinking in state responsibilities is largely a consequence of the expulsion of the state from any constitutive role in the formation of civil society: 'No longer concerned with the maintenance of the whole social body the art of (liberal) governance is instead occupied with the encouragement of the private pursuit of wealth and the protection of private property' (1998, 446). For Colquhoun (and the same might be said for Bentham), however, 'it is not that the discourse of police is displaced by the discourse of political economy and the system of natural liberty ... but that police and political economy are the two sides of the same discursive coin' (Neocleous 2000, 717–18). Colquhoun is credited with seeing that the naturalness of the social order within which market discipline operates is the artificial construction of concerted state action. In order for the market to function efficiently, its acceptance as an inescapable natural fact requires, as a necessary condition, the establishment of a moral consensus precisely as to its non-artificiality. As Dodsworth puts it, the liberal preventive police is itself underpinned by an understanding and recognition of the central role of the state in creating the social order, 'the idea of prevention emerging as part of a detailed regulatory system that sought to actively create the social order' (2007, 451). Or, with Bentham, 'What the legislator and the Minister of the Interior have it in their power to do towards encrease either of wealth or population is as nothing in comparison with what is done of course, and without thinking of it, by the Judge, and his assistant the Minister of Police' (Bentham, UC xvii. 208, 20 August 1801; Bentham 1952–4, iii, 323).

On the one hand, Bentham would agree with Smith on the importance of security, and especially the security of property, to the achievement of prosperity. On the other, he would utterly reject the liberal 'myth of the market', since he was entirely explicit, as against Smith, in recognizing the manner in which the state, through law, was constitutive of civil society: 'I leave it to Adam Smith and the champions of the rights of man … to talk of invasions of natural liberty, and to give as a special argument against this or that law, an argument the effect of which would be to put a negative upon all laws' (Bentham, UC iii. 223; Bentham 1952–4, iii, 258). How might the apparent contradiction be removed? In Bentham's case, simply by deriving the functions of government from their contribution to the goal of maximizing happiness. As Laval notes: 'A spontaneous economic act in Bentham's sense is not in any case the pure exercise of a natural faculty, it is an act authorized and guaranteed by the law' (2003, 51).[23] In his jurisprudential writings, Smith too recognizes the central role of the state, through law, in constituting civil society. As Ron puts it: 'legislators create through the act of legislation conditions that allow the formation of shared expectations regarding the activity of subjects' (2008, 121). In *Wealth of Nations* especially, Smith is content to exploit the rhetorical appeal to 'natural liberty', but his natural liberty covers very much the same ground as Bentham's security. No more than Bentham does Smith think that anything more than a very temporary exercise of natural liberty is conceivable without the protection of law.

To make the point in reverse, the *sponte acta* of Bentham's political economy coincide more or less exactly with Smith's realm of natural or perfect liberty. Bentham defines *sponte acta* as 'Cases in which, and measures or operations by which, the end is promoted, by individuals acting for themselves; and without any *special* interference exercised with this special view on the part of government; any beyond the distribution made and maintained, and the protection afforded, by the civil and penal branches of the Law' (Bentham, UC xvii. 208; Bentham 1952–4, iii, 323). And compare Smith's description of natural liberty: 'Every man, *as long as he does not violate the laws of justice*, is left perfectly free to pursue his own interest his own way, and to bring both his industry and capital into competition with those of any other man, or order of men' (1976, ii, 687, emphasis added). For both men, security, the enforcement of the protections promised by the legal order, plays the crucial role in both wealth creation and the achievement of whatever happiness human beings can attain. Notwithstanding his employment of the rhetoric of natural liberty, Smith himself is perfectly well aware of the potentially positive and extensive role of the state in providing security, in creating and maintaining the conditions in which citizens can live worthwhile lives, and in addressing the inequities liable to result from failing effectively to regulate the rhetorically 'self-regulating' market.

The substance of Bentham's political economy coincides to a large degree with that of Smith. However, the transformation of civil society into an autonomous, self-regulating sphere is not only absent from Bentham's thought, it is explicitly and roundly rejected. Bentham was simply less disingenuous about the constitutive role of law in establishing the conditions in which commercial societies could flourish. In this sense, Smith's political economy succeeds precisely by making the artificial look natural, and by keeping the supporting machinery out of sight behind the curtain. Bentham, as befits 'a theorist of the art and science of government' (Engelmann 2017, 71), that is, of police in its broadest sense, is concerned precisely with making the machinery transparent and evaluating its effectiveness in delivering welfare.

Bentham agreed with Colquhoun on the importance of policing the poor – that is, the vast majority of the population – in the sense of seeking to influence their moral outlook. Bentham's 1799 contribution to this goal will receive detailed discussion in the article's final section, but, given the importance in a British context ascribed by Neocleous to Colquhoun's groundbreaking concept of 'social police', the connection between policing and poverty demands investigation here. For Neocleous, 'Following Malthus rather than Bentham, Colquhoun was a key figure in effecting a conceptual break in the notion of the "labouring poor" that was to become a crucial conceptual device in the class strategies thereafter' (2000, 715). The prevailing opinion of commentators on Colquhoun's efforts to reform the police is that one of his most original contributions was the advocacy of using official channels of intelligence to mould and direct public opinion. Radzinowicz devotes a subsection to Colquhoun's 'Moralizing Police Gazette' (Radzinowicz 1948–86, iii, 296–8), and Neocleous highlights the way in which Colquhoun sought to construct a moral consensus that would contribute to a significant reduction in offences. The major source on which both rely is Colquhoun's *Treatise on Indigence* (1806), a vastly expanded version of a pamphlet first published in 1799(a). This matters because the assertion of this paper is that the moving spirit behind the *Police Gazette* (as it incontrovertibly was behind the conceptual division between poverty and indigence, which Neocleous describes as 'the key to understanding his [i.e. Colquhoun's] idea of the Municipal Police and, as such, his notion of prevention' (2000, 715)) was not in fact Colquhoun, but Bentham.[24]

For Neocleous, it is only in Colquhoun's hands that the distinction informs official attitudes to the labouring poor, and forms the intellectual core of the new poor law enacted a generation later. Besides the fact that this line of causation completely overlooks the role of Edwin Chadwick, who was not only Bentham's secretary in the final years of his life but was completely familiar with Bentham's poor law writings of 1797–8,[25] it also overlooks Colquhoun's own familiarity with those writings, and the intensive cooperation between Colquhoun and Bentham in 1798–9.

It was certainly the case that Colquhoun consistently bemoaned the moral corruption of the poor, which was only exacerbated by the failings of the penal law (1797, 12–13, 33–8, 242–3). It was also true that Colquhoun connected the spread of crime with that of indigence, and in 1799 proposed the establishment of what he called 'pauper police' (1799a, title page). Again, however, Bentham had anticipated him on the importance of preventing the descent from poverty into the indigence that led to crime. In the 1780s, Bentham had noted that 'The police of charity, in drying up the most fecund source of crimes, becomes at the same time police against offences'[26] (Bentham, UC lxii. 20). Ten years later, the entire point of his detailed schemes for the provision of a whole raft of services – pecuniary, medical, itinerary and informational – to the independent poor was precisely to maintain their independence (2001, 66–140; 2010a, 560–608). As Bentham pointedly noted, once the relevant choice became that between committing crime and starvation, no penalty, however draconian, could deter crime: 'Certain death being the lot of innocence, and only a chance of punishment … the lot of criminality, [is it] not to be expected that … a man should seek to relieve himself by whatever means, whether by fraud or force' (2001, 10). There were similarities between Colquhoun's proposals and those that Bentham had advanced in his own poor law writings. Both men wanted to abolish the parochial postcode lottery, where the quality of relief received depended on the budget and the generosity of local overseers. Both also proposed the systematic examination of mendicants, followed, if appropriate (which for Bentham, but not for Colquhoun, it almost always was) by detention in a House of Industry. However, the two men also differed significantly, most notably over Bentham's proposal for the provision of relief by a joint-stock company (Bentham 2010a, lxxxiv–lxxxv).

Bentham would also plead guilty to advocating the commodification of labour, arguing that the process was a necessary condition for the efficient functioning of a commercial society, and that such societies delivered benefits, to the poor as well as the rich, that outweighed the burdens: 'Security stands before equality: because where there is most inequality … the condition of the lowest, is not so bad, but that want of security may make it worse' (Bentham, UC clxx. 51). His attitude is evinced both in his support of agricultural enclosure, which ended the customary practice of gleaning, and in his readiness to cooperate with Colquhoun and the West India merchants in attempting to criminalize the practice of taking home spillage or spoiled goods. In a sadly fragmentary set of 'Elucidations' to his draft of the Thames Police Bill, Bentham took his stand on the necessity of reducing what he insisted was theft (that is, either pilfering or part-payment in kind, depending on whether the respondent was a West India merchant or a dock worker):

> In every different spot over which it passes, the property passing to and from the Thames is subject to diminution, partly from natural and inevitable waste, but in an incomparably larger proportion to artificial diminution and decrease. In comparison of the latter branch, the quantity of the former is so very small, that were this all, and could it be kept separate from the other, it might without any loss or inconvenience worth regarding be abandoned to any such persons to whom their situation gave the requisite facility, and their industry an adequate motive to collect it. (2018, 40 {UC cl. 96})

Bentham argued that since the necessary separation between natural and factitious waste cannot be made: 'In a case like this, even destruction would be better economy than donation or allowance: it would be better economy to destroy the spillings altogether than to give them to, or suffer them to be taken by, any of the individuals who are occupied in or in the neighbourhood of the spot in which they take place.'

The inescapable inference is that if Colquhoun was one major figure in the development of the legal buttressing of capitalism, Bentham has a strong claim to be another. Bentham makes no principled separation, in the sense of dealing with disconnected and mutually exclusive systems, between police and civil society, or between police and political economy, or, most basically, between state and civil society. He recognized that the state, through the means of law in all its forms, played a creative causative role in the formation of the market. However, he concluded, with Colquhoun and Smith, that the security of property, and the endorsement of the inequality that followed on the distribution of rewards by that market, allied to a state-underwritten guarantee that none would be abandoned to starvation, was the best guarantee of two of the three remaining subordinate ends of legislation (subsistence and abundance), and that in its absence, the only achievable mode of the final subordinate end, equality, would be that of universal indigence and misery (1843, i, 311–12).

The police writings: Colquhoun or Bentham?

Before discussing the details of what is presented in the next two sections as the core of Bentham's original contribution to Colquhoun's project of police reform, the question of authorship demands some assessment. It is reasonable to query the extent to which Bentham's writings on preventive police were his own, and to what extent they were simply an exercise in expressing positions that properly belonged to Colquhoun. Contemporary evidence of Bentham's subordinate role is provided by his repeated contrast between Colquhoun as 'the Author of the System' and himself as the 'drawer' or 'framer' of the Bills (2018, 93–6n, 132n {UC cl. 656, 732, 720}). In relation to both the Thames Police Bill and the Police Bill, Colquhoun appears to have equipped Bentham with a brief, outlining the intended substance of the Bills.[27] In addition, Colquhoun appears to have exercised a veto upon the modifications and amendments put forward by Bentham as a sort of menu that Colquhoun might adopt or reject at pleasure, as evidenced by Bentham's comment that two sections he had drafted for the Police Bill 'may be either retained or struck out, as may be deemed most advisable' (Bentham, UC cl. 693)[28] and his comment on another cancelled passage drafted for 'Notes to the Police Bill': 'Not now. Disapproved by Mr Colquhoun' (Bentham, UC cl. 700).[29]

Some specific evidence of Bentham's input, and of the way in which his Bills were the outcome of a dialogue between the two men, is provided by a brouillon for his first draft of the Thames Police Bill (Bentham, UC cl. 323, 17 and 27 May 1798), where he lists 'Additions proposed in Colq's Paper' to the existing Bumboat Act (2 Geo. III, c. 28), all of which were incorporated in one form or another in Bentham's first draft of the Bill. In relation to Colquhoun's suggestion that imprisonment and whipping be substituted for the fines prescribed by the Bumboat Act, Bentham countered: 'No reason why pecuniary punishment should not remain with increase – it might be doubled for each subsequent offence',[30] and added just such a provision, as well as imprisonment at the magistrate's discretion, to the correspondent section of the Bill (2018, 11–12 {UC cl. 91}).

Reflecting on this three years later, Bentham gave a very modest estimate of his involvement in determining the substance of the Police Bill: 'The principle of the System, and therefore of the *Bill*, being extant [i.e. in Colquhoun's *Treatise on the Police of the Metropolis*] ... I may take upon me to state with the less reserve, that neither the merits nor the demerits of it – whatever they may be – belong to me' (Bentham, UC cxx. 169, 15 February 1802). Bentham went on explicitly to withhold his endorsement of the substance of the measure:

> *Whether, on the ground of preponderant utility, and ultimate eligibility, the principle of that Bill* – supposing it comprehensively and consistently followed up, and carried through all the several applications which the end in view would require to be made of it, in order to give it its full range and efficacy – *would upon the whole stand the test of examination, is a question which, from the first to the last, it never seemed necessary or so much as competent[?] to me, to take upon me to grapple with. What I did see in the principle, was – its indispensable tendency to be productive* – and that in a very high degree – *of the effect aimed at by it – the diminution of the habitual mass of criminality, in the most exuberant and pernicious of its shapes. This was a great and indubitable good. A point I did not tax myself, nor so much as permitt myself, to enquire into, was – whether the price which the system required to be paid for this universally extensive good, in the shape of particular, but unhappily but too extensive, as well as intense, vexation – was worth the purchase.* Of coercion in that shape, as in every other shape – of the thus proposed exercise of the imperative powers of Government ... I need scarcely observe ... that it consists altogether in doing evil, in hopes that good may come. *Of the two opposite masses – the evil done and the good hoped for – which promises to be the greater, is a calculation, which, in the instance the thus proposed measure, as of all other measures of government, requires to be made. In the present instance I do not take upon me to say – I never have taken upon me to say – for there never was any call upon me of any sort to enquire – on which side the ballance would be found to incline.* When I took up the system, it was on the footing suited to the humility, and studied as well as natural obscurity, of my situation, not to speak of the

mediocrity of my intellectual powers. (Bentham, UC cxx. 170–1, 15 February 1802, emphasis added)

If this judgement were taken at face value, the degree of Bentham's input would appear to be very small. However, in his 1799 'Elucidations relative to the Police Revenue Bill', Bentham had been more positive:

> In contemplating the several occupations which for one reason or another had presented themselves as proper to be included in the proposed licencing system for the purposes of Police, it was impossible either for the original Author of the System or for the Drawer of the present Bill … to be insensible to the … opportunities which from time to time presented themselves … for the deriving from the same subject matter an accession in one way or other to the Revenue. The idea of union of these two designs appeared throughout as being uniformly attended with one very considerable and prominent head of recommendation: viz. that of purchasing, at the expence of one and the same mass of *vexation* … two separate and independent masses of benefits: so that, in short, under favour of this combination of views, one of two very good and necessary things, each of which could not be obtained, if aimed at alone, without a very considerable degree of vexation, might thus be obtained *gratis*, and without the payment of any such price. … Happily so close, so natural will the alliance between these two great branches of Government, *Revenue* and *Police*, be found to be, that there is perhaps scarce an instance in which, from the measures suggested in the first instance as necessary by the one, a collateral help may not be afforded to the other. (2018, 132–3n {UC cl. 720–1})[31]

In addition, there are at least three areas in relation to which Bentham's role appears to have been more significant than his later assessment implies. First, in relation to the policing of the Royal Dockyards, Bentham's draft 'Mode of disposing of old Stores' (2018, 44–51 {UC cxlix. 37–45}), which contains all the reworkings and revisions typical of his process of composition, seems a very likely source for the substance of reforms in organization of the sale of naval stores proposed by Colquhoun in a pamphlet published in October 1799 (1799b, 27–32), which was itself reprinted in the sixth edition of *Treatise on the Police of the Metropolis* (1800, 249–87). Second, Bentham himself asserts that the idea of extending the proposed reforms to include 'Arms Police', and to regulate the manufacture, trade and ownership of weapons and ammunition, was his own, and the same appears true of the text he drafted on the subject for 'Elucidations relative to the Police Revenue Bill' (2018, 94–5n, 96–109 {UC cl. 732, 733–50}). Nothing of this nature appears in any publication by Colquhoun. Third, and most centrally for the purposes of this paper, the evidence suggests that if Bentham made a substantive contribution to the Police Bill, it is above all in relation to Part VI. *Gazette* and *Calendar* that it is to be sought. In this regard, it is relevant to note that the *Police Gazette*, a paper to be published by the Board of Police, and intended to disseminate information enhancing the chances of 'detecting and bringing to justice persons guilty of offences' (Bentham 2018, 195 {UC cl. 266}), makes no appearance in early editions of *Treatise on the Police of the Metropolis*, and that discussion of it in later editions is fleeting at best,[32] in contrast to the 25 folios devoted by Bentham to notes to the sections of the Bill that concern the same subject.[33]

The *Gazette* does appear in Colquhoun's evidence to the Finance Committee of 1798, where he outlined its primary role as a conduit of information, before mentioning a supplementary function 'as a Means of conveying Instruction to the innocent … respecting Frauds and other criminal Devices' (Lambert 1975, 56–7). There is good evidence, however, that the author of Colquhoun's published response to the Committee's question,[34] in which he introduces discussion of the *Police Gazette*, was not in fact Colquhoun, but Bentham, since Bentham's autograph draft of that discussion, bearing all the hallmarks of composition, and presumably composed and inserted at proof stage, survives (Bentham, UC cliv. 589–90).[35] Bentham also summarized the first proofs of Colquhoun's three examinations by the Finance Committee, and added, after a summary of the response in question as originally given: 'Here might come in the *Police Gazette* for Correspondence' (Bentham, UC cl. 323ᵛ). The obvious implication is that the *Gazette* had not featured at all in Colquhoun's original evidence, and that therefore, in the absence of Bentham's intervention, the importance attached by Colquhoun to the *Gazette* would have been even more negligible than it appears at first glance.

In relation to the *Calendar of Delinquency*, an annual statement to be published by the Central Board of Police, containing 'information of the number of offences known or suspected to have been committed, under each head of delinquency in each year, in the several parts of this … United Kingdom, together with the result, of each act of delinquency, in respect of punishment or impunity' (Bentham 2018, 79 {UC cl. 163}), a similar pattern emerges. The *Calendar* does not appear in *Treatise on the Police of the Metropolis* until 1800, nor does the name '*Calendar of Delinquency*' appear in Colquhoun's evidence to the Finance Committee, although the substance of the proposal for an annual statement of offences and the outcomes of legal process does (Lambert 1975, 57).[36] In his summary of Colquhoun's evidence, Bentham noted: 'Being asked about a regular annual account of expenditure as a check, he approves of it, and adds a proposal for a Calendar of Delinquency' (Bentham, UC cl. 323^v). If Bentham thus probably invented the name, he might also reasonably be credited with recognizing the importance of regularizing an annual statement of the incidence of crime. In his own 'shadow' draft of the Committee Report, in outlining the functions of the Board of Police, Bentham notes the potential benefits of a 'List of delinquencies committed, with their attendant damage' (Bentham, UC cl. 411), and goes on to emphasize that while a single incidence of such a list or 'picture' would provide much useful information, what was necessary for the purposes of comparison and evaluation of policy was 'a series of such pictures, following one another in regular order at the conclusion of each year' (Bentham, UC cl. 412). No trace of such emphasis appears in Colquhoun and, once more, the idea receives little or no attention from Colquhoun, in contrast with the 34 folios that Bentham devotes to notes to the sections of the Bill concerning the same subject.[37]

The *Calendar of Delinquency* and moral calculation

The *Calendar of Delinquency*, an annual statement of offences committed, including offences unprosecuted, and identifying the outcome of any legal process arising from those offences, was to be presented to Parliament by the Board of Police, which was also to 'suggest all such regulations as in their judgments shall appear best calculated for augmenting the efficacy or, without prejudice to the efficacy, mitigating the severity, of the penal branch of the Law … and for diminishing … the expence' (Bentham 2018, 84 {UC cl. 170}). Data for the *Calendar* would come from the *Police Gazette*, and from returns made by magistrates, police surveyors and jailers. As to its substance, it represented a classic Benthamic demand for the use of evidence in the formulation and evaluation of policy. As he put it in 'Notes to the Police Bill':

> As *Finance* has its annual Budget, so (it is conceived) ought *Police*. The proposed *Calendar of Delinquency* would be the main article

in the Budget of Police. It is by an instrument of this nature, and by this alone, that any explicit index or measure can be afforded, of the demand for improvement in this line at the outset, or progressively of the result … of such exertions as … come to have been made, in that view. (2018, 333 {UC cl. 596})

Bentham contrasts policymaking in matters of police and political economy, arguing that the former does not suffer from the weakness of the latter, in which government intervention was usually a matter of robbing Peter to pay Paul: 'Capital can not be given to one branch of industry without being taken from another: but reductions may be made in the number of offences of any one class committed within the year, without any addition made to the number of any other.' The *Calendar* would allow the evaluation of policy according to its effects, so that it 'will be, to penal legislation, what the *thermometer* is to Chemistry' (Bentham 2018, 334 {UC cl. 598}). It would make rational policymaking based on cost–benefit analysis possible:

> Abstractedly considered, it is easy enough to devise measures that in one shape or other would be serviceable in the way of Police. But will the advantage in each case afford sufficient payment for the vexation and expence? On that question depends the eligibility of each measure: and to that question it is only from the *Calendar of Delinquency* that a substantial and perfectly satisfactory answer can be deduced. (Bentham 2018, 335 {UC cl. 600})

Bentham works through an example of calculation in evaluating a hypothetical proposal that a *Marechausée*, or national watch, be instituted to reduce the incidence of highway robbery. His approach is noteworthy on several counts. First, it seeks to use the proxy of money value to measure the value of a range of variables on a single metric. Second, it is entirely consistent with the method he had set out for estimating the value of pleasures and pains in *An Introduction to the Principles of Morals and Legislation* (1970a, 38–41). Third, it recognizes the limitations of the method and frankly admits that significant relevant variables do not admit of precise measurement. Finally, and notwithstanding those limitations, it cleaves to this method as the only rational means of evaluation.

Using money as a metric offered two major advantages. In the first place, it avoided all of the problems of seeking to measure intensity, the dimension of sensations that Bentham admitted throughout his career to be 'imponderable' – that is, incapable of direct objective measurement (1998, 254). For pains and pleasures that could be translated into money terms, this difficulty was surmounted indirectly. Second, it reduced all values to commensurability on a single metric (Quinn 2014, 77–89). Thus, the estimated cost of the *Marechausée* was assumed to be £40,000, while the *Calendar of Delinquency* was assumed to reveal that the annual value of property lost through highway robbery was £20,000. It seems that the pain of the taxation necessary to fund the watch easily outweighs the potential benefit, especially since the assumption that the watch would completely eliminate highway robbery is likely to prove over-optimistic, so that the alleged benefits will actually amount to something less than £20,000, while the *Calendars of Delinquency* for the years following the implementation of the measure would supply an objective indication of the amount of the reduction. However, although the measure was aimed primarily at deterring highwaymen, it would in all probability deter other offences as well, for instance, smuggling, and its effects on these also required to be taken into account, and, by reference to successive *Calendars of Delinquency*, these effects too might be expressed in money terms. Further, as Bentham had always stressed (1970a, 144–7), to estimate the mischief of offences accurately, the secondary mischiefs of danger (the objective chance of suffering from a similar offence in future), and especially of alarm (the subjective apprehension of danger), had to be added to the primary mischiefs suffered by the victim and their connections. In relation to highway robbery, 'the general apprehension in the neighbourhood of a road on which robberies are frequent, and the restraint on travelling which, to a certain degree, will be the result of such apprehension, remain to be added to the account'. At this point, utilitarian calculation became less precise:

> These *items*, unfortunately, are not to be had in figures. And hence, but hence only, arise those incommensurable quantities by the amount of which the conclusions deducible from this source of information will fall short, in point of certainty and precision, of those which rest in their whole extent on the basis of mathematical demonstration. (2018, 336 {UC cl. 601})

Bentham does not expand on this brief comment, but it is a significant concession to the imperfections of moral calculation. At the minimum, it could be construed as merely a reference to the fact that data on alarm were not intended to be collected by the *Calendar of Delinquency*, and were, therefore, 'not to be had in figures'. However, the reference to 'incommensurable quantities' makes it much more plausible to interpret it as a frank recognition that not every pain or mischief could be accurately expressed in money terms, an admission that Bentham had made early in his career, and never repudiated.[38] Equally important is Bentham's response, which is to move directly from the concession to a qualification, but by no means a retraction, of the claim made early in the discussion that 'nothing can be clearer than the results that may be afforded, nothing more conclusive than the inferences' derived from the *Calendar of Delinquency* (2018, 334 {UC cl. 597}). Utilitarian calculation might be less exact than one would wish, but it remained the only defensible approach for those seeking a rational criterion for the evaluation of rules or institutions.

The 'moralizing *Police Gazette*'

The primary function of the *Police Gazette* was the dissemination of knowledge. As Bentham noted in 'Bill for the establishment of a Board of Police':

> it might contribute in an especial degree to the bringing of offenders to justice, if a channel of appropriate intelligence were established, in such sort that, in and by means thereof information of predatory and other offences might immediately, and without expence, be received from persons aggrieved and others, and convey'd in the same manner to all persons throughout this United Kingdom to whom … opportunity might occurr of contributing to the discovery or apprehending of the Offender, (Bentham 2018, 194 {UC cl. 266})

The idea of a *Police Gazette* was not itself new. Sir John Fielding, principal magistrate for Westminster for more than 25 years, had consistently used newspaper adverts to broadcast descriptions of wanted fugitives, and in the early 1760s submitted to government a general plan of police for London, which argued for 'a Paper established by Law, in which every Thing, relative to the Discovery of Offenders, should be advertised, and that all Persons be bound to take Notice of whatever is advertised therein' (Radzinowicz 1948–86, iii, 478). In 1772, in a series of circulars addressed to magistrates and mayors, he proposed a coordinated national system of reporting and disseminating information relevant to crime, and published and distributed to magistrates and jailers the first issues of the paper he had envisaged, *The Quarterly Pursuit* (Styles 1983; Radzinowicz 1948–86, iii, 47–54, 479–84). In 1773, Fielding succeeded in convincing government to cover the cost of publication and distribution, and the paper continued publication, under several different titles,[39] and was offered to public sale from 1793. Thus, though neither explicitly says so, Bentham and Colquhoun were seeking to build directly on Fielding's work, while a publication that sought to address the need for intelligence which they identified was already in existence.

The *Gazette* of Bentham's Police Bill was to be published weekly or more often, was to be free of stamp duties, and would be distributed without charge to all magistrates, all pub licensees, all licensees under the new system, and all parish officials, both of the Church of England and of dissenting congregations. Bentham estimated this '*factitious* or *forced* circulation' at 100,000 (2018, 324 {UC cl. 580}). The *Gazette* was also to be offered to general sale at a low price, while its cheapness and the combination of natural interest in issues of personal security, and that human prurience that delights in 'true crime', might increase the readership to some 500,000 (Bentham 2018, 325 {UC cl. 581}).

In terms of its content, the *Gazette* was to contain 'all such intelligence, *and such intelligence only*, as … shall be … contributory to the detecting and bringing to justice persons guilty of offences' (Bentham 2018, 195 {UC cl. 266}). More specifically, it would contain intelligence of crimes:

> The ground work – the standing ground work – of it, is composed of the events of the day: – in a word, of *news*: of all species of information the most generally and strongly interesting: and of that species of news which – with reference to the understanding and affections of … the most numerous classes of society – is of all species of news the most interesting. (Bentham 2018, 323 {UC cl. 579})

It was thus primarily a tool for the dissemination of information between understanding and understanding, and thus not dependent for its efficacy on the employment of affective appeals to emotional or political bias. It would facilitate at once reciprocal exchange between public officials charged with the investigation of offences on the one hand, and between members of the public and those officials on the other. In this mode, it was effectively an extension of Fielding's paper, and a direct anticipation of Edwin Chadwick's similar proposal made 30 years later (1829). Fielding had predicted that such dissemination would reduce crime by reducing the power of criminals, who would no longer be able to escape justice (and remain free to undertake new depredations) by the simple expedient of quitting the neighbourhood where the crime was committed.

As noted above, Neocleous identifies the moralizing agenda of Colquhoun's *Police Gazette* as the crucial factor that differentiates it from Fielding's prototype. However, Colquhoun makes absolutely nothing of the *Gazette* as a means of moral instruction before the period of his intense cooperation with Bentham, or indeed for several years after it. As also noted, the *Gazette* does appear in Colquhoun's evidence to the Finance Committee, where he outlined first its primary role as a conduit of information (Lambert 1975, cxii, 59) and then a supplementary role as follows:

> The same Publication might also prove highly useful as a Means of conveying Instruction to the innocent and well disposed Part of the Community, respecting Frauds and other criminal Devices, for the purposes of putting them on their Guard, and occasionally serve as an Instrument for the Promulgation of such Laws, as might not otherwise come within the Knowledge of those whose Conduct they are designed to regulate. (Lambert 1975, 59)

Despite the use of 'instruction' here, the content of that instruction remained limited to factual information: that is, information of a sort that Bentham himself had advised the legislator to disseminate in 'Indirect Legislation', and which he described as 'Furnishing the people with cautionary instructions putting them on their guard against several modes of defraudment and other species of delinquency' (Bentham, UC lxxxvii. 153). Of moral instruction, in the sense of transmitting substantive judgements about right and wrong, there is no hint in Colquhoun's evidence.

In support of the assertion that Colquhoun wished the *Gazette* to be a moralizing force, Neocleous relies on the 1806 edition of *Treatise on Indigence*, published seven years after the composition of Bentham's 'Notes to the Police Bill'. In 1806, Colquhoun does indeed stress the role of the *Gazette* in moral reformation, recommending that it should include 'Occasional short essays, conveyed in familiar language, enlivened and rendered interesting by the introduction of *narrative*, as often as circumstances will admit' (1806, 98). Among the subjects to be covered were 'Religious and moral Duties', under which head 24 sub-themes were listed, including 'sloth and idleness, and lounging in ale-houses', 'frugality and sobriety', 'patience under adversity', 'the commendable pride of rearing a family without parish assistance' and 'the great advantages arising from the provident care of the earnings of labour during early life' (1806, 98–100). It seems probable that Colquhoun's focus on the role of the *Gazette* in reforming the moral outlook of the poor owed something to the influence of Bentham. As early as 1782, in discussing the 'culture of the moral sanction' in 'Indirect Legislation', Bentham had advised that government might sponsor morally improving works of literature, featuring 'virtue represented as amiable, vice in odious, colours: the former rewarded; the latter punished' (Bentham, UC lxxxvii. 18).

Bentham's own focus on the moralizing influence of the *Gazette* emerges in his 'Notes to the Police Bill'. When he begins to offer examples of the additional benefits provided by the *Gazette*, he first offers uses that exemplify the importance of disseminating factual information, and which he had used almost 20 years before in 'Indirect Legislation', namely the prevention of escapes, desertion and double-enlistment, and he cannot forbear proposing that identity tattoos might be rendered compulsory for members of the armed services, though clearly not anticipating a positive response (Bentham 2018, 320–1 {UC cl. 572}). It is in his next suggestion, involving the distribution of the *Gazette* to non-conformist congregations, that Bentham moves from transparent communication of fact between understanding and understanding, to the far from transparent collection of information about specific subgroups of the population:

> *Government will open to itself a channel through which, without committing itself, it will be able to address itself at any time to the various classes of non-conformists.* ... From the occasion of transmitting the papers in question to those several congregations, an exact and constant acquaintance with the numbers and situations of them will be obtained *without the appearance of being sought, and the attention of the local Surveyors of the Board will be pointed to the numbers and deportment of the individuals of whom these congregations are respectively composed.* (2018, 321–2 {UC cl. 574}, emphasis added)

Not only would the *Gazette* generate information about minorities whose loyalty could not be taken for granted, but the gradual acceptance of the *Gazette* as an interesting but objective source of information would make possible the undetected transmission of preferences and of will, by exploiting a cognitive gap – an asymmetry in knowledge about the functions of the *Gazette* – between government and its readers:[40]

> And when, for purposes not exposed to repugnance or suspicion, this sort of channel of communication has once been established in the several assemblies, and the minds of the members have become familiarized with the use of it, it will be easy, if on any occasion it should become desirable, *to make use of it for the purpose of conveying any impressions which it may be wished to produce with a view to the execution of justice or the preservation of the public peace.* (2018, 322 {UC cl. 575}, emphasis added)

Indeed, Bentham goes on to identify the use of the *Gazette* in the 'capacity of being employed as an instrument for the propagation and maintenance of social dispositions and affections, and for the preservation of tranquillity, harmony, and loyalty among the great body of the people', as a use 'though but collateral, and *not proper to be mentioned in the Bill, … still more important, perhaps, than even the direct one*' (Bentham 2018, 322 {UC cl. 576}, emphasis added). The intended audience of Bentham's commentary on the Police Bill were decision-makers in government. It seems reasonable to assume that among the reasons for the omission of this use from the Bill itself was that it is difficult to successfully manipulate the sentiments of people who you have just made aware of your intention.

Bentham noted that reports of the apprehension and punishment of offenders, which, if all went well, would increasingly constitute the bulk of the *Gazette's* contents, were in themselves 'a perpetual lesson of morality and of submission to the laws':

> But besides this, though precluded from the circulation of every thing *else* that can bear the name of *news*, it need not be, nor ought it to be, expressly precluded (and if not *expressly*, it will not be regarded as *virtually* precluded) from administering useful instruction and exhortation of the moral, and, upon occasion, the political cast, in whatever forms may from time to time present themselves as best adapted to the purpose. (Bentham 2018, 323 {UC cl. 576}, emphasis added)

Since newsworthy events do not happen at regular intervals, all newspapers are liable to suffer from slow news days. Fortunately, 'inequalities of this kind are what all newspapers are in the habit of supplying, for the purpose of exhibiting on each day of publication a paper of a uniform size'. In consequence, in the *Gazette* this 'collateral part' would 'pass not as a novelty, nor as directed to any special end, but as coming in as a matter of course, in conformity to the custom of the trade':

> The occasional superstructure, the *didactic* part, will have at any rate the circumstance of contiguity, to cement the idea of it in the mind with the idea of the other part, and thus obtain for it a portion of the same favour: and by grafting it upon the other, as the moral is upon the fable, the sermon upon the text – or (to come nearer) the *observation* part in a newspaper upon the intelligence part which gives occasion to it – the association will be rendered still more intimate and indissoluble. (2018, 323–4 {UC cl. 579}, emphasis added)

Bentham thus explicitly advises government to add moral to fable, sermon to text, conscious direction of moral and political preferences to provision of factual information. The communication of will to will is facilitated by familiarity with the *Gazette*, and the (mis)identification of it purely as a channel of communication of understanding to understanding. To the *Gazette's* ostensible role, as a conduit of factual information, is added an esoteric role as the shaper of opinions, and it is precisely the establishment and general acceptance of its fulfilment of the former role that creates the opportunity to exploit its potential for the latter. In a draft that was omitted from his final text, Bentham was candid about the duplicity involved:

> But the sort of Sermon which might be practised, and practised without ceasing in the *Police Gazette*, this *unannounced and unsuspected Sermon, cautiously, sparingly, and in a manner imperceptibly, though at the same time unremittingly, insinuated into a publication composed principally, and to appearance exclusively,* of that sort of matter which, so long as man is man, can never lose … its hold upon the affections – especially of those otherwise untutored minds, for whose direction it is more especially designed – there would be neither end nor limit to its influence. (Bentham, UC cl. 279ᵛ, emphasis added)[41]

Bentham anticipates an objection that moral lectures are not an appropriate feature of a government newspaper, since such lessons ought to be read rather in the Bible: 'In a Newspaper (who does not know it?) a man will read, and read throughout, what he would not so much as look at elsewhere. … In his Bible, a man can *not* be made to read the *Police Gazette*: but in the *Police Gazette* he *might* be made to read his Bible' (2018, 330 {UC cl. 589}). Once more, he describes the unique strength of the *Gazette* as the manner in which its declared function – the dissemination of factual information – paves the way for its undeclared function – the manipulation of moral and political preferences. No self-declared propaganda sheet could aspire to such influence:

> No paper bearing a name of party on its title-page – though it were the party of the country – *No paper which aimed avowedly at this object, can act in pursuit of it with nearly equal advantage and effect. Hanging out such a sign, it presupposes on the part of its customers the presence of those very dispositions the absence of which is the cause that produces the demand for it. Addressing itself to none but those whose affections are already engaged, and deeply engaged, on the same side, it gives warning to those on the other side to shut their doors against it, and to those who are neutral or indifferent, to put themselves upon their guard against its influence.* (2018, 329 {UC cl. 587}, emphasis added)

The *Gazette* would do better:

> Five hundred thousand forms … but a part – of the audience to which the sort of *sermon* in question would be preached weekly and as much oftener as was thought fit, addressed to ears the attentiveness of which would not be subject to those causes of failure which affect the efficacy of other sermons. Not a nook nor a cranny in which this antidote would not be sure to meet whatever poisons of the moral or political kind either actually are or ever can be administered: and beyond that, the antidote would preoccupy and preserve thousands and thousands of minds, in places into which the poison … can never hope to penetrate. (2018, 325 {UC cl. 581})

I have argued elsewhere that some of the expedients of 'Indirect Legislation' presented by Bentham seem to fly in the face of his commitment to transparency (Quinn 2017, 29–32). In discussion of the *Police Gazette*, he repeatedly urges government to exploit its ostensibly objective nature, and the public perception of its objectivity, to pass off substantive moral judgements and condemnations as equally objective. Needless to say, a government-inspired moral catechism that declared itself to be a moral catechism would do nothing but alert the 'neutral or indifferent, to put themselves upon their guard against its influence'. The contrast with 'Transparency Bentham', the apostle of the conjunction of rule with rationale, and of the exposure of all exercises of public power to unremitting public scrutiny, could hardly be more stark. In 1782, in 'Indirect Legislation', Bentham had written:

> There are but two plans of dealing with the people that bear any tolerable colour of propriety: perfect mystery or perfect unreserve. To exclude the people perfectly and absolutely from the knowledge of their affairs, or to give them as perfect a state of them as possible: to shut the door of intelligence altogether, or to throw it open as wide as possible: to keep them from forming any judgment at all, or to enable them to form a right one: in a word, to deal with them like beasts or to deal with them like men. (Bentham, UC lxxxvii. 110)

How might this tension be reduced, or at least explained? The short answer is fear. It has been a commonplace for many years that the 1790s was a decade during which Bentham wrote some very unBenthamic things. Ideally, communication should take place between understanding and understanding, on the basis of facts, but, noted Bentham in 1794, 'The people are all *will* – they have no reason, no understanding. ... A proposition must be extremely simple or their minds can not take hold of it – and when they do, it can only be through the medium of their affections' (Bentham, UC xliv. 2). A year before drafting the Police Bill, Bentham hoped to interest government in his plan for the reform of the poor laws, partly by the promise therein contained to deliver loyal, docile subjects, who might provide a dependable supply of manpower to supplement the armed forces (2010a, 193–6, 613–16). In 'Notes to the Police Bill', Bentham goes so far as to describe Pitt's Seditious Meetings Act (36 Geo. III, c. 8), which proscribed political meetings of 50 persons or more unless licensed by magistrate, as 'a second *Magna Charta*, preserving against attacks still more destructive that security which the first had formed' (2018, 327 {UC cl. 585}). However, the Seditious Meetings Act had failed to regulate the written word, while the *Police Gazette* is presented as a gentle alternative to explicitly licensing the press (2018, 328 {UC cl. 586}). Again, dissembling on the part of government is explicitly recommended, to the end that an exercise in political indoctrination might be passed off as the dissemination of news. This is the same Bentham who had been arguing for 20 years that freedom of the press was among the defining characteristics of a free state (Bentham, UC lxxxvii. 18; 1977, 485; 2002, 54–61).

If the obvious cause of Bentham's embrace of duplicity was the continuing threat from Revolutionary France, the specific (if undeclared) purpose of the *Police Gazette* was to defeat the enemy within:

> The French may be the most conspicuous, but they are by no means the most determined nor the most formidable enemies of national repose: the most formidable enemies by far which the country has are in her own bosom. Of these the country can not be cleared by any power or by any industry: all that can be done ... is *to guard the minds of the susceptible and thoughtless multitude* against the poisons which it is their incessant endeavour to disseminate. Against dangers of this kind (the source of every other) the force of arms and hands is unavailing: for combating pens or tongues, pens or tongues are weapons altogether indispensable. (2018, 326 {UC cl. 584}, emphasis added)

The vipers lurking in the body of the state were those who had imbibed the democratic and egalitarian ideas popularized by Tom Paine. Schofield notes that one consequence of the French Revolution was to delay political reform in Britain 'by delaying the creation and propa-gation of the utilitarian case for democracy' (2006, 108). When he finally made that case in private in 1809 – it would be published only in 1817 – Bentham admitted in a draft passage: 'In the endless catalogue of calamities and mischiefs of which the French revolution has been the source, not the least is that which consists in the severe and hitherto paralizing check given to peaceable and rational reform in every shape imaginable' (Bentham, UC cxxvii. 47, 18 August 1809).

The later Bentham believed that only the systematic exposure of all exercises of public authority to public scrutiny, combined with the institutionalization of dislocability and thoroughgoing democratic accountability, could avert the dangers of misrule. To the Bentham of 1799, however, the preservation of property, and thereby of security, against a radicalized majority of non-proprietors justified not only the exclusion of the latter from the franchise, but the surreptitious effort to manipulate their moral attitudes and thus stave off mob rule, mass expropriations and the destruction of the security of all. Both Benthams are utilitarian, while the crucial difference between them concerns the level of the threat to security posed by the poor, and the consequent justification of manipulating their political preferences for their own good. The Bentham of the preventive police writings, who identified democracy as a clear and present danger to security and the maintenance of the social order, is a very different animal from the newly radical Bentham who reflected sadly 10 years later: 'Scared out of our wits by distant anarchy, we have been drawn into the ever open arms of domestic despotism' (Bentham, UC cxxvii. 47, 18 August 1809).

Notes

1   The first volume in the new edition was published in 1968 (Bentham 1968), and to date 33 of a projected 80 volumes have been published. For further details, see the Bentham Project website at https://www.ucl.ac.uk/bentham-project/.
2   A pre-publication version of *Preventive Police* is available at http://discovery.ucl. ac.uk/10055084/.
3   Part I. Writings on Marine Police contains Bentham's first draft of the 'Thames Police Bill' (i.e. 'A Bill to explain and amend an Act intituled An Act to prevent the committing of Thefts and Frauds by persons navigating Bum-boats and other Boats, upon the River of Thames') and a partial 'Contents' thereof; two précis of his revised and expanded version of the Bill; an incomplete set of 'Elucidations' of the revised Bill; and a discrete discussion of the best means of disposing of unserviceable naval stores. Part II. Writings on the Police Bill contains an early précis or 'Heads' of the Bill (i.e. *'Heads* of the *Draught* of a *Bill* to be intituled A Bill for the granting to his Majesty certain duties on Licences, for the establishment of a Board of Police Revenue, for the suppression of divers Offices, and for the more effectual prevention of Larcenies and other Offences, by the regulation of divers trades and occupations, and the establishment of a system of prompt and all-comprehensive Correspondence for Police purposes'); an essay for which Bentham's working title was 'Preliminary Observations', but that he eventually entitled 'Elucidations relative to the Police Revenue Bill'; a set of 'Introductory Observations' (followed by an Appendix containing an incomplete discussion of coin police); the full text of the Police Bill (i.e. 'A Bill for the establishment of a Board of Police, and for the suppression of divers Offices:—or else, A Bill for the establishment of a Board of Police, for the suppression of divers Offices, and for the more effectual prevention of predatory and other offences, by the licencing and regulation of divers trades and occupations'), as revised early in 1799 (followed by an Appendix containing a 'Table of Precedents'); and finally a set of 'Notes to the Police Bill: containing Reasons, Precedents, and other Elucidations' (followed by an Appendix, 'Anonymous Information', drafted for but excluded from 'Notes to the Police Bill').
4   *Preventive Police* is the first volume in the *Collected Works* to benefit from the efforts of the volunteers of Transcribe Bentham, the award-winning crowdsourcing transcription initiative established in 2010. For further details visit https://www.ucl.ac.uk/bentham-project/transcribe-bentham.
5   This work, first published in 1796, went through six editions by 1800, while the seventh, published in London in 1806, appears to have been a reprint of the sixth. Except where otherwise indicated, references are to the fourth edition. Colquhoun had first developed proposals for licensing dealers in second-hand goods in 1793, and outlined a Bill for the purpose in 1794, documents relating to which survive among Bentham's papers at

University College London: see 'Reasons offered in favour of the Bill for establishing Regulations for the purpose of preventing frauds and embezzlements by obliging certain Classes of Dealers who are generally Known to be Receivers of Stolen Goods to take out Licences' (Bentham, UC cxlix. 12–13), 'Explanatory Observations' (Bentham, UC cxlix. 14–22) and 'Queries, Answers and Observations' (Bentham, UC cxlix. 23–7) on an identical or very similar Bill.

6   For the use of the word 'policy' in this context in the 1790s, see, for instance, William Pitt's comment on 21 February 1798, in debate on the first 22 reports of the Select Committee on Finance, that he intended to transfer the functions of the Commissioners of Hawkers and Pedlars to 'another Board', but deferred any motion 'on the question of policy' (Great Britain, Parliament 1797–1802, v, 313).

7   Hanway (1775, 93) defined police as 'good regulations for the œconomy and preservation of the people, who are all entitled to one common freedom, so long as they act properly in their several stations'.

8   Smith (1978, 5) defined the first design of government as justice, and the second as police, while 'Whatever regulations are made with respect to the trade, commerce, agriculture, manufactures of the country are considered as belonging to the police'. Sir William Mildmay (1763) published a discussion of the police of France, which on the one hand disseminated awareness of the continental understanding, but it may also have contributed to its connection with the administration of despotic states.

9   A recognizance, similar in effect to a bail bond, was a formal acknowledgement undertaken before a court of a debt to the Crown, which debt was voided if certain behavioural conditions were satisfied by the undertaker. If the undertaker breached the conditions, he was obliged to settle the debt named in the recognizance. In his unpublished essay 'Indirect Legislation', Bentham described recognizances as a 'striking and masterly provision ..., so justly celebrated by the Author of the Commentaries' (Bentham, UC xcix. 256). In his 'Notes to the Police Bill', however, Bentham criticizes the recognizances employed in licensing publicans as 'a contrivance for obtaining by force of law, a forced consent to a penalty, which, being fixed and the same in the case of every transgression, has infinity to one against its propriety in each instance that occurs: at the same time that without any such consent it is equally in the power of the law to subject a man in each case of transgression to a penalty adapted in quality as well as quantity to the nature of the case' (Bentham 2018, 265 {UC cl. 500}).

10 The full sentence runs as follows: 'Time out of mind the military department has had a name: so has that of justice: the power which occupies itself in preventing mischief not till lately, and that but a loose one: for the power which takes for its object the introduction of positive good, no peculiar name, however inadequate, seems yet to have been devised.' *An Introduction to the Principles of Morals and Legislation* was largely printed in 1780, but was not published until 1789 (Bentham 1970a). In 1782, Bentham also wrote three additional chapters in continuation of this text, the first two of which expanded to book length. The first – 'Of the Limits of the Penal Branch of Jurisprudence', which was edited by H. L. A. Hart as *Of Laws in General* and appeared in the *Collected Works* in 1970 (Bentham 1970b), before being revised by Philip Schofield and reissued under its original title – focuses on the question of what is to be understood by a complete law, and mentions police only briefly (Bentham 2010b, 165–7). A preliminary text of the third, 'Place and Time', appeared in a collection of *Selected Writings* in 2011 (Bentham 2011, 152–219). A preliminary text for the second, 'Indirect Legislation', was prepared by Charles F. Bahmueller in the early 1980s, but lack of funding to complete the editorial work has thus far prevented its appearance in the *Collected Works*.

11 In quotations from Bentham's manuscripts, his spelling and capitalization are retained in most instances, although some discretion is exercised with regard to his punctuation, which is often inconsistent and sparse.

12 In *An Introduction to the Principles of Morals and Legislation* (1970a, 263n), Bentham listed potential offences against national, as opposed to public, wealth (idleness being the first listed), and against population (emigration, suicide, procurement of impotence or barrenness, abortion, unprolific coition, celibacy).

13 See also UC lxxxviii. 7: 'The business of legislation, so much of it at least as we are now considering, is to exclude mischief. Now there are two methods by which the business of excluding mischief may be endeavoured to be compassed: 1. by preventing the acts from

which mischief is expected to arise: 2. by excluding the mischief itself, although the acts from which it might otherwise arise, should happen to have taken place.'

14 The discussion (Bentham, UC lxxxvii. 29–38) is headed 'Indirect', and subheaded 'Political', the latter being a reference to the political, as opposed to the physical, moral or religious sanctions.

15 The full title of this projected work is 'Projet d'un corps de loix complet, à l'usage d'un pays quelconque: avec les principes et les raisons tant générales que particulières sur lesquelles chaque disposition aura été fondée' (Bentham, UC xcix. 156) (i.e. 'Project of a complete body of laws for the use of any country: with principles and reasons as much general as particular on which each disposition will have been founded').

16 Bentham's original draft of this passage (Bentham, UC lxii. 20) differs significantly from Dumont's version, in providing not one but two enumerations of the functions of police. The first, differentiated according to the end in view, consisted of seven functions, which Bentham notes might be divided into 'police de nécessité' (police of necessity) and 'police de surérogation' (police of supererogation). The second, differentiated according to the species of article with which a particular branch was concerned, consisted of 13 branches, which Bentham notes might be divided into 'police des villes' (town police) and 'police de la campagne' (countryside police).

17 The original reads: 'Police, c'est un appellative des plus vagues: il y en a plus, et plus intractables[?]: on ne trouve de quoi le fixer, ni dans l'etymologie, ni dans l'usage même. Cependant, il faut s'en server toujours, car quelque mauvaise que soit une langue, il ne depend pas d'un particulier de le corriger.'

18 The single occurrence in the text comes in an incomplete discussion of 'Coin Police' (Bentham 2018, 143 {UC cxlix. 178}): 'In the tracing out the several separate links in a chain or fluxion of acts or transactions thus connected is one of the resources of what may be termed *indirect legislation*: to create proofs of the criminative consciousness above spoken of, or even to give birth to the perception[?] itself, is another, but of this a little farther on.' In a related brouillon (Bentham 2018, 144n {UC cl. 171}), in a list of 'Topics *Tractandi* per J.B.', the following appears: '6. Indirect legislation, by subjecting to Inspection and exposing to observation the practice of innocent arts the products of which are easily transferable to this criminal purpose.'

19 The classes were: '1. Dealers in Old Naval Stores not used for the purpose of making Paper 2. Wholesale Dealers in Naval Stores, Hand Stuff, Rags &c. 3. Retail Dealer in Rags, Hand Stuff &c for making paper. 4. Dealers in Second-Hand Wearing Apparel &c. 5. Itinerant Dealers in wearing Apparel &c. 6. Pawn Brokers and Salesmen Selling unredeemed Pledges privately 7. Wholesale Dealers in Iron and other Metals 8. Retail Dealers in Old Iron and other Metals. 9. Manufacturers purchasing Metals of persons not Licensed 10. Founders and Others having and using Crucibles, Melting Pots &c. 11. Persons being Licensed Dealers Keeping Draught Carts for Conveying Stores, Rags, Metals &c. 12. [Persons being Licensed Dealers Keeping] Truck Carts for the above purpose.'

20 Colquhoun's iterations of lists of classes to be licensed are often difficult to compare directly, in that, for instance, sometimes trades are divided into retail and wholesale branches, and sometimes not.

21 The omitted class was 'Pawn Brokers and Salesmen selling unredeemed Pledges privately'. A further list of 14 classes (with the addition of 'Horse-slaughterers, Livery-Stable keepers and Auctioneers') was contained in 'Appendix A' to the Report, 'Copy of a Letter from Patrick Colquhoun and Charles Poole, Esquires, to George Rose, Esquire, relative to the Establishment of a Central Board of Police Revenue' (Lambert 1975, 39–44, at 43).

22 On 18 October 1798 Bentham compiled a 'Police Bill Contents' (Bentham, UC clvii. 9), which identified the following 34 'Classes of Trades and Occupations [proposed to be] subjected to Licence': '1. Dealers in Second-hand Household Goods &c. 2. Wholesale Dealers in Rags and Cordage for Paper-making. 3. Retail Dealers in Rags and Cordage for Paper-making. 4. Dealers in Second-hand Apparel, Made-up Piece Goods and Remnants. 5. Itinerant Dealers in Second-hand Apparel, Made-up Piece Goods and Remnants. 6. Dealers in Second-hand Naval Stores. 7. Wholesale Dealers in Second-hand Metals. 8. Retail Dealers in Second-hand Metals. 9. Purchasers of Second-hand Metals for working up. 10. Metal Founders. 11. Dealers in Second-Hand Building Materials. 12. Cart-Keepers for Second-hand Goods. 13. Hand-Cart-Keepers for Second-hand Goods. 14. Forfeited-Pledger Seller[s]. 15. Water-Hawkers and Bumboat-Keepers. 16. Purchasers of Ship's Stock. 17. Master or Principal

Lumpers. 18. Common Lumpers. 19. Horse Dealers. 20. Post-Horse Letters. 21. Stage-Coach Keepers. 22. Gunpowder-Makers. 23. Wholesale Gunpowder Dealers. 24. Retail Gunpowder Dealers. 25. Makers of Fire-Arms. 26. Dealers in Fire-Arms. 27. Artillery Founders. 28. Makers of edged and pointed weapons. 29. Dealers in edged and pointed weapons. 30. Livery Stable Keepers. 31. Slaughterers, Flayers, and Boilers. 32. Letters of Lodgings ready-furnished of the 1st Class. 33. – of the 2^d class. 34. – of the 3^d class.' In 'Elucidations relative to the Police Revenue Bill' (Bentham 2018, 91–3n {UC cl. 729–30}), he indicated a total of 31 classes that had been considered by either Colquhoun or himself for inclusion in the licensing system. Twenty-eight classes appear in both lists, while each includes three classes not found in the other, and the variation in the total number arises from differences on whether and how far to subdivide two classes common to both. With the exception of the omission of '10. Metal-Founders', the first 14 classes in the list of 18 October 1798 coincide in name and order with the 13 classes of '*Licentiandi*' in Bentham's 'Bill for the establishment of a Board of Police'. The earlier drafted 'Heads of the Police Bill' had also included classes 15–18 and 31 of the list given in 'Elucidations relative to the Police Revenue Bill', that is, Water-Hawkers and Bum-boat Keepers, Purchasers of Ship's Stock, Master-Lumpers, Working Lumpers and Slaughterers. The progressive reduction in the number of classes appears to have been tactical, and intended to reduce possible sources of opposition by reducing the scope of the Bill, with a view to the passage of up to five additional Bills in due course: see Bentham's explicit discussion of this tactic in 'Introductory Observations relative to the Board-of-Police Bill' (Bentham 2018, 137–8 {UC cl. 126–7}).

23 The French text reads: 'Un acte économique spontané, au sens de Bentham, n'est en aucun cas l'exercice pur d'une faculté naturelle, c'est un acte autorisé et garanti par la loi.'

24 Colquhoun appropriated the distinction wholesale (Bentham 2001, xix–xx; Poynter 1969, 200–2). It is true that the distinction appears in Colquhoun's *State of Indigence*, written in 1799 (1799a, 18), but that was more than two years after he had encountered it in Bentham's 'Essays on the Poor Laws' (2001, 1–140, at 3–5), which Bentham sent to him in December 1796 (Bentham 1981, 349). In 1806, Colquhoun restated the distinction, without attribution, in precisely Bentham's terms (1806, 7–8). Bentham himself had introduced the central definition of indigence as early as the mid-1780s, when drafting material in French on civil law (Bentham, UC xxxii. 42): 'By the indigent, I mean all those who find themselves outside the condition of supplying themselves with necessaries. By relief to their needs, I mean the supply of these same necessaries.' (The original reads: 'Par indigens, j'enten[d]s tous ceux qui se trouvent hors d'état de se fournir à eux-mêmes le necessaire. Par subvention à leurs besoins, j'enten[d]s la fourniture de ce même necessaire.')

25 Edwin Chadwick edited Bentham's 1797 work 'Observations on the Poor Bill' (Bentham 2001, 217–63) for private circulation in 1838 (Bentham 2001, xlvii–xlix).

26 The original reads: 'La police de charité, en tarissant la source la plus féconde des crimes, devient en même temps police contre délits.'

27 In relation to the Thames Police Bill, Bentham referred twice to 'Colquhoun's Paper' (Bentham, UC cl. 323 [17 and 27 May 1798], 314 [May 1799]), which is likely to be identified with a set of propositions for the reform of the Bumboat Act drafted by Colquhoun for circulation within government. See UC cl. 315, headed 'Observations on the marginal Annotations written in pencil on the margin of the original draught of Mr Colquhoun's "*Propositions*" intended for the Admiralty &[c.]'. In relation to the 'Bill for the establishment of a Board of Police', he refers several times in 'Notes to the Police Bill' to 'the Instructions' given by Colquhoun (2018, 286, 287, 294 {UC cl. 529, 530, 538}). Unfortunately, neither document has been located.

28 §§ 30–1 of Bentham's 'Heads of the Police Bill' empowered the Police Board to regulate the dress and working hours of Lumpers and Water-Hawkers. In the event, since both classes were omitted from the revised Bill, so were these two sections. Bentham's 'Short Heads of a Bill for the more effectual prevention of depredations on the River Thames', § 17 (2018, 26 {UC cxlix. 146}), contained a similar provision in relation to Lumpers.

29 The note in question concerned a proposal to limit the geographical range of licences issued to 'Walking Purchasers of Second-hand Apparel &c'.

30 Colquhoun (1797, 69) had argued that the fines imposed by the Bumboat Act were ineffective, since they were paid from a subscription fund arising from the profits of trade in stolen goods.

31 It should also be noted that Bentham's 1802 comment referred to a version of the Bill that he had not finally approved, and which he was thus in no position to endorse in detail: 'The copy ... was one that had never passed under my review. How far it may be a correct one, was accordingly, and still is, a matter of entire uncertainty to me' (Bentham, UC cxx. 174–5, 9 March 1802).

32 The *Police Gazette* does not appear in the first five editions of *Treatise on the Police of the Metropolis*, published between 1796 and 1797, but is first mentioned by Colquhoun in his 1798 evidence to the Finance Committee (Lambert 1975, 59). The *Gazette* also appears once in Colquhoun's 1799 pamphlet *General View of the National Police System* (Colquhoun 1799c, 5–6), in the form of a quote from the Committee report. As late as 1800, in the sixth edition of *Treatise on the Police of the Metropolis* (Colquhoun 1800, 539), Colquhoun devotes exactly three lines to the *Gazette*, once more in quoting from the report.

33 That is, UC cl. 571–95 (Bentham 2018, 319–33). §§ 45–7 of Bentham's Bill (2018, 194–9 {UC cl. 266–71}) dealt with the *Police Gazette*.

34 The question to which Colquhoun was responding was 'What are the Ramifications of your Plan of Police with respect to the Country? Whom do you look to as the Correspondents of your Central Board; and who do you propose should grant the Licences to the different Traders in the Country?' (Lambert 1975, 56).

35 Bentham has noted in the margin in relation to the passage quoted 'Quere', while he follows it with the following passage, which he has bracketed for possible deletion, and of which he has noted 'To be inserted or not?': 'and by proper warnings[?] to the memory it might be made to act as an antidote to moral corruption of every sort'. A further fragment in Bentham's hand, headed 'Police Revenue Report' (Bentham, UC cl. 421–2), contains a discussion of the *Police Gazette* that is similar in substance to that at UC cliv. 589–90, and may be an earlier version of it. Yet a third version of Colquhoun's response, in a copyist's hand, is at UC cl. 422^v. The published version of Colquhoun's response is not identical to Bentham's draft at UC cliv. 589–90, but with the exception of the addition of a final paragraph, the differences are minor. A fair copy of Colquhoun's third examination, as published, is at UC cl. 308–11. Bentham's discussion of the *Police Gazette* for his own draft of the Committee report is at UC cl. 387–90.

36 The Committee reported the proposal as 'deserving the attentive Consideration of the House' (Lambert 1975, 33). The term '*Calendar of Delinquency*' appears twice in *General View of the National Police System* (Colquhoun 1799c, 5, 10), though seemingly with reference simply to the annual aggregate of offences, rather than to any specific formal annual statement thereof. The expression appears four times in the sixth edition of *Treatise on the Police of the Metropolis* (Colquhoun 1800, 341, 539, 543, 638). Of these, the second and third are verbatim repetitions of the *General View of the National Police System* references, while the other two both use the plural form, and again seem to refer simply to the annual total of offences rather than to any proposed formal annual statement thereof.

37 That is, UC cl. 596–629 (Bentham 2018, 333–54). §§ 48–51 of Bentham's Bill (2018, 199–206 {UC cl. 272–83}) dealt with the *Calendar of Delinquency*.

38 Bentham frankly admitted the incommensurability between the pleasure of monetary gain and of the satisfaction of ill will (2010b, 204–5): 'A man falls upon you and beats you: what pecuniary loss is there that you could be sure would give him just so much pain as the satisfaction of giving vent to his ill-will promised to afford him pleasure. It is plain that, between quantities so incommensurate, there is no striking a sure balance.'

39 From 30 September 1797 it appeared under the title *Police Gazette, or Hue and Cry*.

40 Bentham took the opportunity to reprise another theme that had figured in 'Indirect Legislation' (Bentham, UC lxxxvii. 23–4, 181–4), namely the unquestionable utility, in Catholic countries, of the buttressing of the political sanction with the religious by the institution of the *monitoire*, whereby communicants withholding information of specific crimes were threatened with excommunication.

41 In his alternative draft of the Finance Committee Report, Bentham also added the following 'Note to be inserted in a private letter': 'Though what is called news must necessarily be excluded, yet this is not the case with Essays. – These might slide in *sub silentio*: and by means of the universality of circulation compared with that of all the democratic newspapers put together, these might be of unspeakable use in combating without intermission the raging malady of the times' (Bentham, UC cl. 421).

References

Bentham, Jeremy. (UC). University College London collection of Bentham manuscripts, boxes i–clxxvi (UC). Roman numerals refer to the boxes in which the manuscripts are placed, Arabic to the folios within each box. Where individual manuscripts are dated, the date is provided in the reference.

Bentham, Jeremy. 1802. *Traités de législation civile et pénale, Volume 3*, edited by E. Dumont. Paris: Bossange, Masson & Besson.

Bentham, Jeremy. 1817. *Plan of Parliamentary Reform, in the Form of a Catechism, with Reasons for Each Article, with an Introduction, Shewing the Necessity of Radical, and the Inadequacy of Moderate, Reform*. London: R. Hunter.

Bentham, Jeremy. 1843. *Works of J. Bentham, Published under the Superintendence of His Executor John Bowring, Volume 11*. Edinburgh: William Tait.

Bentham, Jeremy. 1952–4. *Jeremy Bentham's Economic Writings, Volume 3*, edited by W. Stark. London: George Allen & Unwin.

Bentham, Jeremy. 1968. *The Correspondence of J. Bentham, Volume I*, edited by T. L. S. Sprigge. London: Athlone.

Bentham, Jeremy. 1970a. *An Introduction to the Principles of Morals and Legislation*, edited by J. H. Burns and H. L. A. Hart. London: Athlone.

Bentham, Jeremy. 1970b. *Of Laws in General*, edited by H. L. A. Hart. London: Athlone.

Bentham, Jeremy. 1971. *The Correspondence of J. Bentham, Volume III*, edited by I. R. Christie. London: Athlone.

Bentham, Jeremy. 1977. 'A Fragment on Government'. In *A Comment on the Commentaries and a Fragment on Government*, edited by H. L. A. Hart and J. H. Burns, 391–551. London: Athlone.

Bentham, Jeremy. 1981. *The Correspondence of J. Bentham, Volume V*, edited by A. T. Milne. London: Athlone.

Bentham, Jeremy. 1983. *Constitutional Code, Volume I*, edited by F. Rosen and J. H. Burns. Oxford: Clarendon Press.

Bentham, Jeremy. 1998. 'Codification Proposal, Addressed by Jeremy Bentham to All Nations Professing Liberal Opinions'. In *'Legislator of the World': Writings on Codification, Law and Education*, edited by P. Schofield and J. Harris, 241–384. Oxford: Clarendon Press.

Bentham, Jeremy. 2001. *Writings on the Poor Laws, Volume I*, edited by M. Quinn. Oxford: Clarendon Press.

Bentham, Jeremy. 2002. 'France'. In *Rights, Representation and Reform: Nonsense upon Stilts and Other Writings on the French Revolution*, edited by P. Schofield, C. Pease-Watkin and C. Blamires, 1–61. Oxford: Clarendon Press.

Bentham, Jeremy. 2010a. *Writings on the Poor Laws, Volume II*, edited by M. Quinn. Oxford: Clarendon Press.

Bentham, Jeremy. 2010b. *Of the Limits of the Penal Branch of Jurisprudence*, edited by P. Schofield. Oxford: Clarendon Press.

Bentham, Jeremy. 2011. *Jeremy Bentham: Selected Writings*, edited by S. G. Engelmann. London: Yale University Press.

Bentham, Jeremy. 2018. *Writings on Political Economy, Volume III: Preventive Police,* edited by Michael Quinn. Pre-publication version. Online. http://discovery.ucl.ac.uk/10055084/ (accessed 20 April 2021).

Blackstone, William. 1765–9. *Commentaries on the Laws of England, Volume 4*. Oxford: Oxford University Press.

Chadwick, Edwin. 1829. 'Preventive Police', *London Review* 1: 252–308.

Colquhoun, Patrick. 1797. *A Treatise on the Police of the Metropolis, Explaining the Various Crimes and Misdemeanours which at Present Are Felt as a Pressure upon the Community; and Suggesting Remedies for Their Prevention*. 4th ed. London: C. Dilly.

Colquhoun, Patrick. 1799a. *The State of Indigence, and the Situation of the Casual Poor in the Metropolis, Explained; with Reasons Assigned Why the Prevailing System, with Respect to this Unfortunate Class of the Community, Contributes, in a Considerable Degree, to the Increase and Multiplication of Crimes: with Suggestions, Shewing the Necessity and Utility of an Establishment of Pauper Police, Immediately Applicable to the Casual Poor, under* the Management of Responsible Commissioners, with Their Functions Explained. London: H. Baldwin & Son.

Colquhoun, Patrick. 1799b. A General View of the Causes and Existence of Frauds, Embezzlements, Peculation and Plunder, of His Majesty's Stores in the Dock Yards, and Other Public Repositories, and in the Naval Department in General; with Remedies Humbly Suggested for the Purpose of Preventing These Evils and Abuses. London: H. Baldwin & Son.

Colquhoun, Patrick. 1799c. A General View of the National Police System, Recommended by the Select Committee of Finance to the House of Commons; and the functions of the Proposed Central Board of Police Revenue: with Observations on The Probable Effects of the General Designs in the Prevention of Crimes, and in Securing the Rights of the Peaceful Subject. London: H. Baldwin & Son.

Colquhoun, Patrick. 1800. A Treatise on the Police of the Metropolis. 6th ed. London: Joseph Mawman.

Colquhoun, Patrick. 1806. A Treatise on Indigence; Exhibiting a General View of the National Resources for Productive Labour, with Propositions for Ameliorating the Condition of the Poor, and Improving the Moral Habits and Increasing the Comforts of the Labouring People, Particularly the Rising Generation. London: J. Hatchard.

Dodsworth, Francis. 2007. 'Police and the Prevention of Crime: Commerce, Temptation and the Corruption of the Body Politic, from Fielding to Colquhoun', British Journal of Criminology 47: 539–54.

Dodsworth, Francis. 2008. 'The Idea of Police in Eighteenth-Century England: Discipline, Reformation, Superintendence, c. 1780–1800', Journal of the History of Ideas 69: 583–604.

Engelmann, Stephen. 2017. 'Nudging Bentham: Indirect Legislation and (Neo)Liberal Politics', History of European Ideas 43: 70–82.

Great Britain, Parliament. 1797–1802. The Parliamentary Register; or, History of the Proceedings and Debates of the Houses of Lords and Commons, Volume 18. London: J. Stockdale, J. Debrett.

Hanway, Jonas. 1775. The Defects of Police, the Cause of Immorality, and the Continual Robberies committed, Particularly in and about the Metropolis, with Various Proposals for Preventing Hanging and Transportation. London: J. Dodsley.

Hume, L. J. 1981. Bentham on Bureaucracy. Cambridge: Cambridge University Press.

Lambert, Sheila (ed.). 1975. 'Twenty-Eighth Report from the Select Committee on Finance &c. Police, Including Convict Establishments'. In House of Commons Sessional Papers of the Eighteenth Century, Volume 45, edited by D. E. Wilmington: Scholarly Resources, cxii, 3–216.

Laval, Christian. 2003. J. Bentham, les artifices du capitalisme. Paris: Presses Universitaires de France.

Mildmay, William. 1763. The Police of France: Or, An Account of the Laws and Regulations Established in that Kingdom, for the Preservation of Peace and the Prevention of Robberies. London: E. Owen & T. Harrison.

Neocleous, Mark. 1998. 'Policing and Pin-Making: Adam Smith, Police and the State of Prosperity', Policing and Society 8: 425–49.

Neocleous, Mark. 2000. 'Social Police and the Mechanisms of Prevention: Patrick Colquhoun and the Condition of Poverty', British Journal of Criminology 40: 710–26.

Poynter, J. R. 1969. Society and Pauperism: English Ideas on Poor Relief, 1795–1834. Toronto: University of Toronto Press.

Quinn, Michael. 2014. 'Bentham on Mensuration: Calculation and Moral Reasoning', Utilitas 26: 61–104.

Quinn, Michael. 2017. 'Jeremy Bentham, Choice Architect: Law, Indirect Legislation and the Context of Choice', History of European Ideas 43: 11–33.

Radzinowicz, Leon. 1948–86. A History of English Criminal Law and Its Administration from 1780, Volume 5. London: Sweet & Maxwell.

Ron, Amit. 2008. 'Modern Natural Law Meets the Market: The Case of Adam Smith', European Journal of Political Theory 7: 117–36.

Schofield, Philip. 2006. Utility and Democracy: The Political Thought of Jeremy Bentham. Oxford: Oxford University Press.

Schofield, Philip. 2009. Bentham: A Guide for the Perplexed. London: Continuum.

Smith, Adam. 1976. An Inquiry into the Nature and Causes of the Wealth of Nations, Volume 2, edited by R. H. Campbell, A. S. Skinner and W. B. Todd. Oxford: Clarendon Press.

Smith, Adam. 1978. *Lectures on Jurisprudence*, edited by R. L. Meek, D. D. Raphael and P. G. Stein. Oxford: Clarendon Press.

Styles, John. 1983. 'Sir John Fielding and the Problem of Criminal Investigation in Eighteenth-Century England', *Transactions of the Royal Historical Society* 33: 127–49.

Part II
Extracts

4

Extracts from Jeremy Bentham's Board-of-Police Bill

Selected and edited by
Philip Schofield
and
Scott Jacques

Introduction

The following extracts, based entirely on the original manuscripts in the Bentham Papers at University College London Library, are intended to illustrate the main themes of Bentham's 'Board-of-Police Bill' or, as he usually termed it in the headings to the manuscripts, his 'Police and Revenue Bill'. The first extract is taken from 'Introductory Observations relative to the Board-of-Police Bill' and gives a brief overview of the different parts of the Bill. The second reproduces a variety of sections from the draft Bill itself, while the third contains a selection of the 'Notes' to the relevant sections of the draft Bill. A number of notes have, therefore, been excluded from the sections reproduced here, though the original note numbers have been retained.

Thanks are due to the Leverhulme Trust for its financial support of the editorial work undertaken by the Bentham Project on Bentham's police writings. The current editors are extremely grateful to Michael Quinn for his editorial work on the preparatory version of Bentham's *Writings on Political Economy, Volume III*. The current editors have checked and made amendments to the text and its presentation and substantially revised the editorial footnotes for the purposes of this volume.

The manuscripts on which the extracts are based, and which do not present any difficulties in terms of their order, having been carefully arranged by Bentham himself, are as follows:

Extract	Manuscripts (UC)
Introductory Observations	cl. 642–3; cxlix. 149–52, 155–6
Police Bill Preamble	cl. 180–1
Police Bill § 1	cl. 182–5
Police Bill § 7	cl. 200–2
Police Bill §§ 32–4	cl. 245–8
Police Bill §§ 45–51	cl. 266–83
Police Bill § 53	cl. 286
Note {1}	cl. 429–30
Notes {3–5}	cl. 434–9
Note {28}	cl. 467
Note {30}	cl. 468
Notes {35–6}	cl. 470–4
Note {101}	cl. 571–89
Notes {106–9}	cl. 595–618, 620–9
Notes {112–13}	cl. 640

In the first two extracts, short rules have been inserted where longer passages have been omitted. In all three extracts, the omission of short passages is marked by three dots within square brackets. Bentham's square brackets have been rendered as curly braces.

In referring to Acts of Parliament, Bentham used the collection known as *Statutes at Large*. The later collection known as *Statutes of the Realm* is regarded as more authoritative. Discrepancies between the two collections in the numbering of statutes and their clauses have been recorded in the editorial footnotes.

Inconsistencies and inaccuracies in Bentham's numeration of the notes have been silently corrected.

The following abbreviations have been adopted:

MS Original manuscript reading

[to] Word(s) editorially supplied

| | Space left in manuscript

UC Bentham Papers, University College London Library; Roman numerals refer to boxes and Arabic to folios

Introductory Observations relative to the Board-of-Police Bill

The Bill for which the explanation of which the ensuing pages are intended will of course, if presented to Parliament, make its appearance, like all other Bills, without any other Divisions than the accustomed Division into Sections: but in the mean time, for the purpose of exhibiting the plan and design of it, and of stating the grounds on which it rests throughout in point of reason and precedent, it will be impossible to avoid considering it as subjected to an intermediate division into *Parts*.

1. Part the first (distinguished by the title *Licence-Duties*)[1] occupies itself with the establishment of a system of Licence-Duties, to be imposed on 13 different classes of persons, all of them comprizable under the general denomination of *Purchasers of Second-hand Goods for Sale*.

2. Part the second (intituled **Board**)[2] occupies itself with the establishment of a new Board, under the name of the *Board of Police*, having for its functions the collection of the above duties—the superintendence of the classes of Dealers on whom those Duties are imposed, together with other functions which will presently be mentioned.

3. Part the third (intituled **Licensing**) comprehends divers provisions relative to the mode of proceeding in relation to the granting of the licences.

4. Part the fourth (intit[u]led **Regulations**) occupies itself about the establishment of divers regulations relative to the mode of carrying on the several occupations subjected to the controul of a licence—and operating in some instances by the actual establishment of regulations relative to the points in question, in other instances by investing the Board with powers for establishing regulations relative to such and such points.

---

1   See pp. 85–6 below, where this Part of the Bill is entitled *Licentiandi*, i.e. 'those to be licensed'.
2   See pp. 87–8 below.

5. In Part the 5th (intituled *Penalties and Procedure*)[3] are collected together the several necessary provisions by which Penalties are appointed for offences committed against the Act, and the jurisdiction and mode of Procedure for the recovery of those Penalties is prescribed.

6. In Part 6th (intituled *Gazette and Calendar*)[4] are contained such provisions as relate to the *Gazette* proposed to be published for Police purposes by the authority of the Board, the Annual Calendar of Delinquency proposed to be framed from documents furnished to and collected by the Board, the authority proposed to be given to the Board to report any such amendments as may appear to be suggested by the consideration of the facts exhibited by the Calendar of Delinquency, and the transfer to be made to the Board of the functions of the two existing Offices (the Hawkers and Hackney Coach Offices) proposed to be abolished.

———————

The provisions of the present Bill embrace a part, and but a part, of a more extensive plan,[5] the remaining parts of which will be brought forward or not, according to the determination of those to whom it belongs to judge.

The main feature of it comes under the head of Police: and consists in the idea of applying a new check to depredation in all its forms, by opposing fresh difficulties and dangers to the faculty of disposing of the fruits of it. The principal means employed is the subjecting to a discretionary licence, as in the case of Public Houses,[6] such occupations as, by reason of the mode of dealing in them, joined to the nature of the articles dealt in, have a peculiar tendency to afford facilities for that purpose.

Another feature of it consists in the idea of extracting, from the measures necessary [and] directed more particularly to the prevention

3   See pp. 88–90 below.
4   See pp. 91–102 below.
5   P. Colquhoun, *A General View of the National Police System, recommended by The Select Committee of Finance to the House of Commons; and the Functions of The proposed Central Board of Police Revenue: with Observations on the Probable Effects of the General Designs in the Prevention of Crimes, and in Securing the Rights of the Peaceful Subject*, London, 1799, lists, in addition to the present Police Bill, a Bill for preventing the counterfeiting of coin, a Bill for preventing depredations on the River Thames, and a Bill for the prevention of frauds, embezzlements and depredations on naval stores. Bentham had drafted material for all four Bills.
6   A series of statutes dating back to 1552 required keepers of alehouses to apply to Justices of the Peace for an annual licence.

of offences, a collateral advantage referable to the head of revenue, as also a stock of political or statistical information, a secondary acquisition in its nature alike serviceable, or capable of being rendered alike serviceable, to both these primary purposes. Three objects are accordingly pursued, and pursued in conjunction, throughout the whole—Prevention of crimes—augmentation of Revenue—and procurement of information.

Using the word economy in the most extensive sense, this is carrying economy to the highest pitch: compassing sometimes two, sometimes three ends, at an expence not greater than what would have been necessary to the attainment of one of them, if pursued by itself. If, then, there be any one of them in the instance of which the advantage obtained affords an adequate equivalent for the expence, the other, or the two others, may thus be said to be obtained *gratis*.

The expence here in question may be distinguished into what is commonly meant by expence, viz: pecuniary expence—and *vexation*; which, if not strictly included under the acceptation of the term expence, can no otherwise be estimated (as is intimated by Adam Smith) than by reference to the expence which a man would willingly be subjected to, rather than undergo it.[7]

All measures of the coercive cast—that is all legislative measures but those which consist in the modification or abrogation of existing ones—involve what may be termed vexation (for all coercion is productive of vexation) in their result: avoidance of vexation being absolutely impossible, there remains only this problem—viz: from a given necessary quantity of political vexation, to extract as much political advantage as possible, in all imaginable shapes.

Between Police and Revenue there is happily a sort of natural connection, which requires only to be improved: insomuch that, from the quantity of vexation necessary to be produced for the sake of one of these objects, there either accrues without contrivance, or by contrivance may be made to accrue, a quantity of advantage referable to the other. In the association between the two connected objects, sometimes it is one, sometimes the other, that is the principal one. In some instances, a measure presents itself as necessary on the score of finance: and there the thing to be done is to consider, whether at

---

7   See Adam Smith, *An Inquiry into the Nature and Causes of the Wealth of Nations* (first published in 1776), ed. R. H. Campbell, A. S. Skinner and W. B. Todd, 2 vols, Oxford, 1976 (*The Glasgow Edition of the Works and Correspondence of Adam Smith*), Bk V, Ch. II, ii, 827: 'though vexation is not, strictly speaking, expence, it is certainly equivalent to the expence at which every man would be willing to redeem himself from it'.

the same expence, or with a small addition to the expence (vexation and pecuniary expence taken together), an advantage referable to the head of Police may not be obtainable from the same measure. In other instances, it is by some view of Police that the measure is suggested in the first instance; and then comes the consideration whether and in what degree the measure necessary for that purpose may be turned to account and improved for the purpose of Finance.

There is again another bond of connection not only between measures of finance and measures of police, but between measures of finance and measures conducive to the purpose of obtaining political information. A stream of revenue, drawn from any subject-matter, gives a degree of efficacy and stability to a measure suggested in the first instance by one or both of these other considerations: a deficiency in a set of returns required with a view principally or wholly to political information, or a want of execution in regard to measures suggested primarily by considerations of police, neither of these deficiencies either shews itself in so determinate and palpable a shape, or is equally capable of exciting that attention which is necessary to the application of an effectual remedy, as where a defect in point of revenue is seen to flow at the same time from the same source. The advantage derivable to the revenue, the money to be got up by the stopping of the gap, wherever it happens to be, operates as a sort of premium to the man of finance (the most powerful among public men) for whatever assistance he may lend in such a case to his neighbours, the *statisticalist* and the man of police. Hence it is, that whatever be the projects that happen to originate with either of these two, policy joins with economy in suggesting to them the advantage that may be gained in point of vigilance, and that efficiency which is the fruit of it, by calling in the man of finance, and taking him, as it were, into partnership, and letting him in for a share in the profits of the business.

———

What may be regarded as the second part of the Bill,[8] is occupied in the collection and exhibition of an assemblage of useful facts. In respect of the nature of the provisions contained in it, it bears little or no resemblance to the first part. The bond of connection between them is no more than this. A particular set of political hands, a particular Board, would be necessary for either purpose, were it to be pursued

8   i.e. Part 6, as distinguished from Parts 1–5, listed at pp. 79–80 above.

alone. But the same set of hands that will serve for the one, will suffice for that and the other [too].[9] As far as pecuniary expence, therefore, is alone concerned (vexation being a separate consideration), by joining the two, either of them may be considered as being compassed *gratis*. And not only one set of hands will suffice for both tasks, but, by engaging in either, any set of hands is rendered the better qualified for the performance of the other.

The information of which it is the business of this second part of the Bill to provide for the collection and preservation consist[s] of two branches perfectly distinguishable in themselves, tho' both pointing to the same end:—the one particular and casual: intelligence of individual acts of delinquency as they come to light in this or that part of the country:—the matter of the proposed *Police Gazette*:—the other periodical and aggregate: information of all acts of delinquency committed in all parts of the kingdom in the course of the Year, accompanied with an intimation of the operations they have respec-tively given birth to on the part of Justice.[10] That both branches of information are of an interesting nature, and that [both] promise to be useful in various points of view, will be apparent upon the bare mention of them: the particular utilities they are pregnant with will be stated with precision and in detail in the particular Notes of which they are respectively the subject. By pursuing still the same fundamental principle of economy—viz: that of extracting from a given mass of expence the greatest possible mass of advantage in each of the greatest possible number of shapes, a distinct and collateral use presented itself as capable of being derived from the *Police Gazette*, viz:—the guarding and preserving the public mind from impressions dangerous to the public peace. Of this likewise, a particular statement will be given in a Note to the Passage by which a provision for that purpose is made in the Bill.[11]

9   MS 'two'.
10   i.e. the Calendar of Delinquency.
11   See Note 101, pp. 114–21 below.

A Bill
For the establishment of a Board of Police, and for the suppression of divers Offices; —or else,

A Bill
For the establishment of a Board of Police, for the suppression of divers Offices, and for the more effectual prevention of predatory and other offences, by the licencing and regulation of divers trades and occupations{1}[12]

General Preamble.

Whereas by the natural facilities administered by divers trades and occupations to the receipt and advantageous disposal of goods stolen or otherwise unlawfully obtained, great and manifest encouragement is afforded to Larceny and other species of depredation, to the reproach and injury of the fair trader, as well as to the insecurity of property in general, which encouragement might be done away and such unlawful dealings in a great degree repressed, and his Majesty's revenue at the same time augmented, were the exercise of the said trades and occupations subjected by means of licence duties to proper regulation and controul; And whereas great difficulties are daily experienced in investigating and pursuing the traces of

---

12 The bold numerals in braces constitute cross-references to 'Notes to the Police Bill', pp. 103–41 below. For note {1}, see pp. 103–4 below.

delinquency for want of an all-pervading system of national Police, having its chief seat or central point in the Metropolis, and from thence maintaining a close and connected chain of correspondence, by receiving information from, and communicating the same with regularity and promptitude to, all parts of this United Kingdom, by a permanent authority which, in consideration of the continually accumulating fund of information and experience so collected and preserved, might moreover stand charged in an especial manner with the business of devising, selecting, and from time to time reporting to his Majesty in Parliament, such measures as shall appear conducive to the more effectual prevention of predatory and other offences and to the attainment of the several ends of penal justice:—*or thus*[13]—to the lessening the demand for punishment, to the diminishing the expence and alleviating the burthen of prosecution, to the turning the hearts or arresting the hands of evil-doers, to the preservation of the untainted, and the forewarning of the unwary, and to the attainment of the various particular ends of penal justice.

Part I. Licentiandi.[14]

§ 1. We your Majesty's most dutiful and loyal Subjects, the Commons of Great Britain in Parliament assembled, as well for the furtherance of the designs abovementioned as for the contributing towards raising the necessary supplies to defray Your Majesty's public expences, and making a permanent addition to the Public Revenue, have freely and voluntarily resolved to give and grant to Your Majesty the several Duties hereinafter mentioned; and do most humbly beseech Your Majesty that it may be enacted, and Be it enacted by the King's most excellent Majesty, by and with the advice and consent of the Lords Spiritual and Temporal in this present Parliament assembled, and by the authority of the same, that the several classes of persons respectively exercising the several trades and occupations following shall, at the several times and places herein after appointed for that purpose, take out, each person, a licence, empowering him or her to exercise such his or her trade or occupation, and shall pay each of them for every year during which such his or her licence shall be in force, such sum or sums as are in that behalf hereinafter specified, differing in divers instances according as

1. Classes to be licenced—Licence-Duties and Inscriptions—London Police District—Country Police Districts.

13   Bentham goes on to present an alternative conclusion to the General Preamble.
14   i.e. 'Those to be licensed'.

the place at or in which such person shall be empowered to exercise such his or her occupation shall be situate within the District composed of the several Parishes and places in, to and from which Letters are at present delivered by the Post called the London Penny Post,[15] according to the list thereof contained in the Schedule marked {A}[16] and hereunto annexed (which District shall be termed the *London Police District*),{3}[17] or elsewhere in that part of Great Britain called England, that is to say in any of the Districts or Divisions{4}[18] hereinafter described (which Districts or Divisions shall respectively be characterized by the common appellation of *Country Police Districts*), and shall moreover, during the time comprized in each respective licence, keep constantly exhibited, in durable and conspicuous characters, each of them, over the principal door or doors, of such his or her place of trade or occupation, as also, in the several instances hereinafter in that behalf specified, in some conspicuous part of the cloathing worn, or of the carriages employ'd, in the exercise of such occupations respectively, inscriptions expressive of the name of such person at length, the occupation which by such licence such person shall be empowered to exercise, together with such other particulars as in the several cases are hereinafter respectively mentioned, subject nevertheless to all such lawful regulations touching the situation, number, form and contents of the said inscriptions as, in virtue of the powers hereinafter given, shall from time to time have been made by the Commissioners hereinafter mentioned: the descriptions of which said several classes, together with the inscriptions by which the same may and shall for the aforesaid, and for all other, purposes be respectively directed, are as follows, that is to say:[19]

---

15 The Post Office (Revenues) Act of 1711 (9 Ann., c. 10), § 6 [*Statutes of the Realm* c. 11, § 7], fixed the scope of the Penny Post, which had been established in 1680, to a radius of 10 miles from the General Letter Office in Lombard Street.
16 None of the Schedules appears to have survived in the Bentham Papers.
17 See pp. 104–7 below.
18 See p. 107 below.
19 Bentham goes on to list the following 13 classes of dealers: 1. Purchaser of Second-hand Houshold and other goods for sale; 2. Wholesale Purchaser of Rags and Cordage for Paper-making; 3. Purchaser of Rags and unserviceable Cordage for sale to Paper-Makers; 4. Purchaser of Second-hand Apparel, made up Piece-Goods, and remnants for sale; 5. Walking Purchaser of Second-hand Apparel, made-up Piece-goods and remnants for sale; 6. Purchaser of Second-hand Naval Stores for sale; 7. Wholesale Purchaser of Second-hand Metals for sale; 8. Retail Purchaser of Second-hand Metals; 9. Purchaser of Second-hand metals of persons in general for working up; 10. Purchaser of Second-hand Building Materials for sale; 11. Keeper of Draught Carts for Second-hand Goods purchased for sale; 12. Hand-Cart Keeper for Second-hand Goods purchased for sale; and 13. Seller of Forfeited-Pledges.

Part II. Board.

§ 7 . And be it further enacted, that, for the granting of the several Licences abovementioned, to the several classes of persons respectively abovementioned, for the collection of the duties so to be paid by the several classes of persons taking out such licences respectively as aforesaid, and for the exercise of divers other functions hereinafter mentioned, it shall be lawful for his Majesty, from time to time, by Commission under the Great Seal, revocable at pleasure, to constitute and appoint Commissioners in such number as to his Majesty may seem meet,[a]{28}[20] and therein to specify and declare what number less than the whole number of such Commissioners shall be necessary and sufficient to constitute a Board for all purposes generally, or for such and such purposes in particular, as also for what days{30}[21] and during what hours such Commissioners shall collectively or severally be bound to give attendance, with such Salaries and other Emoluments for themselves and their subordinates herein after mentioned as his Majesty may from time to time be pleased to appoint, which said Commissioners shall be stiled *Commissioners of Police*, and the fund formed for the purpose of defraying the expences of the Police by and out of the produce of such Duties as aforesaid shall be termed the Police Fund, and after defraying the expence of such Salaries and Emoluments and other expences created or provided for by this Act, the surplus of such product shall from time to time be paid into his Majesty's Exchequer, and be carried to and made part of the Consolidated Fund,[b] and in so far as the situation of the House, Shop, Warehouse, Yard, or other place of trade or occupation, in respect whereof any such licence is so to be taken out, shall be comprized within the said *London Police District,*

§ 7. Commissioners of Police—their appointment—functions—Emoluments—Local authority—Police Fund.

---

[a] 5 W. c. 21. Stamps; 9 An. c. 23. Hackney Coaches; 9 & 10 W. c. 27. Hawkers; 1 An. Stat. 1. c. 21. § 26. Salt.[22]

[b] 38 G. 3. c. 89. § 137. *Salt.*[23]

---

20 See pp. 107–8 below.
21 See p. 108 below.
22 The Stamps Act of 1694 (5 & 6 Will. & Mar., c. 21), § 7 [*Statutes of the Realm* § 5], the Stamps Act of 1710 (9 Ann., c. 23), § 1 [*Statutes of the Realm* c. 16, § 1], and the Salt Duties, etc. Act of 1702 (1 Ann., Stat. I, c. 21), § 26 [*Statutes of the Realm* 1 Ann., c. 15, § 23], each empowered the Crown to appoint Commissioners, while The Hawkers Act of 1697, § 2, empowered the Treasury to do so.
23 The Salt Duties Act of 1798, § 137, prescribed that 'all Monies arising by the said Duties by this Act granted or imposed (the necessary Charges of raising and accounting for the same excepted) shall from Time to Time be paid into the Receipt of his Majesty's Exchequer, and shall be carried to and made Part of the Consolidated Fund'.

such licences shall be granted by the said Commissioners, who for that purpose shall hold their Office{35}[24] in some convenient part of the said District:{36}[25] and in so far as the situation of such place of trade or occupation as aforesaid shall be in any such Country District, as aforesaid, such Licences shall be granted in manner as hereinafter mentioned by the same Justices by whom, under the laws in being, licences are granted to Alehouse keepers: and if it shall happen that one and the same such place of dealing or occupation as aforesaid shall be situated partly within and partly without the said London Police District, or if one and the same person shall have in his or her occupation two or more such places of dealing or occupation as aforesaid, of which one or more shall be situated within the said London Police District, and one or more without the same, then and in every such case such licence or licences respectively shall be granted by the said Commissioners alone and not by such Justices as aforesaid: and in respect of the granting of such several licences, the said Commissioners and such Justices as aforesaid shall respectively have and exercise the same authority and discretion as, under the laws in being, are exercised by such Justices in respect of the granting of such licences to Alehouse keepers as aforesaid.

———

Part V. Penalties and Procedure.

§ 32. Penalty for dealing without licence—and for infringing regulations made by the Board.

§ 32. And be it further enacted, that if, in any District or Division in which a Meeting shall have been duly holden for the granting of licences as aforesaid, any person who, by reason of any occupation exercised by him or her, is hereby required to take out any such licence as aforesaid under and by virtue of this Act shall, at any time after the said 29th of September next ensuing (save and except in case of any such adjournment as is herein above allowed for inquiry into character) exercise such occupation without having duly taken out and received such his [or her] licence (whether such default took place for want of due application made for such licence, or by reason that on such application such licence was refused), every such person so offending shall, on conviction before any one Justice

---

24 See pp. 108–10 below.
25 See pp. 110–12 below.

of the Peace, forfeit and pay any sum not less than { } nor more than { }: and every such licenced Purchaser as aforesaid who shall offend against any regulation which shall have been lawfully made and published by and by the authority of the said Board of Police, in virtue and pursuance of the powers herein in that behalf above given to the said Board, shall for every such Offence, on conviction before any one Justice as aforesaid, or before the said Board, as the case may be, forfeit and pay any such sum not exceeding {£5} or any such sum not exceeding the said sum of {£5} as shall in each case have been appointed in that behalf by and by the authority of the said Board.

§ 33. And be it further enacted, that when and so often as there shall be reasonable cause for suspecting that any person, not being duly licenced under and by virtue of this Act as a Purchaser of Second-hand Houshold and other goods for sale, a Wholesale Purchaser of Rags and Cordage for sale to Paper-makers, a Retail Purchaser of Rags and Cordage for sale to Paper-makers, a Purchaser of Second-hand Apparel, Piece-Goods and Remnants for sale, a Walking Purchaser of Second-hand Apparel, Piece-Goods and Remnants for sale, a Purchaser of Second-hand Naval Stores for sale, a Wholesale Purchaser of Second-hand Metals for sale, a Retail Purchaser of Second-hand Metals for sale, a Purchaser of Second-hand Metals of persons in general for working up, a Purchaser of Second-hand Building materials for sale, a Cart Keeper for Second-hand Goods purchased for sale, a Hand Cart Keeper for second-hand goods purchased for sale, or a Seller of Forfeited Pledges, has in his or her possession, for the purpose of sale, any goods or articles in respect of which [he or she] ought to have taken out any such licence as aforesaid, or, that any person, though duly licenced as aforesaid, in respect of certain sorts of goods or articles, has in his or her possession, for the like purpose, any goods or articles in respect of which he or she shall not have been so licenced as aforesaid, and proof of such reasonable cause shall have been made upon oath before and to the satisfaction of any Justice of the Peace, it shall be lawful for any and every Constable and other such Peace-Officer, upon warrant duly issued by such Justice, at any seasonable hour in the day time, to enter into, and make search in, any Dwelling-House as well as any Warehouse, Shop, Yard or other place in which such goods or articles shall so have been suspected to be, as aforesaid; and if any such goods or articles be thereupon found in such place, or in the act of being removed to or from the same, then and in such case to seize

§ 33. Powers of search for goods dealt in without licence.

and secure any and every such article so possessed for the purpose of sale without licence as aforesaid, or such thereof as shall be necessary and sufficient to be produced in evidence for the conviction of the Offender, and to convey the same, as soon as conveniently may be, before some Justice or Justices of the Peace, before whom information of such Offence so committed shall be lodged.

§ 34. Power of search for goods stolen.

§ **34.** And be it further enacted, that upon reasonable cause (proved by Oath) for suspecting that any goods or other valuable articles, stolen or otherwise feloniously or fraudulently obtained, are concealed or lodged in any House, Outhouse, Building, Yard or other place, whether the same be in the occupation of any person who shall have taken out or shall have been bound to take out any licence under and by virtue of this Act, or in the occupation of any other person or persons whatsoever, it shall be lawful for any Constable or other Peace-Officer, upon warrant duly issued by any Justice of the Peace, to make search for such goods or valuables in any such Building, Yard or place, at all seasonable hours in the day time, as also in the night if thereto specially authorized in and by such warrant, and moreover, in case of necessity, to enter into and upon the premises, and therein make search for such goods or valuables by force, and for that purpose to break open doors, locks and packages, if thereto specially authorized in and by such warrant as aforesaid: and if, upon such search, any such goods or articles as aforesaid be found, to seize and detain or carry off and secure the same, and the same to convey before the same or any other Justice, according to the said Warrant, together with all such persons in whose possession such goods or articles shall be found to be, or who, knowing the same to be stolen or otherwise feloniously or fraudulently obtained, shall appear to be privy to their being so concealed or lodged, to the end that and untill such goods, articles or persons respectively shall be dealt with and disposed of in due course of law.

———

Part VI. Gazette and Calendar &c.

§ **45.** And whereas it might contribute in an especial degree to the bringing of offenders to justice, if a channel of appropriate intelligence{101}[26] were established in such sort that, in and by means thereof, information of predatory and other offences might immediately, and without expence, be received from persons aggrieved and others, and convey'd in the same manner to all persons throughout this United Kingdom to whom, by means of their respective Offices, professions, trades, occupations, or otherwise, opportunity might occurr of contributing to the discovery or apprehending of the Offender, Be it further enacted, that it shall and may be lawful to and for the said Commissioners, and they are hereby authorized and required, so soon as conveniently may be, to cause to be printed and published on such day or days of the week as they shall from time to time think fit a paper of appropriate intelligence, to be stiled the *Police Gazette*, in which shall be inserted free of all Stamp-Duties and circulated free of all duty or other charge of postage all such intelligence, and such intelligence only, as in the judgment of them the said Commissioners shall be in the nature thereof subservient and contributory to the detecting and bringing to Justice persons guilty of offences against any of the Laws or Statutes of these his Majesty's realms: which said Police Gazette shall be printed at some place within the said London Police District, as also at such other place or places, if any, as the said Commissioners in their discretion shall appoint, regard being had to the number of copies requisite to be printed and the speed which it may be necessary and practicable to use in the circulation of the same; and the said Police Gazette shall be furnished *gratis* to every such Country Police Commissioner or Country Police Magistrate as aforesaid, as also to every one of his Majesty's Justices of the Peace who, having 'sued out his Majesty's Writ or Commission of *Dedimus potestatem*',[27] shall signify to the said Commissioners his desire to be supplied with the said Gazette, and to all Members of Corporations possessing the authority of a Justice of the Peace in virtue of their respective Offices; as also to every person belonging to any of the several Classes of persons required to take

§ 45. Police Gazette to be published by the Board—free of stamps and postage—and furnished *gratis* to Justices and Licenced persons.—Penalties for malitious information, and for anonymous malitious information.

---

26 See pp. 112–21 below.
27 A writ of *dedimus potestatem* [i.e. 'we have given the power'] was issued by the Chancery in order to authorize the swearing in of a new Justice of the Peace: see Richard Burn, *The Justice of the Peace, and Parish Officer* (first published at London in 1755), 2nd ed., 2 vols, London, 1756, ii, 88.

out licences under and by virtue of this Act, or to such of them as to the said Commissioners it shall from time to time seem meet to fix upon for that purpose; as also to every person who under any law in being shall take out any licence for retailing Ale, Wine, Sweets, Spirituous liquors, or any other fermented liquors, Tea, Coffee,[28] or any other liquor to be drunk at the house of such licenced person; and the said Police Gazette shall be sold to all other persons at one penny each number, or some such other low price, to be from time to time fixed by the said Commissioners: and the expences of the printing and publishing of the said Gazette shall be borne by and charged upon, and the receipts on account thereof 'carried to and made part of',[29] the said Police Fund: and every person who malitiously, and with intent to create trouble, alarm or other suffering in the minds of persons in general, or any undue trouble, alarm, loss, disgrace or other injury to any person or persons in particular, shall cause or attempt to cause any false information to be received by the said Commissioners, knowing the same to be false, or without having any probable cause for believing or supposing the same to be true, shall forfeit and pay any sum not exceeding £10, recoverable as any other of the penalties of this Act are made recoverable, over and above all such penalties or damages as such offender may already be liable to by law: and if any person with any such malitious intent as aforesaid shall cause or attempt to cause any such false information as aforesaid to be received as aforesaid, knowing the same to be false, or without having any probable cause for believing the same to be true, and in so doing shall omitt to sign or otherwise declare his or her true name, or his or her place of abode, so described as that he or she may with ordinary diligence be found thereby, or shall subscribe, use or declare any false or fictitious name or abode, or use any other device, for the purpose of preventing its being known that he or she was the person or causing it to be believed that any other person was the person, or one of the persons by whom such information was so communicated or attempted to be communicated, every such person so offending and being convicted thereof on indictment shall be punished by fine and imprisonment, and may moreover be set in the Pillory for such number of times, and for such lengths of time, and in such place or places, as the Court in which such offender shall have been convicted shall appoint.

---

28   Retailers of each of these items were required by statute to take out licences.
29   See p. 87 & n. above.

§ 46. And be it further enacted, that towards the defraying such part of the expence of and concerning the said Police Gazette as shall be occasioned by the furnishing thereof to the several classes of licenced persons in that behalf abovementioned, it shall and may be lawful to and for the said Commissioners of Police from time to time, at their discretion, to add any such sums as shall appear to them to be sufficient for the said purpose, to the amount of the several licence-duties{106}[30] herein before made payable by the several classes of persons required to be licenced under and by virtue of this Act, in such proportion, in the instance of each such Class, as to them the said Commissioners, in their discretion, shall seem meet, provided that the amount of such additional duty shall not in the instance of any one such class exceed the sum of {5^s} in any one year: and it shall moreover be lawful to and for the Commissioners of Excise, by order from the Lord High Treasurer or Commissioners of the Treasury, at the instance of the said Commissioners of Police, to add to the duties annually payable on each Excise licence for the retailing of Beer, Ale and other exciseable liquors made from grain fermented and not distilled, any sum not exceeding {2^s 6^d} in any one year, and to the duties payable on each Excise licence for retailing British made Wines or Sweets, to be drunk in the House of the person taking out the same, any sum not exceeding {2^s 6^d}: and to the duties payable on each Excise licence for retailing distilled Spirituous liquors or strong waters, any sum not exceeding {2^s 6^d}: and to the duties payable on each Excise licence for retailing Foreign Wines, any sum not exceeding {2^s 6^d}: and every provision contained in every law made or to be made in relation to licence-duties payable in respect of any of the exciseable liquors aforesaid shall be in force (so far as the same are respectively applicable) in relation to every such additional duty as, in virtue of the powers last above given, shall be added to such respective duties under and by virtue of this Act;[a] Provided always, that a separate account shall be kept by the said Commissioners of Excise of the produce of all such additional duties as shall have been so imposed: and such produce shall be carried either to the Fund called the Consolidated Fund, or to the said Police Fund, as the Lord High Treasurer or Commissioners of the Treasury shall from time to time think fit.

§ 46. Expence of supplying Publicans and other Licenced persons with the Police Gazette, defrayable by additional Licence-Duties.

[a] 30 G. 3. c. 38. § 19.[31]

30 See p. 121 below.
31 The Retail of Liquors Act of 1790, § 19, prescribed that all powers relating to the retailing of wine contained in former Acts, unless altered by the Act, were to continue in force.

§ 47. Ministers
of Congrega-
tions—Post-
Masters—and
Town-
Magistrates
shall publish
Notices &c.
transmitted
to them from
the Board.—
Penalties for
neglect—and
for defacing
&c. Notices
when stuck
up.

§ 47. And be it further enacted, that for the circulating of any number or numbers of the said Police Gazette, or of any intelligence proper to be inserted in the same, in any particular Parish or Parishes, place or places, in which the circulation of such intelligence shall appear to afford any special prospect of contributing to bring any Offender to justice, it shall be lawful for the said Commissioners, and for any person or persons acting by their authority, from time to time to cause to be transmitted to any resident Ministers, Church-wardens, Chapel-wardens or Parish Clerks of any such Parishes or Places respectively, as well throughout that part of Great Britain called England as throughout that part of Great Britain called Scotland, any requisite number of Copies, Extracts or Abstracts of or from any number or numbers of the said Police Gazette, with proper Instructions for the fixing the same or causing the same to be fixed upon a principal door or some other conspicuous part or parts of the Church or Chapel of each such Parish or Place: as also to any Ministers, Priests, Rabbis, or other persons concerned in the management of the affairs of any Chapels, Synagogues, Meetings or other places of religious worship respectively, belonging to Congregations of persons dissenting from the Churches of England and Scotland respectively, with instructions for fixing such papers in like manner upon such places; as also to the Postmasters of any Post Towns; as also to any resident Mayors, Bailiffs, Aldermen, Chief Burgesses, Recorders, Town Clerks or other Magistrates or persons concerned in the management of the affairs of any Towns Corporate respectively, with instructions for fixing such papers against the Post Houses, Town Halls or Market places of such Towns; and if need be, for causing the matter of such papers to be publickly cried within the same; specifying in each case during what length of time such paper, after having been fixed, shall continue unremoved and undefaced; and in the Instructions inserted in any such Paper sent out for the purpose of being made public in any Church or other place of worship, whether used by persons conforming to or dissenting from the rites of the Church of England or the Church of Scotland respectively, it shall be lawful to the said Commissioners, at their discretion, in the case of wilful murder, arson, burglary or robbery accompanied with wounding or any other atrocious crime, to cause to be inserted proper directions for the reading of such Paper or any part thereof by the Minister, Clerk or any other proper person in each such place of worship, in or near the middle of the service performed therein, or at such other time at which the congregation thereof may be reasonably expected to be fully assembled: and if any person, by whom or at whose house any such paper shall have been so transmitted and received as aforesaid, shall wilfully or through negligence omitt to fulfill any such reasonable instruction as shall therein be given for such purpose as aforesaid, or if, before the expiration of the length of time mentioned in such Paper as the length of time for and during which it is intended that the same shall continue in the place where the same shall have been fixed, any person shall be concerned in pulling down, concealing or defacing such Paper or any material part thereof or causing the same to be pulled down, concealed or defaced, every such person so offending shall forfeit and pay any sum not exceeding {40^s} nor less than {5^s}.

§ 48. And whereas it might, by the blessing of providence, be a means of promoting well-grounded, substantial and gradual amendments and improvements in the penal branch of the Law of these his Majesty's Realms, and of exciting and keeping up a due spirit of zeal and vigilance on the part of all persons concerned, by Office or otherwise, in the execution of the same, if the numbers of the several offences known or suspected to have been committed, under each head of delinquency, in each year, in the several parts of this his Majesty's Realm of Great-Britain, together with the result of each act of delinquency in respect of punishment or impunity, were annually collected, digested, and exhibited to view, Be it further enacted, that it shall and may be lawful to and for the said Commissioners, and they are hereby authorized and required, so soon after the end of every Year as conveniently may be, to prepare and frame, or cause to be prepared and framed, and to present to his Majesty and both Houses of Parliament, a Report or Reports containing a Table or set of Tables to be named and stiled *The Calendar of Delinquency*,{107}[32] in and by which shall be delineated and exhibited the General State of the Nation for such Year as touching the matters and things aforesaid, under the set of heads contained in or indicated by Schedule { } annexed to this Act[33] or under such other or further heads as in the judgment of the said Commissioners shall from time to time appear best adapted to the said purpose: And for the purpose of obtaining the several documents or materials requisite for the composition of the said Calendar of Delinquency, the said Commissioners of Police are hereby authorized and required, so soon as conveniently may be, and so from time to time as there shall be occasion, to frame or cause to be framed and transmitt or cause to be transmitted to the Registering Clerk or Clerks or other proper Officer

§ 48. Calendar of Delinquency to be annually published.— Materials for it to be furnished to the Board by Judges &c. and Justices.

32 See pp. 121–33 below.
33 For the proposed Schedules to the Bill, see p. 86 n. above.

or Officers of every Court exercising criminal jurisdiction, or having cognizance of any penal action, or possessing the authority of inflicting Ecclesiastical censure, in any part of Great Britain, a competent number of blank forms or schemes for Returns to be made from time to time of the several proceedings had, and of the several instruments issued or signed in, by, or before each such Court, in virtue of such its jurisdiction, cognizance or authority as aforesaid: which said blank forms or schemes may respectively contain such heads as are exhibited in the Schedules marked F.1, F.2,[34] and so forth, and herewith annexed, or any such other or further heads as in the judgment of the said Commissioners shall from time to time appear best adapted to the aforesaid purpose: and such blank forms or schemes shall respectively be accompanied with any such reasonable Instructions touching the filling up thereof as the said Commissioners shall think fit: and every such Clerk or other Officer shall, within such reasonable time as shall have been limited by the said Commissioners, return every such blank form or scheme duly filled up, according to such Instructions: and 'all Judges and Justices in the respective Courts aforesaid are hereby authorized and required, at the request of the said Commissioners, to make all such Orders, and do all such other matters and things'[a] as shall be requisite and necessary to the due and compleat filling up and returning of the said blank forms or schemes when so transmitted as aforesaid: and every such Clerk or other proper Officer who shall neglect, or without reasonable and sufficient excuse omitt, to fill up in any particular or to return according to such instructions, within such reasonable compass of time as shall have been therein limited, any such blank form when so transmitted as aforesaid, shall, for every such offence, forfeit and pay the sum of {£10}, to be recovered with costs of suit by Action in the Court of King's Bench at Westminster, in which no Essoign, Privilege, or Protection, nor more than one Imparlance, shall be allowed,[35] or in the Court of Exchequer at Edinburgh, as the case may be, by him that will sue: one moiety thereof, together with costs of suit, to be paid immediately after the receipt thereof by the Officer

---

[a] Taken from Stamp Act, 5 W. c. 21. § 12.[36]

34 For the proposed Schedules to the Bill, see p. 86 n. above.
35 These were stages of legal procedure that might be employed to delay the trying of cases.
36 See the Stamps Act of 1694 (recte 5 & 6 Will. & Mar., c. 21), § 12 [Statutes of the Realm § 10]: 'the Judges in the several Courts, and such others to whom it may appertain, at the Request or Requests of the said Commissioners, ... shall make such Orders in the respective Courts, and do such other Matters and Things, for the better securing of the said Duties, as shall be lawfully and reasonably desired in that Behalf'.

receiving the same to such Informer for his own use, the other moiety, within one week after the receipt thereof in England, and within three weeks after the receipt thereof in Scotland, to the said Receiver General of the said Police Fund, to be by him carried to and made part of the same: and the said Commissioners shall in like manner frame and from time to time and as often as there shall be occasion transmitt or cause to be transmitted to and for the use of every one of his Majesty's Justices of the Peace, who, by having sued out his Majesty's Writ or Commission of *Dedimus Potestatem*,[37] shall have intitled himself to act in the execution of the said Office, a set of blank forms or schemes in competent number, exhibiting a daily Calendar or Register of all proceedings had by and before such Justice on every information laid before him touching and concerning any offence for which the offender may be convicted either before any one such Justice or before any two or more such Justices out of General Sessions, under any Statute then in force: as also another set of blank forms or schemes exhibiting a daily Calendar or Register of all proceedings had by and before such Justice, either singly or in conjunction with any other number of Justices out of General Sessions, touching and concerning all felonies and other Offences in respect of which the power of convicting shall not have been given to any such Justice or Justices; And every such Justice, to whom any such blank form or scheme shall have been transmitted as aforesaid, is hereby directed and required, by the General or Penny Post, as the case may be, or by some other safe conveyance, to return the same, properly filled up, as soon as conveniently may be, after the proceeding, of which such form or scheme is designed to give account, shall have been had, according to such reasonable requests and Instructions as shall from time to time have been transmitted to him in that behalf by the said Board: and in particular, so often as it shall happen to such Justice to make out any Warrant for the commitment of any person to any Jail or other place of lawful confinement, or for the discharge of any person from such Jail or place of confinement, or for the making Distress and Sale on the goods of any person, or for making search in any House or Place for any person, or for any article or articles therein supposed to be contained, and as often as it shall happen to such Justice to take any Recognizance from any person on any occasion, whether civil or criminal, whatsoever, such Justice is hereby directed and required to cause a memorandum thereof and of the cause thereof, and other particulars relative thereto, according to

37 See p. 91 n. above.

such form as shall have been transmitted to him as aforesaid for that purpose, to be returned,{108}[38] by the filling up and transmitting of such blank form or otherwise, by the then next post if possible, or at the latest within one week thereof: and every such Justice shall, upon letter of request by him transmitted to the said Commissioners, be intitled to receive *gratis* and free of postage from them the said Commissioners a Copy of the said Police Gazette, as also of the said Calendar of Delinquency, as often as the same shall respectively be made public, as also of all such other printed papers as shall from time to time have been made public by authority of the said Board; such alone excepted, if any, as the Lord High Treasurer, or Commissioners of the Treasury for the time being, shall have forbidden to be so circulated, in consideration of the expence{109}[39] or otherwise.

§ 49. Further materials for the Calendar of Delinquency.— Returns from Jails.— Penalties for neglect.

§ 49. And be it further enacted, that the said Commissioners shall from time to time prepare or cause to be prepared and transmitt or cause to be transmitted, by the Post or some other equally convenient conveyance, to the Keeper of every Jail and other place of lawful confinement within this United Kingdom (such places included as are or then shall be in use for the confinement of the insane) a competent number of Blank Forms or Schemes with instructions for the filling them up respectively in such manner as to exhibit a memorandum of and concerning the receipt of each person who shall have been received into custody in each such Jail or other place of confinement, together with the date and cause of the commitment of such person and any other proper particulars relative to such person or such commitment: as also another set of Blank Forms or Schemes for exhibiting in like manner a memorandum of and concerning the departure of each such person respectively who shall have departed out of such custody, together with the date of such departure, and the cause or manner thereof, whether the same happened by death, escape, discharge, or otherwise, and any other proper particulars relative thereunto: as also another set of Blank Forms or Schemes, with proper and sufficient Instructions for the filling up the same, in such manner as that the same shall exhibit each of them a Register or Calendar of all persons who shall have been so received into, and of all persons who shall have so departed out of, such custody in the course of each Yearly, quarterly, monthly or other such proper and convenient period as shall from time to time have been appointed for that purpose by the said Commissioners, and of

38 See pp. 134–5 below.
39 See pp. 135–40 below.

all persons remaining in such custody at the end of each such period so appointed: and every such Jailor or Keeper, to whom any such set of Blank Forms or Schemes with such Instructions as aforesaid for the framing any such memorandums of receipts and departures respectively as aforesaid shall have been transmitted, from or by authority of the said Commissioners, shall, by the next post after each such receipt or departure shall respectively have taken place, transmitt or return to the said Board a proper and sufficient memorandum of and concerning such receipt or departure respectively, expressed by the filling up of some such blank form or scheme as aforesaid, or in some other equally proper and sufficient mode: and every such Jailor or Keeper, to whom any such Blank Form or Scheme with such instructions as aforesaid for the framing of any such periodical Register or Calendar shall have been transmitted as aforesaid, shall, within such reasonable time, after the expiration of each such period, as shall have been appointed or limited by the said Commissioners, transmitt or return to the said Board, by the Post or otherwise, a paper, expressive of such Register or Calendar, by the filling up of the heads contained in such Blank Form or Scheme so framed for that purpose, or in some other equally proper and sufficient mode, according to such Instructions as shall have been so transmitted to him as aforesaid in relation thereunto: and every such Jailor or Keeper as aforesaid, who, having received from the said Commissioners as aforesaid any such Blank Form or Scheme with instructions thereunto relating as aforesaid, shall wilfully or through negligence omitt to make any such return as shall be required in and by any such Instructions, shall forfeit and pay any sum not exceeding {10ˢ} nor less than {1ˢ} for every day during which such omission shall have continued: and every such Jailor or Keeper as aforesaid who, in and by any such return so made by him as aforesaid, shall wilfully or through negligence omitt to make true and perfect answer to any such lawful and reasonable question, or to comply with any such lawful and reasonable requisition, as shall be contained in any such Instructions relative thereto, or shall wilfully or through negligence make any false answer to any such question, shall forfeit and pay for every such Offence any sum not exceeding {£5} nor less than {5ˢ}.

§ 50. And be it further enacted, that every Constable or other such Peace-Officer, and every other person to whom any Warrant, Summons, Order or other precept or authority in writing shall have been delivered by any Justice or Justices of the Peace, to the end that such Warrant or other authority may be executed by such Constable or other person, shall by the then next post, or so soon as conveniently may be, transmitt or cause to be transmitted by the Post (or otherwise according to such appointment as from time to time shall be made in that behalf by the said Commissioners) a true copy of every such Warrant or other authority; such Warrants or authorities excepted as the said Commissioners shall have thought fit to except; with a signature expressive of the name and abode of such Constable, together with a figure or figures expressive of some number, whereby the copy of each such warrant or other authority may be distinguished from every other, the series of such numbers commencing with the first of such copies so transmitted by each such Constable or other person, and continuing to the end of the Year of our Lord in which such transmission shall be made by the same person: and each such Constable or other person, so soon as he shall have executed, or in part executed, such Warrant or other authority, according to the nature of the business therein required to be done, shall moreover transmit or cause to be transmitted in manner aforesaid a paper or papers containing a memorandum or statement of the business so done and executed, as, for example, the arresting of the body of some person, the producing of the same before some Justice, the conveying of the same to some Jail, the making search in any House for any person or any goods, the arresting of any person thereupon, or seizing any goods, and producing him, her, or them before any Justice as aforesaid, the making Distress on the goods of any person, the making sale of the goods of any person in consequence of any such Distress, and so forth, in such convenient form and according to such reasonable Instructions as from time to time shall be framed and made public by the said Commissioners: and in regard to such business as any such Constable or other person shall not have been able to execute, or shall not have executed notwithstanding such warrant or authority, every such Constable or other person shall from time to time give notice and make return thereof, and in case of non-execution as aforesaid, then also of the cause or causes of such non-execution, at such yearly, quarterly, monthly or other proper periods, and shall repeat the same for such reasonable number of successive periods in each year, as the said Commissioners shall from time to time have appointed and made public as aforesaid: or, in lieu of a copy at length of such Warrant or authority in each instance, every such Constable or other person shall transmitt or cause to be transmitted as aforesaid, according to such reasonable instructions, if any, as shall from time to time have been given in that behalf and made public by the said Commissioners, an Abstract of the contents of such Warrant or authority, under such heads as shall be contained in a blank form or scheme or any convenient number of blank forms or schemes, to be provided and duly transmitted by the said Commissioners; and for the due making of such returns and fulfillment of such Instructions as aforesaid, all Justices of the Peace are hereby required at all convenient times to give all proper and needful aid, assistance and advice to every such Constable or other person as aforesaid; Provided always, that for the transmission of any such Return as aforesaid, no such Constable or other such person shall be obliged to travel any further than to the Post Town nearest to his abode, nor to any such Post Town oftener than once in every week, if such Post Town be more than one Mile distant from such his abode; And every such Constable or other person, who, having received any such warrant or other authority as aforesaid, shall, for two whole weeks after the receipt thereof, have omitted to transmit to the said Commissioners the Copy or Abstract thereof as aforesaid, as also every such Constable or other person, who, having received any such warrant or authority, shall have omitted to make return of or concerning the execution or non-execution thereof, as aforesaid, at the next periodical time so appointed for the making of such Returns as aforesaid, shall forfeit and pay any sum not exceeding {10^s} nor less than {1^s} for every such Copy or Abstract so omitted to be returned, and for every Return so omitted to be made of or concerning such execution or non-execution, with the cause of such non-execution, as aforesaid.

§ 51. Provided always, and be it further enacted, that it shall not be lawful for the said Commissioners to cause or wilfully suffer to be made public in and by the said *Calendar of delinquency*, or by any other ways and means, the name of any person so convicted of, under prosecution for, or suspected of, any offence under the rank of Felony, except persons convicted of Forgery, Perjury or Conspiracy, and persons absconding from justice by reason of any offence, for the special purpose of causing him or her to be amenable thereunto, unless by a special Order of the Board made in relation to each such person taken singly, or unless a special Order for such publication shall have formed part of or been added to the judgment or Order by which such person shall have been convicted: and the said Commissioners are hereby authorized and required to take such course for the purpose of preventing such divulgation as is hereby prohibited, as in their judgments shall seem most effectual and best adapted to the said purpose.

§ 51. Names of Delinquents not to be divulged— except as excepted.

---

§ 53. Board
to make
Reports to
Parliament—
stating
proceedings
—and
suggesting
improvements.

§ **53.** And be it further enacted, that the said Commissioners, so soon as they shall have collected the information sought for by the Returns aforesaid, or sooner if need be, shall *'from time to time, at their discretion, or as often as they shall be thereunto required, give an account of their proceedings, in writing under their hands and seals, to the King's Most Excellent Majesty, and to both Houses of Parliament':*ᵃ{**112**}[40] and shall moreover from time to time *'suggest all such regulations'* as in their judgment shall appear best calculated for augmenting the efficacy,{**113**}[41] or, without prejudice to the efficacy, diminishing the severity, of the penal branch of the Law, or any part or parts thereof, and for diminishing, without prejudice to the efficacy of the law or to the security of the unoffending, the expence (whether to individuals or to the public) incident to the execution of the same.

ᵃ 20 G. 3. c. 54: Account; 25 G. 3. c. 19: Fees; 26 G. 3. c. 87: Crown Lands.[42]

40 See p. 140 below.
41 See pp. 140–1 below.
42 Bentham is paraphrasing the Audit of Public Accounts Act of 1780, § 5, and the Crown Lands Revenues, etc. Act of 1786 (26 Geo. III, c. 87), § 1, which required the respective Commissioners periodically to give accounts of their proceedings and to suggest reforms to Parliament, and the Inquiry into Fees, Public Offices Act of 1785 (25 Geo. III, c, 19), § 1, which required the Commissioners to give accounts and to suggest reforms to the Privy Council.

Notes to the Police Bill: containing Reasons, Precedents, and other Elucidations.

{1} Page 84.[43] Title.

1. Title—which title to prefer—the longer or shorter.

The objects that appear to have been aimed at in the framing of *Titles* to Bills are—

1. The giving a name whereby, when passed into a Law, the Act may be distinguished from other Acts, and referred to in succeeding Acts.

2. The affording a general indication of the contents, to avoid the inconvenience that has some times been observed to result, where, a provision being buried in a quantity of matter to which it bears little or no relation, the very existence of a provision to that effect may come to be forgotten and unknown, and even where the existence of it is known, a man may not know where to find it.

3. To operate in recommendation of the Bill, by the indication of the species of utility expected to result from it.

For the first of these purposes, the words *'An act for the establishment of a System of Police'* would be sufficient; for the second, it may perhaps be thought fit to add *'and for the suppression of divers Offices'*: especially as the indication of this part of the business of the Act may be attended in some degree with the other effect of contributing to recommend the Bill to the favour of the House.

The quantity of room occupied by the Titles of Acts, when referred to in the usual way by their Titles in other Acts, is an enormous inconvenience:—and, should this Bill pass into a Law, the occasions for referring to it in future Acts seem not likely to be unfrequent. Usage apart, the thing to be desired seems to be—that every Act, at least every Act the contents of which are in any degree multifarious, should have, as it were, *two* titles, one for mere reference, the other for the indication of the topics touched upon in it. To the

---

43 The numerals in braces and the page numbers refer to the note-makers and the pages on which they appear in 'Bill for the establishment of a Board of Police', pp. 84–102 above.

former purpose, nothing can be better adapted than the extempore titles by which Bills are denominated in the common Newspapers. These, short as they are, never fail to give some general intimation of the contents, which would not be done by a mere indication of the numbers expressive of the Year and the place occupied by the Act in question in the series of the Acts of that Year, nor even with the help of the recent improvement, by which the month and day of the passing of the Act are added;[44] besides that mere numbers are extremely liable to error, for want of that check which is afforded by the import of the context in other cases.

With these observations, how much of the title here proposed shall be suffered to stand, and whether any thing more shall be added to it, is submitted to those to whom it belongs to judge.

Part I. Licence Duties

3. Penny Post District—why taken for the standard in point of extent.

{3} § 1. Page 86. {*London Police District*}.

As to the extent here proposed to be given to the London Police District, the indications afforded by abstract utility, precedent being laid out of the question, can not be expected to be very determinate. In one point of view, the more extensive the better, because the more extensive it is, the more compleatly it will embrace the great field of depredation, and the great market for the fruits of depredation, viz: the Metropolis, and such part of the surrounding country, as may be regarded as being readily accessible to, and lying within the beat of, the London Thieves. Whatever may be regarded as the extent of this ideal district, there will be an evident advantage in subjecting the whole of it to the inspection of one and the same set of eyes:—and as the Metropolis and its vicinity is the great and principal theatre of the dishonest branch of the trade in second-hand goods, so is it of the honest branch: insomuch that, within this expanse, the scale of dealing may be regarded as being susceptible of greater extent than in the distant parts of the Country, or even any provincial Town: whence (as already observed)[45] the reason for encreasing the rate of duty within the compass of this circle: and

44 The Acts of Parliament (Commencement) Act of 1793 (33 Geo. III, c. 13) prescribed that Acts of Parliament, unless otherwise specified within the Act itself, were to be endorsed by the Clerk of the Parliaments with the date on which they received the Royal Assent and were to come into force on that day. Acts had previously been deemed to have come into force on the first day of the Parliamentary session in which they had been passed.
45 See pp. 85–6 above. Bentham proposed that the fees for dealers in the London Police District should generally be twice those for dealers elsewhere.

for the describing of it, the *radius* taken from the distance travelled by the Penny Post seems not too great.[46] On the other hand, a consideration the tendency of which is to set limits to the extension of this circle, is—that the distance ought not to be so great, as to raise to an oppressive pitch the trouble and expence of journeys, to Candidates for the licences and persons whose testimony may be recurred to for their characters: but on this head it is to be observed, that as, between the Metropolis and the instance of any place situate at a given distance from it, the occasions of passing to and fro are more frequent than between any other two places at an equal distance, so are the facilities.

This being considered, possibly for the sake of regularity and simplicity, it may be thought adviseable to include within this *Home District*, the whole of the County of Middlesex, no part of which is above 17 miles or thereabouts from London (reckoning from the place from which the miles are counted), and that only in the three projecting corners towards Colnbrook, Harefield and South Mims:[47] or if this should appear too great a distance, the list of the Parishes in the London District might at any rate be so far extended as to take in the broken remainders, if any such there should prove to be, of every licencing Division, which, upon the other plan of division, would be so far cut into as to be reduced to a portion of territory so small as not to be worth forming into a Division by itself.

As to the mode of demarcation, to say—*for such a number of miles round a given point* ('*five miles round Temple Bar*', for example, as in the Act 24 G. 3. sess. 2. c. 27. § [8],[48] which appoints the limits within which Carts are to be registered)[49] would not so well answer the purpose, for want of pre-established limits running in the direction of the circumference of a circle. The boundaries of Parishes (how irregular soever the boundary line) are generally, if not universally, determined with a degree of precision sufficient for every legal purpose. Precision is

---

46 i.e. a radius of 10 miles from the General Letter Office in Lombard Street: see p. 86 n. above.
47 Colnbrook was on the western edge, Harefield on the north-western edge, and South Mims (today spelt South Mimms) on the northern edge of the County of Middlesex. Distances from London were often measured from the start of the relevant road. South Mims, for instance, was reckoned to be about 15 miles from Hick's Hall, the start of the Great North Road: see *The Traveller's Pocket-Book; or, Ogilby and Morgan's Book of the Roads, Improved and Amended, In a Method never before attempted*, 24th ed., London, 1794, 33.
48 MS '7'.
49 See the Hackney Coaches Act of 1784, § 8, which prescribed that no one who had not registered their names and places of abode with the Commissioners for licensing Hackney Coaches should drive a cart in London, Westminster, Southwark, within the Bills of Mortality, and within 5 miles of Temple Bar. For the Bills of Mortality, see p. 123 n. below.

necessary under this head not only with reference to questions of *jurisdiction*, but for the sake of determining without litigation whether this or that man shall be liable to pay the *London* or only the *Country Duties*, and in what Houses the London Surveyors, and in what the Country Surveyors, are to exercise the several powers here given to that Office. In referring to the District of the Penny Post, it was necessary to speak of the *present time*: since, as far as *law* is concerned, the limits of that establishment have no description more determinate than what is given to them by the first Post-Office Act, 9 A. c. 10. § 6:[50] viz: '*ten miles from the General Letter Office in London*': and whatever fixation they have received has been given to them solely by the authority of the Postmaster General, by which same authority (by 34 G. 3. c. 17. § 6) they have been declared to be variable any time,[51] and may come hereafter to be varied for reasons which would not apply to the business of the Police. The existing list of the places included in that District will either serve without alteration for the list of places included in the proposed London Police District, or, if it does not give the names of the Parishes in every instance with sufficient precision for the present purpose, it will at any rate afford a sufficient clew to the discovery of those names.

In the case of the Excise, though the words employ'd by the Act {12 C. 2. c. 24. § 46}[52] in the description of the District within which the Head Office shall be situated are '*in the City of London or within ten miles thereof*' (a circle without a center), those by which, in the same Statute {§ 48},[53] the limits are marked out with a view to local authority and jurisdiction, are expressive of the same plan of demarcation as that which is *here* proposed to be adopted—'*All parts* of the Cities of London and Westminster, with the Borough of Southwark, and the several Suburbs thereof'.

It is, perhaps, no uncommon case for the same house to be part in one parish and part in another: but the boundaries of the two Parishes are not the less determinate; and the case is provided for in a subsequent clause. [...]

It is an obvious question—why make the rate of duty double in the London District? but the answer is little less obvious: viz: because

---

50 i.e. the Post Office (Revenues) Act of 1711.
51 The Post Office Act of 1794, § 6, authorized the Postmaster General, at his discretion, to extend the limits of the Penny Post beyond 10 miles from the General Post Office in Lombard Street.
52 i.e. the Statute of Tenures of 1660 [*Statutes of the Realm* § 33].
53 *Statutes of the Realm* § 36.

in and in the neighbourhood of the Metropolis, the *field for dealings* of the sort in question, and thence *the scale of dealing*, is so much more extensive than even in the largest country towns. *The Royal Dock Yards* afford an equally obvious exception to the general rule: and it is on this account that they are here proposed to be charged [...] with the London Duties. The practice of making a distinction between the Metropolis and the country, in regard to the rate of licence duty, is indeed not universal, but it has many precedents: upon turning to the annexed Table it will be found that, in *seven* or *eight* instances, out of about *two* or *three and forty*, the distinction is observed.[54] [...]

{4} § 1. Page 86. {*Districts or Divisions*}.

The Divisions here adopted are the Divisions into which the several Counties are already cast for the purpose of the business of granting licences to Public Houses [...]. They are termed *Divisions*, as being already known by that name: they are termed Districts with a view to the purposes of this Act, and that the common appellative thus given to them, may match with the appellative *London Police District*; in which case the word *Division* could not be employ'd, that District including a considerable number and variety of Public House licencing Divisions, and not being exactly commensurate, perhaps, with any number of them.

5. Terms *District* and *Division*, why both employ'd.

Part II. Board

{28} § 7. Page 87. {*In such number as to his Majesty may seem meet*}.

Fixing or limiting the number by Statute may be attended with inconvenience. It seems difficult to say before hand how much time the business of this new-created Office may come to occupy: if no division of the business is allowed, encrease in the number of the persons taking a part in it tends, it is true, rather to retard than to accelerate the progress of it; but, if the quantity of the business made it requisite, means might probably be found of making a division of

28. Commissioners— number why made variable.

---

54 Bentham annexed a 'Table of Precedents' to these Notes, but does not give examples there of different rates of duty for London and elsewhere. He does so, however, in a related brouillon, headed 'Police Bill Precedents', at UC cvii, 190–1, where he lists 41 professions for which licences were required by statute, and noted different rates of duty in relation to five, namely auctioneers, watch-makers and dealers, hatters, tanners, and tobacco and snuff dealers.

that sort without inconvenience. These are matters of experience and matters for experiment: and the latitude necessary for the making of such experiments should not be withholden from the executive government.

30. Attendance Days, why made variable.

{30} § 7. Page 87. {*For what days*}.

The proper proportion of the number of days of Attendance in the Year to that of the days of non-attendance will vary according to the quantity of business which presents itself to be done. This, therefore, is another point which should (it should seem) be left open to change. The practice of the different Boards in relation to this point appears to admitt of great diversity:—a diversity produced in good measure by the differences in regard to the number of days observed as Holydays. In the existing Hawkers and Pedlars Office, the whole business demands no greater space of time than what is comprized in the compass of about a fortnight in the Month of June.[55]

Over and above what concerns the whole Board in common, there may be good reason why it should be left to the discretion of the Executive Department to accept of different degrees of constancy in regard to attendance from different individuals. It may on these terms be able to obtain at less expence than ordinary, or without any expence, for particular purposes and on particular occasions, the assistance of particular persons whose whole time could not be to be purchased or to be spared.

35. *Office* where to be holden—shall the above points be mentioned or not in the Bill?

{35} § 7. Page 88. {*Shall hold their Office . . . in . . . the said District*}.

This provision, though scarcely necessary, is copied from the Act establishing the Excise—12 C. 2. c. 24. § [46].[56] [...]

---

55   See 'Tenth Report from the Select Committee on Finance, &c. Hawkers and Pedlars', 19 July 1797, in *House of Commons Sessional Papers of the Eighteenth Century*, ed. S. Lambert, 145 vols, Wilmington, Delaware, 1975, cviii, 319–33 at 321, stating that 'The official Attendance of the Commissioners is very inconsiderable' and 'An Account of the Official Attendance of the Commissioners and other Officers belonging to the Office for Licensing Hawkers, Pedlars, and Petty Chapmen; stating the Days in each Week, and the Hours in each Day', Appendix B. 2, in ibid., 330, that the Commissioners attended 'Every Day in the Week in the Month of June' from 11.00 a.m. to 2.00 p.m., for other meetings of the Board when required, and that one Commissioner was 'always resident'.

56   MS '§ 26' is a slip. The Statute of Tenures of 1660, § 46 [*Statutes of the Realm* § 33], prescribed that the principal Office of Excise should be established 'in the City of *London*, or within Ten Miles thereof'.

Possibly it may be thought still more advisable to make no mention at all in the Bill of any of the above points relative to the Constitution of the Board—viz: Quorum number—Days and Hours of attendance—Salaries and Place of sitting: because in that case, all these points would fall of themselves (it should seem) within the discretion of the Crown. One advantage, however, may arise from the mention of them in the Act—viz: that it will serve to direct the attention of the Executive power to the several points, and will appear to call for express regulations on the subject to be made by Order of Council, grounded on some determinate considerations: whereas otherwise the course taken with regard to these several points might pass, as it were, *sub silentio*, and be the work, not so much of reflection as of chance.

The Crown being intrusted by the constitution itself with the power of stationing the Courts of Law (all but the Common Pleas) wherever it pleases, and even the two Houses of Parliament themselves,[57] it were strange indeed if there could be any danger in intrusting it with the power of conforming to the dictates of convenience, in the instance of a particular Board of Revenue or Police. The Stamp Office affords an instance of the inconvenience that may result from the tying the hands of the Crown in regard to a point so little exposed to abuse—tying them unawares and without any particular object in view. On the first establishment of the Stamp-Duties, a place was found for the Office for the collection of those Duties—it does not appear precisely where, nor is it worth enquiring. Whether the business was become too great for the building, or for what other reason, towards the latter end of Queen Ann's reign, it was thought necessary to find out another building for it, upon which occasion it was, or upon some subsequent one, that it was thought proper to place it in Lincoln's Inn, from whence it was removed a few years ago to the General Receptacle for Public Offices erected on the site of Somerset House.[58] But, upon turning to the original Stamp Act, 5 W. c. 21, it was found that, by a clause in that Statute (§ 7), the situation of the Stamp Office had been confined—not to a circle in which the Cities of London and Westminster were included, but to the two unconnected

---

57 Although the superior courts and the Houses of Parliament in practice had in effect gained a permanent home in the Palace of Westminster, only the Court of Common Pleas was obliged to sit in a permanent location by Magna Carta, c. 17 (1215) (see *English Historical Documents 1189–1327*, ed. H. Rothwell, London, 1975, 319): 'Common pleas shall not follow our court, but shall be held in some fixed place.'

58 From its establishment in June 1694, the Stamp Office had been accommodated in Serle Court (later known as New Square), Lincoln's Inn. In December 1787 it had moved, along with many public offices, into the newly rebuilt Somerset House.

spots occupied by those Cities themselves:[59] and Lincoln's Inn (or the situation, if any, to which the Office was removed before it was set down in Lincoln's Inn) not being in either of those Cities, it was found necessary to apply to Parliament to untie the knot, and accordingly, in the long and prolific Revenue Act of the 10th A. c. 19, a clause was inserted (§ 181) for no other purpose than that of completing the above circle, by throwing into it a few of the adjacent Parishes, together with the Inns of Court.[60]

36. Oath of Office—why none inserted.

{36} § 7. [Page 88.][61]

Judging from custom, here might appear to be a place for the appointment of an *Oath of Office*, to be taken by the Commissioners, with or without the same or another Oath for their Subordinates. But, to confess the truth, the sort of Oath called an Oath of office is, in every instance that has happened to fall under my observation, so pure a piece of old-womanism—so perfect a chip in porridge, that I could not prevail upon myself to make use of it. Besides those profanations which are but too frequent on the part of individuals, there are two species of profanation (for such they have appeared to me) which are but too frequent on the part of the Legislator. The first and most abominable is the imposing an oath containing an asseveration such as (it is known) is seldom or ever true, or a promise such as (it is known) is seldom or ever performed: of this kind are the Oaths called *Custom House Oaths*, and many others.[62] The other is the sort here in question: the putting into a man's mouth, under the name of an oath,

59 The Stamps Act of 1694, § 7 [*Statutes of the Realm* § 5], had prescribed that the Commissioners of Stamps should 'keep their Head Office in some convenient Place within the Cities of *London* or *Westminster*'.
60 The Customs and Excise Act of 1711 (10 Ann., c. 19, § 181 [*Statutes of the Realm* § 197], permitted the Stamp Commissioners to keep their Head Office 'in any Part of the four Inns of Court' or the parishes of Saint Andrew Holborn, Saint Clement Danes, Saint Paul Covent-Garden, or Saint Giles in the Fields', although these places were outside the cities of London and Westminster.
61 Bentham is explaining an omission from the Bill and hence gives no corresponding quotation.
62 See, for instance, Edmund Overal, 'A Short View of those National and Personal Sins which call for Humiliation and Repentance', in *Memoirs of the Life and Writings of Mr. William Whiston. Containing, Memoirs of several of his Friends also*, 2 vols, London, 1749–50, ii, 410–22 at 411–13, complaining that 'a Custom-House Oath is become a proverbial Expression, for a Thing not to be regarded' and that a variety of oaths sworn in the Universities of Oxford and Cambridge meant that 'there is not a Man in either of our Universities who is not forsworn'. See also [Henry Home, Lord Kames,] *Loose Hints upon Education, chiefly concerning the Culture of the Heart*, Edinburgh, 1781, 362: 'custom-house oaths now a-days go for nothing. Not that the world grows more wicked, but because no person lays any stress upon them.'

a form of words which, amounting to nothing, can not bind a man to any thing. The habitual imposition of Oaths known to be habitually false is certainly the most crying scandal of the time, and does most towards the bringing the obligation into contempt: but the continual practice of giving a man to mumble upon his entrance into office, as a matter of course, a form of words calling itself an oath, and promising to do what is right and proper, is such an instance of legislative indifference as, though not in so high a degree, has a tendency of the same kind.

What I mean by this is—not to reprobate Oaths of Office as a species of supposed obligation necessarily impotent, and incapable of being applied to any use. On the contrary, it appears to me [that][63] in the instance of the office in question, as well as of every other office, it might, if constructed as it might and ought to be, be made of the highest use. But seeing before me nothing under this name but what is nugatory, I should deem it an act of imprudence to come forward on such an occasion with any thing that shall not be nugatory: it would be unusual—innovational—utopian: and, in proportion as it promised to be efficient if adopted, it would be in danger of appearing ridiculous when proposed. Unhappily for candour, veracity and moral honesty, the practice of feeding old and young with false oaths has been taken for one of the pillars of religion: and that of imposing trifling ones is too near of kin to it, not to have come in, tho' perhaps unperceived, for a corner of the same mantle.

It is going very far, if not too far, on so delicate a ground, to suggest, even in the most general terms, the complexion that an Oath must wear in order to be of use. It must not confine itself to generals, for then it is inefficacious—nor yet apply itself to such points of duty of the breach of which a man may be convicted by legal evidence, and for the purpose of legal punishment, for then it is superfluous: it should bear specifically upon particular points of duty, but upon such points the infraction of [which] is scarcely or not at all susceptible of being ascertained for the purposes of penal or coercive law, though at the same time not altogether unsusceptible of being ascertained for the purpose of exposing a man to the censure of the world at large. While thus employ'd, an oath of office may be regarded as a most useful and irreplaceable supplement to a set [of] penal regulations; it may serve at once as a guide to discretion, as a check upon private interest and affection, and as a buckler against external sollicitation. The following

---

63 MS 'than'.

may serve as an example of the purposes to which it might be applied in the present instance. Abjuration of personal interest and favour in the choice of subordinates—promise to have regard to active and intellectual fitness, as well as to moral innocence. Abjuration of ill-will on the one hand, and personal tenderness and favour and external influence and sollicitation on the other, on questions relative to the punishment or dismission of a subordinate. Abjuration of considerations of both kinds—personal favour as well as personal enmity—on questions relative to the granting or refusing licences.

At one time, attempts (though none of the happiest) appear to have been now and then made to give something like the particular sort of *bearing* here spoken of, to Oaths of Office: but, of late Years, all such curious labour seems to have been given up; and when an Oath of Office has been put in, it has been copied, *mutatis mutandis*, from an Oath of the nugatory cast, as a matter of course, and stuffed into the Act, to match with other surplusage.

Should an oath of the serviceable cast be at any time thought fit to be called for, for the use of the proposed Office, the responsibility will not be shrunk from, nor the trouble grudged: but at the present conjuncture, a production of that sort seems in danger of being premature: the business of the Board must be fully settled and marked out, before an Oath of Office can be properly shaped to it.

Part VI. Gazette and Calendar &c.

101.
Particular and further uses of the Police Gazette.

{101} § 45. Page 91. {. . . *a channel of appropriate intelligence*}.

In addition to the use stated in general terms in the text, it may not be amiss to subjoin a brief intimation of a few particular as well as collateral uses, which might either be derived from it or would result from it of course—

1. Against Desertions and Escapes— Auxiliary preventives indicated.

1. Against Escapes and Desertion, the *Police Gazette* might be made to afford a preservative of peculiar efficacy. *Profiles* are advertised as taken at so low a price as 2^s 6^d apiece: a machine for taking them, at a guinea:[64] of course, in the wholesale way they might be afforded a great deal cheaper. If taken on wood, at the time of commitment or inlistment, a portrait of this kind might be inserted into, and worked

---

64 See, for instance, the advertisements placed by Abraham Jones for 'Perfect Likenesses taken in Miniature Profile, at 2s. 6d.' and for 'Reflecting Mirrors, at One Guinea each' in the *Morning Post*, 25 March 1794, 4, and the *Morning Chronicle*, 18 December 1798, 4.

off with, the verbal description of the fugitive as given in the *Police Gazette*, without any addition to the expence.

Among seafaring men and others, there is a custom, not unfrequent, of *tattooing* the name of the person upon his arm, or some such part of the body usually kept covered, but at any time uncoverable without offence to decency. The mark is made in such a manner as to be absolutely indelible. The writer of this has seen a mark of this sort upon the arm of an Admiral made when he was a Midshipman. Were the receiving a mark of this sort made a condition of inlistment, the act of harbouring any inlisted person bearing such a mark, especially after the appearance of his *description* with his *profile* in the *Police Gazette*, might be made penal without scruple. The near and natural connections of the fugitive, so long as they were not exempt from search, might, without prejudice to justice, be exempt from punishment; all others might be punished without mercy. In that case, Desertion without detection being evidently impossible, it never would be attempted. In the Navy, the Army and the Militia, *Double inlistment*[65] as well as Desertion would thus be at an end. What a scene of misery and fraud and profusion would thus be closed! This practice, as an idle one, is familiar; it is only as a useful one, that it is new. In consideration of the utility, would the novelty be endurable? The question may at least be pardoned:—the answer will be given by the proper judges.

2. Another use of the *Police Gazette*, is the furnishing a stock, and that a compleat as well as authentic one, of materials for several of the aggregate heads comprized in the proposed *Calendar of Delinquency*: viz: 1. Offences known or suspected to have been committed: 2. Offences of which the authors are known or suspected: 3. Amount of pecuniary loss (in cases where property is affected) produced by the several offences:—lists the completion of which will, by the help of the *Police Gazette*, be a mere work of common arithmetic, to the due composition of which any and every body that pleases may act as a witness and a check. Concerning the *Calendar of Delinquency*, and the uses of it, see the Note on the section relative to that head.[66] {2. Affording divers necessary materials for the Calendar of Delinquency mentioned below.}

3. By means of the provisions of the next section but one (§ 47),[67] Government will open to itself a channel through which, without committing itself, it will be able to address itself at any time to the various classes of Non-conformists: all of whom, for the general {3. Affording a channel through which Government}

---

65 i.e. the practice of claiming a second bounty by enlisting, deserting and re-enlisting in a different regiment.

66 See note {107}, pp. 121–33 below.

67 See pp. 94–5 above.

may exert
a salutary
influence over
the Congre-
gations of
Sectaries, as
per § 47.

purposes of Police, that is for the common security of themselves and their fellow subjects, will naturally be disposed to receive the *Gazette* without repugnance when thus sent to them on the particular occasions and for the particular purposes specified in the Bill: and repugnance on the ground of principle being out of the question, the moderate penalty provided in the Bill will be sufficient to secure the communication against any inattention capable of resulting from mere negligence. From the occasion of transmitting the papers in question to those several congregations, an exact and constant acquaintance with the numbers and situations of them will be obtained without the appearance of being sought, and the attention of the local Surveyors of the Board will be pointed to the numbers and deportment of the individuals of whom these congregations are respectively composed. In the case of Catholics, the instrument termed, in the language of the French Monarchical and Ecclesiastical jurisprudence, a *Monitoire* (an exhortation in which the force of the religious sanction is employ'd in engaging individuals to come forward to the assistance of justice by the disclosure of any particulars they may happen to be acquainted with in relation to any particular crime supposed to have been committed)[68] might, perhaps, by these means, be employ'd upon occasion to good effect, and be made to render even to this Protestant Government that sort of service which it has frequently been made to render in so eminent a degree in the Catholic Countries in which the use of it has been established. And when, for purposes not exposed to repugnance or suspicion, this sort of channel of communication has once been established in the several assemblies, and the minds of the members have become familiarized with the use of it, it will be easy, if on any occasion it should become desirable, to make use of it for the purpose of conveying any impressions which it may be wished to produce with a view to the execution of justice or the preservation of the public peace.

4. —as
likewise over
the lower
Orders in
general, with
a view to their
preservation
from the
poisons of

4. Over and above the direct uses of the *Police Gazette*, as already exhibited, another use (which, though but collateral, and not proper to be mentioned in the Bill, may be found still more important, perhaps, than even the direct one) is—the capacity of being employ'd as an instrument for the propagation and maintenance of social dispositions and affections, and for the preservation of tranquillity, harmony and loyalty among the great body of the people. The species of intelligence

68 In *ancien régime* France, a *lettre monitoire* was a type of injunction whereby the clergy of a diocese, at the request of the civil judicial authorities or parties to a criminal lawsuit, ordered any of their parishioners with relevant knowledge to testify to the facts of a case on pain of excommunication.

or *news*, to the circulation of which it is proposed to be appropriated anarchy.—All other means inadequate. (consisting of notices of acts of delinquency committed, accompanied with a display of the punishments and perils to which the authors stand exposed) is of itself, in every line of it, a perpetual lesson of morality and of submission to the laws: and by the turn that, under able and suitable management, might be given to it, this *natural* aptitude to the conveyance of wholesome instruction might be abundantly improved. But besides this, though precluded from the circulation of every thing *else* that can bear the name of *news*, it need not be, nor ought it to be, expressly precluded (and if not *expressly*, it will not be regarded as *virtually* precluded) from administering useful instruction and exhortation of the moral, and, upon occasion, the political cast, in whatever forms may from time to time present themselves as best adapted to the purpose. Something in this way would pass as a matter of course, and even of necessity, rather than choice: for the quantity of matter expressive of the current stock of *intelligence* or *news* would, in its nature, be liable to perpetual inequalities: inequalities of this kind are what all newspapers are in the habit of supplying, for the purpose of exhibiting on each day of publication a paper of a uniform size, and thus giving a pennyworth for every penny.—This collateral part would, therefore, pass not as a novelty, nor as directed to any special end, but as coming in as a matter of course, in conformity to the custom of the trade.

Partly in virtue of its direct uses, partly in virtue of this collateral one, the *Police Gazette* would be a perpetual instrument of good order in the hand of Government: and a more efficient, and at the same time a more gentle, one (keeping multitudes from harm, and doing harm [to] no one) lies not within the sphere of possibility, nor even of imagination.

The ground-work—the standing ground-work—of it, is composed of the events of the day:—in a word, of *news*: of all species of information the most generally and strongly interesting: and of that species of news which, with reference to the understanding and affections of the classes of persons principally in view—that is of the most numerous classes of society—is of all species of news the most interesting. The occasional superstructure, the *didactic* part, will have at any rate the circumstance of *contiguity* to cement the idea of it in the mind with the idea of the other part, and thus obtain for it a portion of the same favour: and by grafting it upon the other, as the moral is upon the fable, the sermon upon the text—or (to come nearer) the *observation* part in a newspaper upon the intelligence part which gives occasion to it, the association will be rendered still more intimate and indissoluble.

As to degree of circulation, the extent of it would, to a degree altogether adequate to its object, be altogether at the command of government. What may be termed the *natural* or *free* circulation is out of the reach of calculation: as far as price is concerned, the difference between a penny, or some such matter, and sixpence, is the advantage it would have in this respect over every other Newspaper.[69] But the *factitious* or *forced* [circulation][70] would (setting day against day) be perhaps not inferior to that of all the other Newspapers put together: it would certainly be many times as great as that of all the Democratical papers put together: for this taint, it is believed, is happily as yet confined, or nearly so, to the Daily papers, of which the circulation is almost confined to the near neighbourhood of the Metropolis: it manifests itself in a much less degree in the every-other-day papers: and in a still less degree, if at all, in the weekly papers, of which, taking the Kingdom through, the circulation (on any given day at least) is greater than that of all the London papers put together. Licenced Public-Houses in the Kingdom, say 50,000:[71] Houses that may come to be licenced under the proposed system, if carried to its full extent, perhaps as many more: total 100,000, the amount of the factitious and certain circulation.

Convey'd to every house of public entertainment—to every place of public meeting for the lower classes without exception, the *Police Gazette* would find its way into the hands, and furnish no small part of the entertainment, of the 500,000 fighting men who have been computed to constitute the population of the Friendly Societies.[72] Five hundred thousand forms, therefore, a part—and but a part—of the audience to which the sort of *sermon* in question would be preached

---

69 Most newspapers were sold at 6d. a copy.
70 MS 'calculation' appears to be a slip.
71 The source for Bentham's estimate may have been Colquhoun, who later published this figure in *A Treatise on Indigence; exhibiting A General View of the National Resources for Productive Labour; with Propositions for Ameliorating the Condition of the Poor, and Improving the moral Habits and increasing the Comforts of the Labouring People, particularly The Rising Generation; By Regulations of Political Economy, calculated To prevent Poverty from descending into Indigence, To produce Sobriety and Industry, to reduce the Parochial Rates of the Kingdom, and generally to promote the Happiness and Security of The Community at Large, by the Diminution of moral and penal Offences, and the future Prevention of Crimes*, London, 1806, 284 and n.
72 The source for Bentham's figure has not been traced, though the total Friendly Society membership for England and Wales was later officially reported as 704,350: see 'Summary of the Totals of the Several Counties of England and Wales, and Grand Total', in 'Abstract of the Answers and Returns Made pursuant to an Act, passed in the 43d Year of His Majesty King George III. Intituled, "An Act for procuring Returns relative to the Expence and Maintenance of the Poor in England"', 10 July 1804, *Commons Sessional Papers* (1803–4), xiii, 717–19.

weekly and, as much oftener as was thought fit, addressed to ears the attentiveness of which would not be subject to those causes of failure which affect the efficacy of other sermons. Not a nook nor a cranny in which this antidote would not be sure to meet whatever poisons of the moral or political kind either actually are or ever can be administered: and beyond that, the antidote would preoccupy and preserve thousands and thousands of minds, in places into which the poison (especially considering the price to which it has lately been raised)[73] can never hope to penetrate.

The effect produced by a publication of any kind upon the body of the people will be in proportion to the number of persons into whose hands it finds its way, and to the magnitude of the interest which each man takes in it:—it will be in the joint ratio of both these two quantities. Euclid never advanced a proposition more irrefragable.[74] In the instance of the *Police Gazette*, the magnitude of this effect lies, therefore, altogether at the command of government. The interest a man will take in the contents is secured by the nature of things: the number of hands into which the paper will find its way is in the inverse ratio of the price, which will be fixed by government. This much with regard to the free branch of the circulation: but the factitious branch, to the amount that has been seen, is still more absolutely at the command of government.

Victories at this moment keep the people in good humour:[75] at the moment and for the moment, in spite of the endless prospect of unprecedented and ever encreasing burthens. But one of these days peace will come: and then at any rate (to say nothing of sinister accidents), there will be an end of victories. Then recommence the attacks upon the vitals of the constitution with redoubled fury, then, when there is nothing to create a diversion in favour of internal quiet. The tide of national ill-humour, of which at this moment so large a portion finds vent by discharging itself upon the foreign enemy, being then pent up within the Country, will return into the old channel, and, if some such means as what are proposed be not employ'd to stem it, will recoil upon government with unexampled pressure.

---

73 The Stamp Act of 1797, § 2, had raised the stamp duty on a typical newspaper from 2d. to 3½d.
74 Euclid (fl. 300 BC), Greek mathematician, author of the *Elements*, which was conventionally structured as a series of propositions, each accompanied by a more detailed demonstration by which it was proved.
75 Bentham perhaps had in mind recent British martial successes in the Mediterranean, notably the Battle of the Nile (1–3 August 1798) and the Capture of Minorca (16 November 1798).

The policy of the Alien Act[76] is sound and necessary, as far as it goes: it is the result of a necessity not likely to be extinguished even by the return of peace.[77] It is a part, indeed, but no more than a part, of what is necessary to be done in pursuance of the same principle. The French may be the most conspicuous, but they are by no means the most determined, nor the most formidable, enemies of national repose: the most formidable enemies by far which the country has are in her own bosom. Of these, the country can not be cleared by any power or by any industry: all that can be done—all that can be so much as attempted—is to guard the minds of the susceptible and thoughtless multitude against the poisons which it is their incessant endeavour to disseminate. Against dangers of this kind (the source of every other) the force of arms and hands is unavailing: for combating pens or tongues, pens or tongues are weapons altogether indispensable.—Of armies there may be no want—*sed quis custodiet ipsos Custodes?*[78] Employ'd with the advantage here proposed—furnished with an all-pervading and inimitable vehicle for their productions—a few able pens—a few of those very pens which, for want of that advantage, are labouring with a degree of effect altogether inadequate—might save more than as many regiments.

That, among the Reviews, the ablest pens and those which find the greatest number of readers are indefatigable in the cause of national destruction has already been remarked. But there is a single Magazine, the influence of which may rival that of all the others put together. Though not yet three years old, the number of copies printed of it every month amount already to five thousand.[79] Rich beyond example in every branch of information as well as entertainment, it leaves all other

---

76 The Aliens Act of 1793, passed on 8 January 1793 shortly before the outbreak of war with Revolutionary France on 1 February 1793, required aliens arriving at British ports to register their personal details and to obtain passports before proceeding elsewhere and restricted their right to import or possess weapons. The Act had been of temporary duration, but had been renewed annually, most recently by the Aliens Act of 1798 (38 Geo. III, c. 50), which had in turn been amended by a second Aliens Act of 1798 (38 Geo. III, c. 77).

77 In the event, peace was restored between Britain and France by the Treaty of Amiens of 25 March 1802, but war was renewed in 1803.

78 See Juvenal, *Saturae*, vi, 347–8: 'But who will guard the guards themselves?' The phrase is now considered to be a later interpolation.

79 The *Monthly Magazine*, founded by Richard Phillips (1767–1840), author and publisher, and edited by John Aikin (1747–1822), physician and writer, had first appeared in February 1796 and, according to Philip Luckombe, *The Tablet of Memory; shewing every Memorable Event in History, from the Earliest Period to the Year 1800. Classed under distinct Heads, with their Dates. Comprehending An Epitome of English History, with An Exact Chronology of Painters, Eminent Men, &c. To which are annexed Several Useful Lists*, 10th ed., London, 1800, 121, by 1797 had a circulation of 5,000.

publications of the same class far behind. But an object it never loses sight of is—to represent the government of the Country as a nuisance ripe for extirpation: and from this passion, objects in their own nature the most remote from politics are made to receive a tinge. Chemistry, Mechanics, Astronomy, Music—every thing is tainted with this venom: Biography, of which there is a constant abundance, of course is full of it. By its *immediate* influence, this publication will seldom (it is true) descend to so low a level as that of the great mass of the people, for whose reading the *Police Gazette* is principally designed: but the minds of those to whom they look up and on whom they depend—their Masters and Employers, will, if it goes on as it has begun, be in a fair way to be formed by it.

The Sedition Act[80] may be regarded as a second *Magna Charta*, preserving against attacks still more destructive that security which the first had formed. (I say *security*: for as to *liberty*, the word is so replete with ambiguity and poison as to be scarce fit for use:—it is as if arsenic were sold at the Grocer's under the same name with Sugar.) The Sedition Act has silenced the mob of inflammatory tongues: but howsoever necessary, and, when considered apart from prejudice, exempt from real danger, it can not be denied to have been a measure of the strongest and most alarming kind. Excellent as far as it goes, it goes, after all, but half way. To pens of the same complexion, the defence it provides does not extend; nor could it receive any such extension, without introducing a licencing system for the press: a measure the bare mention of which would, perhaps, be scarce endured among some of the warmest advocates for the other. To shut up the Court of Public Opinion altogether would be among the most unpopular, not to say the most dangerous, of all attempts: but the simple faculty of being heard is a privilege which no government whatever can, with the least colour of reason, be censured for securing to itself: even if this were the known object of the *Police Gazette*, which it is not proposed to be.—Laying out of the question altogether the press-licencing system, between the Sedition Act and the proposed *Police Gazette*, the difference in point of roughness of operation is as great, as between the strongest *Drastic*, and the most gentle alterative.

If this instrument be not employ'd—all the wit of man can not devise, nor all the efforts of man produce, an equivalent for it. In the

---

80 The Seditious Meetings Act of 1796 (36 Geo. III, c. 8) proscribed the holding of public meetings of more than 50 persons for political purposes, unless publicized in advance and authorized by Justices of the Peace.

shape of a series of Essays, published on the ordinary footing, without other support than its own merits, all the talents in the kingdom or in the world put together could not produce a composition, the circulation of which would amount to more than a few hundreds, or at the utmost a very few thousands, and that but momentary, depending not only upon the ability of the Conductors, but upon the taste and humour of the times. Spectators, Tatlers, Guardians, Freeholders—none of that class of writings, not even the most popular, was ever able to maintain its ground as a periodical composition for more than a very few years:[81] nor have any of these ingenious and polished productions descended low enough for the present purpose. Neither wit nor wisdom can act where it is not: to act every where, a paper must be present every where: but present every where neither paper nor any thing else can be, without those wings, which it is here proposed to construct, and which can not be constructed by any other hand than that of Government. No paper bearing a name of party on its title-page—though it were the party of the country—no paper which aimed avowedly at this object, can act in pursuit of it with nearly equal advantage and effect. Hanging out such a sign, it presupposes, on the part of its customers, the presence of those very dispositions the absence of which is the cause that produces the demand for it. Addressing itself to none but those whose affections are already engaged, and deeply engaged, on the same side, it gives warning to those on the other side to shut their doors against it, and to those who are neutral or indifferent, to put themselves upon their guard against its influence.

All instruments, that for their efficiency depend principally upon the nicety of the workmanship, are essentially incompetent to such a purpose. Worthy by its importance of occupying the ablest hands the country produces or can be made to produce, the instrument presented by the *Police Gazette* possesses the peculiar advantage of being incapable of being altogether spoilt, even by the clumsiest. Dependent within certain bounds, as every work of art must be, upon the hands that frame it, it is beyond all comparison less dependent than any other. Composed of materials always new, and endowed with

---

81 *The Tatler*, a thrice-weekly journal founded by Richard Steele (bap. 1672, d. 1729), writer and politician, ran from 12 April 1709 to 2 January 1711. A prominent contributor was Joseph Addison (1672–1719), writer and politician, and on 1 March 1711 Addison and Steele jointly launched *The Spectator*, which ran daily until 6 December 1712. On 12 March 1713 Steele began another daily journal, *The Guardian*, which ran until 1 October 1713. Addison revived *The Spectator* as a thrice-weekly publication from 18 June to 20 December 1714 and then established *The Freeholder*, which ran twice-weekly from 23 December 1715 to 20 June 1716.

attractions of which the power is inherent and indestructible, it may be superior or inferior to itself, but, at the very lowest, it will be superior to all others put together.

For supplying this additional and perpetual sheet-anchor to the Vessel of the State, the institution of the proposed Board presents such an opportunity, as if now permitted to slip away unimproved, may never be to be recalled.

The Bible (it may be said) is what the people *ought* to read:— there is their best preservative. Be it so:—but is the conclusion just, that because they *ought*, therefore they will *read* it? and that nothing should be done in aid of this preservative? Were this reasoning just, then ought all penal laws to be abolished, since a man ought to live honestly although there were no such laws. No:—the just and only just conclusion is—then let no expedient be left unemploy'd, which can contribute to engage a man to read his Bible. In a Newspaper (who does not know it?) a man will read, and read throughout, what he would not so much as look at elsewhere.—Many a man, who would loath or scorn to read his Bible *in* his Bible, might be made to read it in the *Police Gazette*. In his Bible, a man can *not* be made to read the *Police Gazette*: but in the *Police Gazette*, he *might* be made to read his Bible. The sacred Book itself will not be deprived by it of a single reader:—on the contrary, it may be made to acquire them by thousands.

{106} § 46. Page 93. {*Lawful . . . . to add to the amount . . . . of the several licence-Duties*}.

106. Shall this section be inserted?

Whether this mode of supply towards the expence of the *Police Gazette* shall be adopted—and if so, whether to this or what other amount must be left to the proper judges—and this section will stand or be struck out accordingly.

{107} § 48. Page 95. {*Commissioners . . . to . . . frame a . . . . Calendar of Delinquency*}.

107. Necessity and probably popularity of a Calendar of Delinquency— Analogous publications already existing— Practical use of it as an

As *Finance* has its annual Budget, so (it is conceived) ought *Police*. The proposed *Calendar of Delinquency* would be the main article in the Budget of Police. It is by an instrument of this nature, and by this alone, that any explicit index or measure can be afforded, of the demand for improvement in this line at the outset, or progressively of the result, favourable or unfavourable, of such exertions as from time to time may come to have been made in that view.

National progress, in point of wealth and population, has of late, though comparatively but of late, been thought worthy of being registered and attended to.[82] It seems almost time that the state of the nation in respect of internal security and morality, should likewise be thought worthy of being collected and attended to, with at least equal care. The demand for exertion in this new line is neither less urgent, nor the benefits derivable from it more questionable, than in the other. To remove a portion of wealth and labour into this or that channel out of all the rest is, in but too many instances, the sole occupation of the exertions bestowed by government upon the augmentation of the national stock of industry, and the expence and vexation attending the removal, the sole fruit. Such are the obstacles opposed to the efforts of government in the line of political economy by the nature of things: but the nature of things will not be found to oppose any such obstacle to efforts from the same quarter in the line of penal law. In this latter instance, nothing can be clearer than the results that may be afforded, nothing more conclusive than the inferences. Capital can not be given to one branch of industry without being taken from another: but reductions may be made in the number of offences of any one class committed within the Year, without any addition made to the number of any other. By the number of offences under each head of delinquency for a given precedent period compared with the number of offences for a subsequent period of equal length (distance between period and period such as shall afford time for the experiment), the degree of efficiency of a supposed remedy may be exhibited in figures: and as to such part of the inconvenience of it as consists of expence (for no measure of government whatever, not even the most unexceptionable, can ever be altogether free from inconvenience), the inconvenience of the remedy may be exhibited in figures likewise. This expence and the vexation together (for no measure of the coercive kind—that is no measure at all but those which consist in the simple removal of coercion already applied—can be unattended

82 In 1796 John Rickman (1771–1840), statistician and civil servant, circulated among MPs a memorandum entitled 'Thoughts on the Utility and Facility of a General Enumeration of the People of the British Empire', which led to the passing of the Census Act of 1800 (41 Geo. III, c. 15). For estimates of the progess in national wealth see, for instance, [George Rose,] *A Brief Examination into the Increase of the Revenue, Commerce, and Navigation, of Great Britain, since the Conclusion of the Peace in 1783*, London, 1792, and [George Rose], *A Brief Examination into the Increase of the Revenue, Commerce, and Manufactures, of Great Britain, from 1792 to 1799*, London, 1799. Rose (1744–1818), whose name appeared on subsequent editions of these works, was Secretary to the Treasury 1782–3, 1783–1801, and later Vice-President of the Board of Trade and joint Paymaster-General 1804–6, Vice-President of the Board of Trade 1807–12, and Treasurer of the Navy 1807–18.

with vexation) will give the exact price which the public pays in each instance for the benefit of the measure.

In a word, the *Calendar of Delinquency* will be, to penal legislation, what the *thermometer* is to Chemistry: and by the attentive observation and practical application of it, the improvement in the *moral art*, may come to rival the progress made, and continually making, by the *natural science*. So much additional fuel consumed, so many degrees of additional heat, as indicated by the *thermometer*: so much money or punishment expended, so many units substracted from the sum total of offences as indicated by the *Calendar of Delinquency*.

This, like other contributions to the science of political arithmetic, and not less than any of them, is that sort of acquisition that, from the very nature of [it], promises to be generally acceptable to persons of all parties and descriptions:—a perpetual fund of information, generally interesting and perpetually new. Independently of its utility, it promises amusement, and each individual will reckon upon making his own use of it. Men in Office and men out of office, the speculative and the active, the industrious and the idle—some with one view, some with another—all agree in their appetite for facts.

In the Metropolis and its vicinity, the Calendars or *Bills*, as they are called, of *mortality*, the lists of deaths with their supposed causes, have for a century and more been collected and published, and use has been made of them in a variety of ways.[83] In the present instance, the connection between science and art, between theory and practice, is surely rather more intimate than in that: effects are rather more obedient to the power of human causes: *sin* in every line is but too difficult to prevent, but in no line quite so difficult as *Death*.

Affording a practical test as well as index of the utility of any new measure to which it may be thought fit to apply it, another effect of the *Calendar of Delinquency* will be the operating as a check to crude and half-considered projects in the line of political improvement, as the practice of keeping regular books operates as a check to similar enterprizes in the line of private industry. By holding up to view the idea of profit and loss in perpetual conjunction, by the continual calls it gives to the Statesman to look at both sides of the account, it opposes a powerful corrective to those partial views in which profit alone is taken account of, and loss turned aside from, as if it were not

83 The Bills of Mortality were weekly returns and annual summaries, issued regularly from 1592 onwards, of the numbers of baptisms and burials, with ages and causes of death, that had taken place in the City of London, the City of Westminster and Southwark, and a number of surrounding parishes.

worth thinking of. Abstractedly considered, it is easy enough to devise measures that in one shape or other would be serviceable in the way of Police. But will the advantage in each case afford sufficient payment for the vexation and expence? On that question depends the eligibility of each measure: and to that question it is only from the *Calendar of Delinquency* that a substantial and perfectly satisfactory answer can be deduced.

Let the question—shall a National Watch or *Maréchaussée* for the guarding of the Roads all over the country be instituted?—serve as an example. Proceeding upon the ground [of] theory and analogy, without attending to figures—if a Parish Watch be necessary, so should a City or Metropolitan watch—and if a City or Metropolitan Watch, so should a National. But a National Watch or *Maréchaussée* will not cost less (say for argument sake) than £40,000 a Year. Turning, then, to the *Calendar of Delinquency*, let £20,000 a Year and no more appear to have been the amount of the property lost by highway robbery, within the same space of time: and, to clear the case from complication, let the year be a year of peace. On the face of this account, the evidence given by the *Calendar of Delinquency* in relation to the supposed project of a National *Maréchaussée* will not present itself as operating very strongly in recommendation of the measure. But further still, in cases of this kind, it is scarcely in the nature of any measure whatever, to compass its end to a degree of absolute perfection: say, then, that the effect of such an establishment would be—(or say that it has been)—not to put an end to highway Robberies altogether—for that would be next to a miracle—but to reduce the loss from £20,000 a year to £10,000, or £5,000: that is to strike off £10,000 or £15,000 from the amount of it. On this further view, the indication presented by this channel of investigation appears still less favourable to the supposed measure. On the other hand, neither is highway robbery the only head of delinquency against which the establishment in question would operate as a preservative (though it is certainly by far the most considerable head), nor, in the case of highway robbery, does the sum total of the pecuniary loss constitute the sum total of the mischief of the offence: for the general apprehension in the neighbourhood of a road on which robberies are frequent, and the restraint on travelling which, to a certain degree, will be the result of such apprehension, remain to be added to the account. These *items*, unfortunately, are not to be had in figures. And hence, but hence only, arise those incommensurable quantities by the amount of which the conclusions deducible from this source of information will fall short, in point of certainty and precision, of those which rest in their whole extent on the basis of mathematical demonstration.[a]

An example afforded by a former head may answer the double purpose of illustrating the use of the proposed *Calendar of Delinquency*, and that of displaying still further the conveniency of a practice already recommended and exemplified, viz: that of operating by the creation of powers rather than by regulations ready made—working by a light and handy engine (so to speak), viz: the *Board*, rather than by the great complicated and unwieldy mechanism of Parliament: an advantage, let it never be forgotten, still more conspicuous with reference to the interests of the individual subjected to the power in question than to those of the public at large, for whose benefit it is more particularly designed. Two or more powers being supposed to be created by Parliament, all conspiring to the same end, let that one of them all be first selected and acted upon, which promises to be attended with least vexation to the party, whose liberty is abridged by the exercise of it: this being tried by itself for a year or two, let the *Calendar of Delinquency* be consulted to discover its effects in practice: it being remembered at the same time that the greater the effect and success of the regulation thus pitched upon as least burthensome, the less the demand is that remains for that other, or those others, that are more burthensome. By this means it may happen that the greatest part of the burthen, which, were it not for the sort of attention in question, would have been laid on, as it were, in one heap and in the first instance, may thus be saved. Thus, call the number of delinquencies of a given class occurring throughout the Kingdom in the compass of a given Year 200: and a single one out of a cluster of regulations, for the establishment of which powers are created, being established in the first instance,

---

[a] Might not the employment of the military for this purpose be a means of striking off the greatest part of the expence? Would not a force of this description be more under command, as well as more effective, than any civil force? Would not the subordination as between the component members be more decided, the discipline more strict, and thence the security against abuse of power, as well as any other species of misconduct, more entire? Would not the service they were thus employ'd in against the internal enemies have the additional good effect of forming and keeping up the habits of activity, intrepidity and subordination, and thus keep them in [a] state of constant preparation for service against foreign enemies? Have the aversions that have been entertained against the employment of the existing stock of military force (a measure very different from the encrease of it) any better foundation than that of a superficial prejudice—incapable of standing the test of reason?—Are not this and all other prejudices of the same cast upon the wane? These are topics which it is sufficient thus to glance at—the discussion of them belongs not to the present purpose.

let the number of similar delinquencies in the course of the next Year have sunk to 100. Such being the effect, the utmost force that can be acquired by the accumulation of the most burthensome regulations that can be imagined can produce no greater effect, all of it together, than what shall be equal to the effect produced by the single one in question, and that one the least burthensome: it can not even produce so much: for as *moral* action, how well soever conducted, can never, in point of regularity of effect, be brought to be upon a par with *mechanical* action, the utmost that can be done, by the most consummate wisdom employ'd on such a ground, is to diminish the current of Delinquency in each channel—it can never dry it up altogether.

In the ordinary way of proceeding, all manner of regulations that present themselves as capable, each of them, of contributing any thing towards lessening the frequency of the Offence, are brought forward together, and laid upon the shoulders of the subject in one lump: if the Bill, pregnant with all these burthens, passes, the load thus laid upon the shoulders of the subject is by this means greater than would have been necessary; but an opposite inconvenience which may also happen is—that Parliament takes fright at the magnitude of the burthen, and the whole measure, with every advantage that had been expected from it, falls to the ground.

The *Calendar of Delinquency* can not be considered as an object altogether new or indifferent to the eye of the legislature. Attempts towards the construction of such a Register—attempts, though partial and unconnected—are visible in various parts of the Statute Book. The instances in which *Convictions* (i:e: Records of Conviction) issued by Justices out of General Sessions have been required to be trans-mitted to the General Sessions, and there preserved (*filed* is the term employ'd), are too scattered to be easily collected, and too well known to be worth collecting.[84]

By the last Hawker's Act (29 G. 3. c. 43) [...] every Justice before whom any person has been convicted under that Act is (by § 28) required to transmitt to the Commissioners divers particulars relative to the conviction, under the several heads following; viz:—1. Name of the convicted person.—2. Day when convicted.—3. Offence whereof convicted.—4. Sum paid on account of the conviction: and the Convictions are required to be classed according to the Counties &c. in which they have taken place. To this head of correspondence, the

---

84 Justices of the Peace were routinely required to return records of convictions to the next Quarter Sessions for filing by the Clerk of the Peace.

Commissioners of Police, as representatives of the Commissioners of Hawkers, will succeed of course.

The practice of requiring Convictions to be transmitted and filed, as above, would naturally have been more frequent, not to say universal, if there had been any common repository into which they could have been received, and in which they could have been preserved, for general use. From the receiving them at the Courts of Quarter Session in the several Counties, distributed as they are by that means among more than fifty different Repositories, and thus scattered all over the kingdom, the collection thus made of them can answer very little purpose: so little, that upon the face of the business, the attention paid to these requisitions does not seem likely to be very general among Magistrates. The case would be very different in this respect, under a Central Board, charged with the special duty of compleating the list of these documents from all quarters, and responsible to Parliament and to the public for whatever deficiencies may be found in it.

Of the practicability of a Register of this sort, could any doubt be entertained of it, other exemplifications are not wanting. The Tables of Convictions printed by the Committee of Finance, for offences arising out of the business of the Hackney Coach office[a] (one of the Offices proposed to be merged in the proposed Board of Police) may be referred to in this view.

By the 31 Geo. 3. c. 46. § 8, Returns are required to be made by Jailers.[85] But this provision, though good as far as it goes, does not come up altogether to the present purpose. It extends not to prisoners committed on mesne process. The Returns it prescribes are to be made at no other time than the first day of each Assizes: that is, nowhere more than twice in the Year, and in some places only once. The persons to be comprized in them are such only as compose the existing stock of prisoners of the above description on each particular day. No account

---

[a] 11th Report.[86]

85 The Gaols Act of 1791, § 8, as Bentham goes on to note in more detail below, prescribed that keepers of jails should, on the first day of every Assizes, make a return to the Clerk of the Assizes, among other matters, of the names of all persons in custody, the offences of which they had been found guilty, the court before which they had been convicted, and the sentences imposed.
86 See 'An Account of the Number and Nature of Complaints and Adjudications, made respecting Hackney Coaches and Chairs, during the Year 1796, at the Public Office in Great Marlborough Street', in 'Eleventh Report from the Select Committee on Finance, &c. Hackney Coach Office', 19 July 1797, Appendix C. 4, in *Commons Sessional Papers of the Eighteenth Century* (1797), cviii, 358, which lists five convictions in 1796 of Hackney coach owners and drivers for 'having exacted more than his Fare'.

of intermediate commitments or departures, between one Assize time and another: so that, even among prisoners committed on conviction, individuals in great numbers (by far the greater number of those committed for a few weeks or a few months) must, under this Act, escape notice. Each Jail may have lost nine-tenths of its inhabitants several times over by pestilences or escapes, and no indication of either misfortune be exhibited by these Returns. No such central authority as the proposed Board being then in existence, the persons to whom the Returns in question are required to be made, are the Clerks of Assize at the several Assizes. A Clerk of Assize not being that sort of person who can naturally be expected to feel any great concern about such matters, the persons looked to in that view seem to have been the several Judges of Assize: but even from these great Magistrates, engrossed as their time is by other duties, no very constant or systematical attention to any such documents, or to any uses that may be derivable from them, seems reasonably to be expected.

The following are (in substance) the heads expressive of the information demanded by this Act. 1. Cells, number. 2. Cells, size of each. 3. Prisoner's name. 4. Prisoner's Offence. 5. Court (in case of regular Procedure) in which the Prisoner was convicted. 6. Court—(in the like case) sentence passed by it on the Prisoner, in consequence of such Conviction. 7. Justice or Justices (in the case of summary procedure) by whom the Prisoner was convicted. 8. Prisoner's Age. 9. Prisoner's 'bodily estate'. 10. Prisoner's behaviour.

The following are among the heads, some or all of which, on one account or other, the proposed Board might, perhaps, find reason to add to the above. 1. Prisoner's place of nativity. 2. Prisoner's condition in respect of marriage:—Batchelor or Spinster—Widower or Widow— Married Man or Woman. 3. Prisoner's Occupation at the time of Commitment. 4. Prisoner's occupations from birth down to that time. 5. Prisoner's place of abode (if any) at the time of commitment. 6. Prisoner's places of abode from birth down to that time. 7. Prisoner's children (legitimate), number of them alive. 8. Prisoner's children, illegitimate (if any), number of them, if any, depending on him or her for subsistence. 9. Prisoner's child[ren], sex and age of each. 10. Prisoner's Child[ren], present occupation (if any) and prior occupations. 11. Prisoner's Child[ren]—present and prior places of abode.

From the above additional heads, a variety of indications may be drawn, subservient in a variety of ways to the purposes of Police. Aliens, Irishmen, Scotchmen, Welchmen, North-Countrymen, West-countrymen, Londoners, Soldiers, Sailors, Militia-men, Vagrants,

Gipsies, London and other regular-bred thieves, Suspected Coiners, Suspected Smugglers, would thus be distinguished. The degree in which licentiousness in respect of sexual intercourse is connected with other irregularities would also be observable, and the quantity of family suffering resulting from the delinquency of the father or mother would likewise be display'd. To indicate all the points of information derivable more or less immediately from these heads, with the uses to which these several points of information might be applied in practice, would almost require a volume.

Under favour of the latitude purposely given in the text, the Board would enlarge the number of heads in its blank forms, in proportion to the maturity of its experience and the enlargement of its views. How much better thus, than for Parliament to be tormented for a fresh Act, every time an additional head came to be demanded, for a system of Book-keeping, for this or any other public purpose!

If, in this country as in others, the concerns of the Poor should be considered as constituting a branch of the business of Police, the Returns obtained by Gilbert's Acts,[a] for two temporary and distinct periods of Years, might be required from Year to Year, and be made transmissible to the Board of Police; and the substance of those Acts might be re-enacted for that purpose, with any additions that might be judged expedient. The almost universal compliance with the requisitions of that Act, even without the benefit of any such permanent and appropriate authority as that of the proposed Board for ensuring compliance, may serve, as an example to shew the practicability of obtaining the most extensive set of documents for an adequate public purpose: while the few instances of non-compliance may serve as indications of the still more perfect compliance obtainable by such an authority as that of the proposed Board.

Under Jonas Hanway's Act,[b] Accounts of the state of the Non-adult part of the London Poor are, or at least ought to be, kept under several

[a] 16 G. 3. c. 40; 26 G. 3. c. 56.[87]
[b] 7 G. 3. c. 39.[88]

87 Thomas Gilbert (c. 1720–98), land agent and poor law reformer, MP for Newcastle under Lyme 1763–8 and Lichfield 1768–94, was responsible for promoting both the Poor Act of 1776 (16 Geo. III, c. 40), which required Overseers of the Poor to submit information to Parliament on the operation of the poor laws for the year ending at Easter 1776, and the Poor Returns Act of 1786 (26 Geo. III, c. 56), which required the submission of similar information for the three years ending at Easter 1785.
88 The Poor Act of 1767, instigated by Jonas Hanway (bap. 1712, d. 1786), merchant and philanthropist, made provision for children born in or received into workhouses in parishes in London, Westminster, and within the Bills of Mortality to be removed to

very interesting heads, from Year to Year. No central Repository being *then* to be found, for collecting, arranging and publishing them, the utility derived from them, though considerable, is not what it might be.

Fragments of the same kind—partial collections of documents similar to those of which the compleat collection is here proposed to be regularly formed and published—materials for the proposed *Calendar of Delinquency*—are not altogether wanting under the Scotch Law. By the [8th] Anne ch. [16].[89] § 4, inferior Judges and Magistrates are '.. required ..... to make up particular accounts of such criminal facts ..... as are to be tried within their respective Circuits, containing the names and designation of the Offenders, the facts [connected][90] with the circumstances of time and place, and others that may serve to discover the truth; containing also the names and designations of the Witnesses, and titles of such *Writes'* (pieces of written evidence) 'as are to be made use of at the trials': which documents, after being authenticated by the signature of the Judges and Magistrates therein mentioned, or their Deputies or Clerks, are to be transmitted '.. to the Lord Justice Clerk or his Deputies at Edinburgh, at least forty days before the holding of the respective Circuit Courts' at which the trials are to take place:—and the use, for which these Documents are required, is declared to be—the serving as a ground for the several indictments in each instance.

This (it may occurr) does not come up altogether to the present purpose: since the notion, under which the documents in question are regarded, is that of their being necessary to the rendering of justice, when the time comes, in each particular case, so that they are not designed to serve merely as memorials, shewing, with a view to collateral and distant purposes, what has been done and taken place, in so many past instances.

The following provision, however, is, as far as it goes, precisely in point. By the Act for the abolition of heritable jurisdictions,[a] no person

---

^a 20 G. 2. c. 43. § 19.[91]

rural districts and to be apprenticed at the age of 14. The Act, §§ 16–21 and Schedules B–E, required officers in each parish to maintain registers of the infant poor and a list of apprentices placed out, with the latter sent to the Company of Parish Clerks for collation and printing.

89 MS '16th Anne ch. 17'. There are minor inaccuracies in the rendering of the following passage from the Circuit Courts (Scotland) Act of 1709.
90 MS 'committed' appears to be a slip.
91 The Heritable Jurisdictions (Scotland) Act of 1747 abolished the traditional judicial rights held by Scottish clan chieftains.

'shall be committed .... in order to trial for any assaults, Batteries and' {or} 'small crimes, without a warrant in writing, expressing the particular cause for which such person is imprisoned; which warrant or order shall be entered at large' {by whom?} 'in a Book to be kept for that purpose; and Extracts thereof' {of what nature?—under what heads?—of every such Warrant?—or of some only, and which? &c. &c.} 'shall be transmitted' {by whom?} 'to the Sheriff or Stewart Court of the County or Stewartry in which such Order shall issue or be executed' {which?} 'there to remain on record.'

The end in view *here* was plainly that the existence of the documents in question might, when thus registered, operate by its notoriety as a sort of check upon the authority exercised [under][92] the several warrants. But, in point of strength, what sort of a check can be afforded by either the written Book of Copies, or the written Book of Extracts, or both together—each lying on a single shelf—compared with what would be afforded by the printed and universally-circulated *Calendar of Delinquency*?

In looking out for materials for the *Calendar of Deliquency*, the object has been to find out the several sorts of written, and consequently permanent, *instruments*, which, in the existing state of things, come to be framed and issued in the several lines of penal procedure—the several *occasions* on which they respectively come to be issued—and the several sorts of *persons* into whose hands they must have found their way: since whatever species of instrument must already, for the justification and security of any persons concerned, have been brought into existence, especially if for the same reason it must already have been presented, the transmission of a Copy or Abstract of such instrument is an operation that may be performed with little difficulty or trouble:—with much less than the framing of any new instrument.

In the regular branch of Procedure, such documents exist already in sufficient variety and abundance. In the summary branch of penal procedure, they may be comprized, mostly if not altogether, under five heads—viz: *Informations, Convictions, Recognizances, Summonses* and *Warrants*. In regard to Informations, Convictions, and Recognizances, there is but one public person in whose hands at any time the instrument is necessarily to be found—viz: the Magistrate by whom the memorandum or statement of the transaction, or chain of transactions, in question, is framed. In the case of a Summons or a

107 continued. Method taken for finding out existing materials for the construction of the Calendar of Delinquency.—Use in requiring the same matter from different sets of hands. More convenient for Subordinates to correspond with one another through the medium of the Boards than directly.

---

92 MS 'by'.

Warrant—both of them instruments expressive of an act of the will—a command addressed by one person to one or more other persons, there are, at the least, *two* public persons, and in some instances *three*, in whose hands, at one time or other, the same instrument must have been lodged: the Magistrate by whom the command has been issued, and one or more subordinates, to whom it has been addressed:—in the case of a summons, the Magistrate who issues it, and the Constable who conveys it: in the case of most Warrants, the Magistrate who issues them, and the Constable by whom they are to be executed: in the case of a Warrant of discharge addressed to a Jailor, the Magistrate and the Jailor: in the case of a Warrant of Commitment, the Magistrate, the Constable and the Jailor. The greater the number of public persons thus concerned in the same transaction, so much the better for the present purpose: so many sets of Officers thus connected, so many checks, each to the other, with regard to the punctuality of the expected Returns, and so many securities against neglect on the part of any of them.

To make the most effectual provision possible against deficiencies in the stock of materials requisite for composing the *Calendar of Delinquency*, virtual duplicates, or even triplicates, are necessary to be called for—documents either one or two of which might be useless, if the Return of any one were absolutely certain. That these virtual duplicates or triplicates may not be duplicates and triplicates in point of form and tenor as well as in substance, that is, that they may not be mere *repetitions*, one or two may be a literal Copy or Copies in each instance, the other or others an Abstract or Abstracts under heads: the sort of person of whom the mere Copy is required being the sort of person on whose part the degree of intelligence requisite to the filling up of an Abstract is with least certainty to be expected, viz: the Constable: for the difficulty of getting Blank Forms properly filled up by unlettered and unexperienced hands has in practice been found greater than was expected: the sort of person from whom the Abstract is required being, for the opposite reason, the man of education, the Magistrate.

If then, in the case of the Constable, Copies be required, punctuality of transmission will be more to be depended upon than if Abstracts were required. Making or filling up an *Abstract*, even a single Abstract, is work for the *head*; and if the Abstracts of a number of warrants at a time are to be entered on the same paper, each will be apt to delay the transmission of the rest. Taking a *Copy* is work only for the *hand*: and, there being no convenience to be gained by making any one such copy wait for any other, there will be no obstacle, but distance from the Post-House, to prevent their being sent off, each of them, by the very next post.

The *natural* course of the business (though, not being the necessary course, it would hardly be proper to encumber the Bill with the mention of it)—the course which the business would be apt to run into of itself, seems to be—that the Justice, when he delivers a Warrant to the Constable, should, at the same time, deliver to him a duplicate, for him to transmitt forthwith to the Board, according to the provision in the text:[93] and by using printed Forms on Papers of the same or correspondent size, with a direction to the Board ready printed on the back, the business may be conducted with great simplicity and regularity, and with very little trouble. As blank instruments of all kinds for the use of Justices of Peace are already an object of sale—as the Post-Office is already in the habit of taking charge of small sums of money on the account of individuals—and as the recent and useful establishment of the Paper Office has put into the hands of government the means of supplying itself with that necessary article upon economical terms,[94] the faculty of obtaining from Government the supply requisite for this additional consumption at a reduced price (so it be not less than a little above the cost to Government) is an accommodation which, perhaps, it might not be unreasonable to afford to Magistrates—that is, to servants of the public, serving at their own expence.

Of *summonses*, it seems hardly worth while that copies or even abstracts should be required. An instrument of this class being neither necessary, in the character of a document, to the indicating the existence of a penal suit of the class in question, nor in all cases so much as necessary to either the commencement, the progress or the conclusion of it, the trouble of transmitting so voluminous an addition to the mass of necessary documents, will hardly be thought worth imposing, unless some special advantage, of adequate magnitude, should be pointed out as calling for it. [...]

93 See p. 97 above.
94 The Stationery Office had been established in April 1786 as a department of the Treasury in order to supply paper, parchment, pens, sealing wax and other items of stationery to all public offices.

108. The
notoriety
which the
proceedings
of Magistrates
will thus
acquire will
be a pledge
of their
correctness.

{108} § 48. Page 98. {*Warrant &c. . . . memorandum therof . . . . .
to be returned . . . . .*}.

Of the system of checks thus proposed to be established, the direct
object is—simply to ensure information of the existence of the several
documents, the transmission of which is required. But a collateral
result and additional good effect would be—the putting Magistrates
upon their guard with respect to the propriety of their proceedings,
as exhibited and recorded by these instruments: operating thus in the
character of a preventive system with regard to the several species of
transgression, whether of omission or commission, into which Magistrates, as such, are liable to fall. What the licencing system is with
reference to the traders who are the object of it, this system of communication is (due regard being had to the differences in point of rank,
education and station in life in the two instances) with reference to
the Country Gentlemen of whom the Magistracy is composed. As the
tendency of the licencing system is to diminish the business, and still
more the demand for the business, of the Old Bailey and the Assizes,
so the tendency of this system of communication, with regard to these
materials for the *Calendar of Delinquency*, is to diminish that part of
the business, and of the demand for the business, of the King's Bench,
which concerns informations against Magistrates.

In the course taken for obtaining the requisite body of information,
less ceremony will naturally be used (and accordingly less ceremony
is used by the Bill) in the instance of persons of inferior account, such
as the Clerks in the several Courts of regular procedure, the Jailers
and the Parish Constables, than in the case of the Magistrates, that is
the Country Gentlemen of the greatest respectability in their several
Counties. In the former case, Penalties, though slight, and rather for
shew than use, are avowedly employ'd: in the other case, no mention
of any penalty is introduced, except in as far as a penalty pointed at the
Magistrate's Clerk, if he happens to have one, may be supposed to affect
the Magistrate himself. But the necessary penalties being pointed at the
Officers of inferior account (the Jailers and Constables), these Officers
may, through apprehension of such penalties, be reasonably expected
to furnish with tolerable punctuality the documents required from
them: and by reason of the correspondence and necessary connection
between that branch of information and that which is required from the
Magistracy, no document can be furnished by either Constable or Jailor,
without indicating the demand for a corresponding Document to be
transmitted by some Magistrate. No Magistrate can, therefore, ever be a

defaulter in this respect, without being pointed out as a Defaulter, and in that character applied to by his neighbour the Country Police Commissioner, or the Board, or both: and finally, by the Lord Lieutenant of his County, by whose representation to the Chancellor, he might be left out of the Commission, if nothing less would serve.[95]

{109} § 48. Page 98. {*. . Such . . . excepted . . . . as the . . . Treasury . . . . shall have forbidden, in consideration of the expence*}.

109. Expence of Paper— Expedients for keeping it down— Sources of reimbursement—Poor's and King's share in forfeitures, those on Recognizances included.

In the mere article of paper, the expence that would result from the proposed institution is certainly no trifling object. But by means of the recently instituted *Paper-Office*, the expence will have been reduced to less than half what it might otherwise have amounted to,[96] and there are expedients which might be employ'd with advantage, partly for confining it within its due limits, partly for reimbursing to the public the amount of it.

1. This (as well as other Paper employ'd for Government purposes and at Government expence) might have some distinctive and conspicuous mark, pervading the whole extent of it, analogous to the broad arrow on the King's naval Stores:[97] on which condition it might be made penal to write upon it for any other purpose: especially as any contravention of this law would carry its own evidence upon the face of it: and, as at any rate it would be paid for at a price higher than that of waste-paper, it could not answer to any person to obtain more of it than what he really wanted for a public purpose.

2. The price charged for it should be the natural prime cost—or at least proportioned to the natural prime cost—of the article, deducting the duty paid on it to government. This deduction, though it would not diminish the real expence of the institution to Government, would keep down the apparent, and prevent it from doing what it would otherwise do—exceed by a great amount the real expence. It would be misleading Parliament and the public, if the institution were to be charged with so

---

95 According to Burn, *Justice of the Peace*, ii, 96, 'if a justice will not on complaint to him made, execute his office, the party grieved may complain to the judges of assize, or to the lord chancellor; and upon examination, if it appeareth that the complaint is true, the chancellor may put him out of the commission, and he shall be punished moreover according to his desert'.

96 i.e. the Stationery Office: see p. 133 n. above.

97 A 'broad arrow', a stylized representation of an arrowhead, was widely used to mark the property and stores of the Board of Ordnance, in particular equipment and munitions supplied to the Royal Navy.

many thousand pounds, as if it were costing that sum to Government, while in fact Government was disbursing nothing for the institution on that score but what, on that same score, it already had received: the institution being as fully the cause of the receipt as of the expence.

One help towards reimbursing to Government the real amount of the expence might be afforded by a law giving at once to the Police Fund all shares of forfeitures which, under the several Statutes, are given nominally to the *poor* of the parish:[98] in reality, as every body knows, to the *rich* of the same parish, since, in as far as the forfeitures are levied and applied, the money goes in diminution of the burthen of that tax upon the rich which is called the *Poor Rate*. For the rich of the several Parishes, this relief is no object: to the Police Fund, the aggregate of the sums levied, or at least the aggregate of the sums that might and *then would* be levied, would be a considerable object. This would be a supply—not only applicable to the expence of the *Calendar of Delinquency*—but growing, in a great degree at least, out of the *Calendar of Delinquency* itself: since, among other effects of the supply of information afforded by the returns, would be the information of the supply of money due from a source which otherwise would be apt to lie neglected and unproductive.

A collateral advantage arising out of the same source would be—the restoring the legal audibility of the only persons who in general are likely to have any evidence to give: and thereby doing away one of the most prolific of those causes of artificial inefficiency which are but too abundant in the system of judicial procedure. [...]

A second resource of a similar nature might be the giving to the Police Fund, what is called the King's share, of all forfeitures levied under penal Statutes, under which the whole or any part of the sum forfeited is given to the King,[99] or at least of all forfeitures which, being given to the King, are, under statutes of that description, made leviable by Justices of the Peace. What becomes of these forfeitures at present will be mentioned presently.

A third resource might be, the giving to Justices of the Peace the power of levying the penalty to the extent of a certain amount (say £20, or up to £50) in the case of every recognizance taken before Justices of the Peace: a power which, it is apprehended, might just as well be

---

98 The Imitation of Tea Act of 1767 (17 Geo. III, c. 29), §§ 6–7, for instance, prescribed that one half of all forfeitures made under the Act should go to the poor of the parish where an offence was committed and half to the parish.

99 See, for instance, the Silk Works Act of 1763 (3 Geo. III, c. 21), § 1, the Seducing Certain Artificers to go beyond Sea Act of 1782 (22 Geo. III, c. 60), § 7, and the Customs Act of 1793 (33 Geo. III, c. 70), § 6.

executed by those Magistrates as the power of levying a penalty to the same amount issuing in a more direct way out of the tenor of the law: and the money drawn from this source also might be made payable to the Police Fund. By this means, the intended energy and use might be restored to an instrument which at present is, in one instance, perhaps, out of a hundred, an instrument of ruin to the individual, and in the ninety-nine others a dead letter. [...]

If, from the sources or supposed sources of revenue here proposed to be transferred to the Police Fund, any thing is at present extracted by individuals on the score of fees of office, an annual indemnification, to the amount of the average annual value of the emoluments thus derived, would of course be to be charged on the Police Fund during the lives of the present occupants of the respective Offices: but the charge on this score does not threaten to be very heavy. From fines and forfeitures levied, or which ought to be levied, on conviction before Magistrates, nothing appears to be derived either to the Revenue or to any Officer of the Revenue—'it not appearing by the view of the Estreats that such fines and forfeitures are included therein, there is too much reason to fear they have not been, in many instances, certified by the Magistrates at the Quarter Sessions, and it may be doubtful whether the Surveyor General of the Green Wax[100] has sufficient means of knowing what fines and forfeitures of this kind accrue, and whether there is any compulsory method to oblige the Justices to certify them at the Quarter Sessions, and to pay them into the hands of the Sheriff, which seems the only course of such fines and forfeitures getting into the Exchequer.'[a]

So much for fines imposed and forfeitures declared by Magistrates sitting singly or in Petty Sessions: and the productiveness and efficiency of fines imposed and forfeitures declared in the Courts of General or Quarter Sessions does not appear to stand on a much better footing—'it being, according to the present practice, a period of two years or thereabouts after such Sessions fines and forfeitures are [estreated before any Process is issued for the Recovery of them; and in

[a] 23[d] Rep. of Committee of Finance, p. 218. Appendix O. 3.[101]

100 The Surveyor of the Green Wax was the Exchequer official with responsibility for collecting green wax monies, that is, revenues derived from fines, amercements, forfeitures and other debts owed to the Crown. The name arose from the colour of the seals traditionally used to authenticate the estreats by which such monies were exacted.
101 See 'Return of John Matthew Grimwood, Esquire, to certain Questions respecting the Collection of the Revenues arising from Fines, Issues, Amerciaments, &c', in 'Twenty-Third Report on Finance', 26 June 1798, Appendix O. 3, in *Commons Sessional Papers of the Eighteenth Century* (1798), cx, 219–24 at 224. Bentham's pagination corresponds to that in the original 'Report'.

that Interval it must happen that many of the Fines and Forfeitures are] lost by the death, removal, or insolvency of the parties. How it has happened that the summons of the Green Wax has not comprehended the Sessions Fines and Forfeitures, as well as the others, we are not able to learn; but we do not find that they have been included in that process within the memory of any Officer now living.'[a]

Here, then, we see a branch of the Revenue killed by mere old age, having become rotten at the core. This would of itself be no such great matter: the misfortune is that a branch of justice, having been grafted on this branch of the revenue, is become rotten along with it. What becomes of the money levied, or that should be levied, by Magistrates out of Sessions, it is, at present, impossible to know: the best thing that can happen in any instance is, that the Magistrate should have received it, and put it into his own pocket: punishment is then inflicted where it is due: and whether one person eats the money or another, makes little difference in the suffering of the man who, for his punishment, is deprived of it:—the worst that can happen, and the thing that seems likely to happen oftenest, is, that the Magistrate, not seeing any body to hand it over to, and fearing or disdaining to put it into his own pocket, should forbear to take it, because he does not know what to do with it.

The portion of Revenue and (what is much more) of justice depending for its existence upon Recognizances, requires somebody to watch—not only when the money leviable on this score *is* levied— but when the time is come when it ought to be levied:—that is when it is that any such event happens to take place by the happening of which the forfeiture of the Recognizance is incurred. Recognizances, being of different natures, that is taken for very different purposes, would require to be classed in this view: a task to be executed by or for the Board, and which, if time permitt, may perhaps be executed and subjoined to these Notes.[102] Furnished with the list of Recognizances taken within his District, and invited by a competent share in the penalty, the Police Surveyor of the District would be an effectual Watchman for this purpose. This would be among the fruits of the proposed system of Returns.

The Book-keeping requisite for them is at any rate not without example. In the London Police Offices, accounts can not but be kept of

[a] ibid. p. 214.[103]

102 No such classification has been located.
103 See ibid. 220.

the monies levied on this score, since these monies are to be employ'd, as far as they go, in defraying the expence of those offices. Accounts are by that means kept of the proceedings had, and documents issued, in those several offices, so far at least as is necessary for the purpose of indicating the source from which each sum has been derived. In one of these Offices, a general account is—or at least was—kept of all proceedings: in which, consequently, must have been included a mention in some way or other of each document belonging to the set of documents proposed to be transmitted, either *in terminis* or in abstract, by the proposed Returns. This example serves at least to shew what *may* be done: and what has been done spontaneously in the instance of any one Magistrate, may not unreasonably be expected to be done, when made matter of obligation, by every other: especially when what is required to be done shall have been reduced to a mechanical process—to a mere piece of *Clock-work*, by examples, instructions and blank forms. To execute such a business spontaneously and for the first time required a combination of zeal and talent: to execute it when bidden by law, according to a pattern given by law, will require no other properties than what may reasonably be looked for on the part of every person to whom the authority of a Magistrate has been thought fit to be intrusted.

Should the sources of indemnification thus indicated fail of being approved of, or should an apprehension be entertained that the proposed expence in paper, notwithstanding all indemnifications, would prove too great to be continued, the expence of making the experiment, were it only for a year or two, might surely not be grudged. If, upon experience, it were regarded as overbalancing the advantage, it might then at any time be struck off. In the mean time, the money thus expended would not have been thrown away: any more than the labour and money expended in the temporary obtainment of other branches of information by Committees of Parliament and Commissions instituted by authority of Parliament has been thrown away. And, moreover, though the *Calendar of Delinquency*, with its constituent elements, the proposed Returns from Regular Courts, Justices, Constables, and Jailors, should, after a year or two's trial, be given up, the proposed sources of indemnification, viz: the transfer of the Poor's and the King's share in forfeitures, and the transfer of forfeitures on Recognizances, to the Police Fund, would not, on that account, be to be given up. If proper in themselves, their propriety would not be affected by any opinion that might be formed of the proposed *Calendar of Delinquency*.

Upon the whole, the proposed expence of paper, whatever it may amount to, does not appear to be of that sort which in prudence can be grudged. What would be thought of the economy of the individual, who, to save the expence of Account Books, should resolve not to keep any accounts?

112.
Precedent
pursued—
Reports why
to Parliament
rather than
Council
Board.

{112} § 53. Page 102. {*Commissioners . . . shall . . . give an account . . . . to . . . . Parliament . . .*}.

The words between the inverted Commas[104] are copied from the first of the three Acts of the present reign for appointing Commissioners for the suggestion of improvements, viz: 20th G. 3. c. 54.[105]

The direction to report to *Parliament* is taken from the *first* of the above three Acts:[106] in the second,[a] it was to the King in Council only that the Reports were to be made: Parliament being omitted: but in the last,[b] Parliament was again inserted. The difference is by no means immaterial: Reports to Parliament are Reports to the public, whose eye will be upon the notice taken of them. Reports to the Council Board might sleep upon the shelves.

{113} § 53. Page 102. {*. . Suggest . . . regulations . . . . calculated for augmenting the efficacy . .*}.

The first of the three reforming Statutes, viz: that which concerns the public *Accounts*, speaks of '*defects*';[107] the last, viz: that relative to the Crown Lands, of '*Abuses*'.[108] In the present instance both words may be

---

[a] 25 G. 3. c. [19].[109]
[b] 26 G. 3. c. 87.[110]

104 i.e. in § 53, p. 102 above.
105 i.e. the Audit of Public Accounts Act of 1780, § 5.
106 Again, the Audit of Public Accounts Act of 1780.
107 See the long title of the Audit of Public Accounts Act of 1780: 'An Act of appointing and enabling Comissioners to examine, take, and state the publick Accounts of the Kingdom; and to report .. what Defects there are in the present Mode of receiving, collecting, issuing, and accounting for publick Money'.
108 The Crown Lands Revenues, etc. Act of 1786, § 1, prescribed that the appointed should, among other duties, suggest regulations to Parliament 'for redressing any Abuses in the Management' of the Crown Lands and in the collection of its revenues.
109 MS '74' is a slip. The Inquiry into Fees, Public Offices Act of 1785 (25 Geo. III, c. 19), § 1, prescribed that the Commissioners appointed under it should report to the Privy Council.
110 The Crown Lands Revenues, etc. Act of 1786, § 1, prescribed that the Commissioners appointed under it should, among other duties, suggest regulations to Parliament 'for redressing any Abuses in the Management' of the Crown Lands and in the collection of its revenues.

dispensed with (it should seem) with advantage. Professional men are not fond of hearing of *defects*, much less of *abuses*, in the law, or any branch of it. Under the words used in the text, legal power will not be wanting adequate to any stock of intellectual power that can be pressed into the service.

Part III
Comments

The Influence of Bentham on the Development of Focused Deterrence

Anthony A. Braga and Stephen Douglas

An increasing number of police departments have implemented focused deterrence strategies to control gang violence, disorderly drug markets and repeat individual offending. These strategies seek to change offender behaviour by understanding the underlying violence-producing dynamics and conditions that sustain recurring violence problems, and by implementing a blended set of law enforcement, community mobilization and social service actions (Kennedy et al. 1996; Braga et al. 2001). Focused deterrence strategies are targeted on specific behaviours by a small number of chronic offenders who are highly vulnerable to criminal justice sanctions (Kennedy 2008). The approach directly confronts offenders, informs them that continued offending will not be tolerated and also notifies these groups how the system will respond to violations of these new behaviour standards. The availability of social service assistance to targeted groups and individuals is another defining characteristic of focused deterrence strategies.

Bentham (1982) was a highly influential developer of deterrence theory and, as Quinn (2021) rightly observes, an early proponent of the idea that the police should be focused on crime prevention. Modern scientific evidence suggests that deterrent effects are ultimately determined by offender perceptions of sanction risk and certainty (Nagin 1998). The available evidence suggests that focused deterrence strategies generate large and visible shifts in offender perceptions of apprehension risks that, in turn, reduce criminal offending (Braga et al. 2018; Durlauf and Nagin 2011). This brief comment considers the influence of Bentham's work on two aspects of contemporary focused deterrence strategies that seem to influence their crime prevention efficacy: incorporating utilitarianism and optimizing the influence of sanctions.

Incorporating utilitarianism

Urban violence problems are often concentrated among groups of chronic, often (but not always) gang-involved, offenders. For instance, in 2006, roughly 1 per cent of Boston youth between the ages of 15 and 24 participated in gangs, but these gang dynamics generated more than half of all homicides, and gang members were involved in roughly 70 per cent of fatal and non-fatal shootings as either a perpetrator and/ or a victim (Braga et al. 2008). The key policy insight is that citywide levels of violence could be reduced if the behaviours of a small number of high-risk individuals were modified. Focused deterrence attempts to change the specific sanction risk perceptions of individuals in this small population rather than attempting to change general perceptions of the broader population, who are generally not involved in the targeted serious violent crime problem.

Bentham's original intention regarding the principle of utility was to study institutions in order to maximize the aggregate pleasure and minimize the aggregate pain of the populations they serve (Engelmann 2011). The focused deterrence framework aligns well with Bentham's principle of utility: focusing police resources upon a small, targeted population of offenders for the greater benefit of the entire population. Drawing on Bentham's work, a successful focused deterrence strategy could be viewed as congruent with the principle of utility given that community 'happiness' is augmented by reducing serious crime and community 'pains' are diminished by its highly economical use of criminal justice sanctions. By focusing enforcement efforts on the small number of people actually involved in criminal offending, it reduces the potential for harms to uninvolved community members who might get caught up in indiscriminate enforcement actions applied uniformly across urban settings. The strategy further attempts to minimize potential harms to targeted groups by offering services and opportunities to group members who want to change their life trajectories by halting their continued offending.

Optimizing the influence of sanctions

Bentham is credited with developing the idea that law is an instrument of policy and policy is primarily understood by individuals in terms of cost and benefit (Engelmann 2011). Deterrence theory suggests that crime can be prevented when the costs of committing the crime are perceived by the offender to outweigh the benefits (Zimring and Hawkins 1973). Bentham's (1982) sanction typology suggests there are five sources of 'pain' that influence offenders' decisions to commit crimes: the physical sanction, the political sanction, the moral sanction, the religious sanction and the sympathetic sanction. Although these kinds of sanctions are separate, their effects are intrinsically connected. One of the key elements in applying Bentham's typology to focused deterrence seems to rest on the notion that his sanction types are compatible and work together to create the desired deterrent effect. Focused deterrence strategies can be viewed as an exercise in 'getting deterrence right' by optimizing the possible impacts of these varied kinds of sanctions levied towards changing offender perceptions of continuing their criminal behaviour. This is most directly the case with the strategic application of political sanctions or the punishment of individuals by government officials. However, the inclusion of the other three sanction types in the strategy may also serve to enhance the crime-prevention efficacy of focused deterrence.

Focused deterrence strategies attempt to deter offenders from continuing to commit very specific types of criminal behaviours (e.g. gang-involved gun violence, disorderly street-level drug sales) by increasing the certainty and swiftness of the application of political sanctions. However, focused deterrence strategies are explicitly designed to prevent crime through the advertising of sanctions and the personalized application of deterrence messages through direct meetings with targeted individuals. The communication of political sanctions to relevant audiences is an important step in generating deterrent impacts (Zimring and Hawkins 1973). The approach directly confronts offenders via notification meetings where criminal justice officials inform them that continued offending will not be tolerated and explain how the system will respond to violations of these new behaviour standards. Direct communications, coupled with swift and certain sanctions for violating established behavioural norms, influence offender perceptions of apprehension risk.

Direct communications with offenders also facilitate the inclusion of moral sanctions by community members, religious sanctions by clergy members representing community interests and sympathetic sanctions tied to the pain inflicted on others. During offender notification meetings, community members convey the harms to neighbourhoods and residents generated by continued violent behaviour; clergy describe the intense regret and long-lasting personal anguish they will experience for violating religious commandments against harming others; and mothers of victims communicate the intense loss they feel over losing their children to seemingly senseless violence (Kennedy et al. 2017). The explicit inclusion of these other sources of 'pain' complements the imposition of political sanctions to influence offender decisions to commit crimes.

Concluding thoughts

The concentration of criminal offending among a few high-rate offenders and the associated focus required by focused deterrence strategies fits well with Bentham's embrace of utilitarian principles in considering police crime-prevention activities. Bentham's seminal thinking on how varied kinds of sanctions impact offender assessments of the costs and benefits of crime have been highly influential in designing innovative police crime-prevention strategies such as focused deterrence. Others have made similar observations. For instance, in a qualitative study on the effects of restrictive deterrence upon young, middle-class drug dealers in a suburban area, Jacques and Allen (2014) note that each sanction type has the potential to either intensify or diminish another's effect on offending. They further suggest that an offender's fear of political sanction will be greater when its occurrence is perceived to result in moral sanction (Jacques and Allen 2014). Nevertheless, while the architects of the initial application of focused deterrence in Boston in the 1990s did not explicitly consider Bentham during the design of the intervention (Kennedy et al. 1996), the approach certainly benefited from the same crime-prevention principles advanced by Bentham more than 200 years earlier.

References

Bentham, Jeremy. 1982. *An Introduction to the Principles of Morals and Legislation*, edited by J. H. Burns and H. L. A. Hart, reissued in 1996 with a new introduction by F. Rosen. Oxford: Clarendon Press.

Braga, Anthony A., David Hureau and Christopher Winship. 2008. 'Legitimacy and Criminal Justice: Losing Faith? Police, Black Churches, and the Resurgence of Youth Violence in Boston', *Ohio State Journal of Criminal Law* 6: 141–72.

Braga, Anthony A., David M. Kennedy, Elin J. Waring and Anne M. Piehl. 2001. 'Problem-Oriented Policing, Deterrence, and Youth Violence: An Evaluation of Boston's Operation Ceasefire', *Journal of Research in Crime and Delinquency* 38: 195–225.

Braga, Anthony A., David Weisburd and Brandon Turchan. 2018. 'Focused Deterrence Strategies and Crime Control', *Criminology and Public Policy* 17: 205–50.

Durlauf, Steven N. and Daniel S. Nagin. 2011. 'Imprisonment and Crime: Can Both Be Reduced?', *Criminology and Public Policy* 10: 131–54.

Engelmann, Stephen G. 2011. 'Introduction'. In *Selected Writings, Jeremy Bentham*, edited by Stephen G. Engelmann, 1–27. New Haven: Yale University Press.

Jacques, Scott and Andrea Allen. 2014. 'Bentham's Sanction Typology and Restrictive Deterrence: A Study of Young, Suburban, Middle-Class Drug Dealers', *Journal of Drug Issues* 44: 212–30.

Kennedy, David M. 2008. *Deterrence and Crime Prevention: Reconsidering the Prospect of Sanction*. London: Routledge.

Kennedy, David M., Mark A. R. Kleiman and Anthony A. Braga. 2017. 'Beyond Deterrence: Strategies of Focus and Fairness'. In *Handbook of Crime Prevention and Community Safety*, edited by Nick Tilley and Aiden Sidebottom, 157–82. 2nd ed. New York: Routledge.

Kennedy, David M., Anne M. Piehl and Anthony A. Braga. 1996. 'Youth Violence in Boston: Gun Markets, Serious Youth Offenders and a Use-Reduction Strategy', *Law and Contemporary Problems* 59: 147–96.

Nagin, Daniel S. 1998. 'Criminal Deterrence Research at the Outset of the Twenty-First Century'. In *Crime and Justice: A Review of Research*, Volume 23, edited by Michael Tonry, 1–42. Chicago: University of Chicago Press.

Quinn, Michael. 2021. 'Bentham on Preventive Police: The *Calendar of Delinquency* in Evaluation of Policy, and the *Police Gazette* in Manipulation of Opinion'. In *Jeremy Bentham on Police: The Unknown Story and What It Means for Criminology*, edited by Scott Jacques and Philip Schofield, 35–74. London: UCL Press.

Zimring, Franklin E. and Gordon J. Hawkins. 1973. *Deterrence: The Legal Threat in Crime Control*. Chicago: University of Chicago Press.

Regulating Crime and the International Crime Drop

Ronald Clarke

Quinn's remarkable chapter (2021) includes the revelation that Patrick Colquhoun's *Treatise on the Police of the Metropolis* was strongly endorsed and supported by Bentham, his great contemporary. It appears that Bentham sought out Colquhoun in order to advise him on how to get his ideas into legislation. Ultimately, Bentham's efforts were unsuccessful, but the fact that the greatest English philosopher of the day took Colquhoun's ideas so seriously is of the utmost importance. It is clear from Quinn's chapter that Bentham, in an unexpectedly humble role, regarded himself as merely Colquhoun's assistant. Without Bentham's endorsement, Colquhoun's *Treatise* could easily be dismissed as the ramblings of an obscure London magistrate.

In fact, there were two planks to Colquhoun's *Treatise*. The first was an extraordinarily detailed set of prescriptions for closing the myriad opportunities for crime arising from the varied institutions, agencies, activities and practices of the modern city that was then London. The second plank was a detailed agenda of control for enabling the poor to resist the temptations to crime laid out before them. Unfortunately, it was this second plank that was in tune with the liberal, welfarist ideas of the day and which for the next 150 years guided crime policy. Not only did this plank determine future policy, but it also launched criminology on a determinedly positivist course, whereby individuals' criminality was believed to be inexorably governed by their past.

In a recent chapter for the *Annals* (Clarke 2018), I have argued that in the past four decades the positivist consensus began to unravel with a series of diverse contributions on causation from a variety of scholars, mostly working independently. I go on to argue that this unravelling opens the possibility of returning to Colquhoun's first and more important plank of regulating crime by reducing the opportunities for it to occur. This transition would be aided by a broad range of theory which establishes something that should always have been obvious: that the criminality of individuals is the product of an interaction between individual propensities and situational circumstances and inducements.

In this brief commentary I wish to explore the particular implications of the regulatory course so strongly endorsed by Bentham. In doing so, I will make considerable use of environmental criminology, which has engaged in two joint enterprises that give substance to the idea of regulating crime. The first is an extensive project supported by Marcus Felson's series of five books on *Crime in Everyday Life*. This can be viewed as a modern interpretation and restatement of Colquhoun's original prescriptions for closing the opportunities for crime that arise from the manifold operations, practices and actions of the entire social body, involving numerous governing agencies, whether public or private.

Environmental criminology's second enterprise, pursued in parallel with the first, has been the extensive effort to develop two preventive approaches: problem-oriented policing (Goldstein 1979; 1990) and situational crime prevention (Clarke 1980; 1997). Both approaches seek to identify the crime opportunity structures for highly specific crime categories (not just 'car crime', but, for example, 'stealing hub caps in the inner city' or 'stealing cars for export overseas'). Both situational crime prevention and problem-oriented policing then proceed to curtail the opportunities for these very different thefts, committed by very different groups of offenders. Dozens, even hundreds of case studies have been published (those for situational crime prevention are more rigorously evaluated). There should be no doubt that these can be very effective in reducing crime.

To summarize, environmental criminology has provided the means to make regulating crime a practical enterprise, first, through a careful documentation of the myriad opportunities of the modern state that make crime possible and, second, by developing the technology to close those opportunities. These are contributions of the utmost importance for crime policy. But in the remainder of this commentary I wish to develop some thoughts in my *Annals* article about the impact that these ideas from environmental criminology should have on its parent discipline of criminology.

I am not so naive as to expect criminology to readily abandon positivism and embrace, instead, the bounded rational choice perspective that I have advocated, even if this would result in many benefits for criminology and its students. Too many criminologists have invested too much of their lives in positivist ideas and there continues to be a ready market for them in the hundreds of criminal justice degrees offered by colleges and universities. Even so, I would like the opportunity provided by this commentary to return briefly to two linked ideas that I have previously touched on (Clarke 2016), but which continue to intrigue me.

The first idea is that during the past decades those responsible for protecting their enterprises from victimization have begun to understand that they can expect little help from the authorities, which have neither the resources nor the expertise to undertake this task. They have realized that protecting themselves means they must do it themselves. This could be the source of the 'avalanche' of security that has occurred in every sphere of modern society – shops, banks, schools, colleges, hospitals, offices, transport systems, the airline industry, fast food restaurants, credit card companies, motels and any other business or organization that is open to some form of criminal exploitation – which is all of them. They have all been tightening up their security in ways highly consistent with Colquhoun's original vision.

Very few criminologists have remarked on this idea. On the other hand, several criminologists, such as Jan van Dijk, Graham Farrell and Nick Tilley (van Dijk et al. 2012; Farrell et al. 2014), have seized upon its equally intriguing corollary: could this avalanche of security provide the explanation for the international drop in crime that has been documented for a wide range of Westernized countries? Such an explanation is quite in contrast to those provided in a recent Academies of Sciences review (Rosenfeld and Weisburd 2016) of the reason for the crime drop in America – all of which rest on positivist thinking. It requires no stretch of the imagination to accept that the crime drop is today's foremost criminological phenomenon. That its explanation is readily accommodated by Colquhoun's thinking about regulating crime is a powerful endorsement of his ideas.

References

Clarke, Ronald V. 1980. 'Situational Crime Prevention: Theory and Practice', *British Journal of Criminology* 20: 136–47.
Clarke, Ronald V. (ed.). 1997. *Situational Crime Prevention: Successful Case Studies*. 2nd ed. Guilderland: Harrow and Heston.
Clarke, Ronald V. 2016. 'Criminology and the Fundamental Attribution Error', *The Criminologist* 41: 1–7.

Clarke, Ronald V. 2018. 'Regulating Crime: The Birth of the Idea, Its Nurture, and the Implications for Contemporary Criminology', *Annals of the American Society of Political and Social Science* 679: 20–35.

Farrell, Graham, Nick Tilley and Andromachi Tseloni (eds.). 2014. 'Why Crime Rates Fall and Why They Don't'. Special issue of *Crime and Justice: A Review of Research*, 43.

Goldstein, Herman. 1979. 'Improving Policing: A Problem-Oriented Approach', *Crime and Delinquency* 25: 236–58.

Goldstein, Herman. 1990. *Problem-Oriented Policing*. New York: McGraw-Hill.

Quinn, Michael. 2021. 'Bentham on Preventive Police: The *Calendar of Delinquency* in Evaluation of Policy, and the *Police Gazette* in Manipulation of Opinion'. In *Jeremy Bentham on Police: The Unknown Story and What It Means for Criminology*, edited by Scott Jacques and Philip Schofield, 35–74. London: UCL Press.

Rosenfeld, Richard and David J. Weisburd. 2016. 'Explaining Recent Crime Trends: Introduction to the Special Issue', *Quantitative Criminology* 32: 329–34.

Van Dijk, Jan, Andromachi Tseloni and Graham Farrell. 2012. *The International Crime Drop: New Directions in Research*. London: Palgrave Macmillan.

'An Attention to Domestic Quiet': A Comparative Commentary on the Originality or Otherwise of Bentham's Views and *Writings on Preventive Police* and the *Police Gazette*

David J. Cox

This commentary is based upon research that I have carried out over the past two decades into the work of the Fielding brothers, creators of the Bow Street policing system in the mid-eighteenth century (Cox 2012). It challenges several of the views proposed by Quinn's (2021) chapter in this publication, 'Bentham on Preventive Police: The *Calendar of Delinquency* in Evaluation of Policy, and the *Police Gazette* in Manipulation of Opinion', most specifically on the originality or otherwise of several of Bentham's ideas concerning the formation of an effective preventive police force, with especial regard to the publication of a *Police Gazette*. I was surprised in Quinn's chapter to find little more than passing mention of the role of the Fielding brothers in the creation of a fully fledged preventive (and indeed detective) policing system. The commentary below aims to explore the links between Bentham's musings and the work of the Fielding brothers in more detail.[1] It argues that many of Bentham's (and by extension, Colquhoun's) ideas on preventive policing owed a great (and in Quinn's chapter, largely unrecognized) debt to the prior work and publications of Henry and Sir John Fielding. Preventive policing was alive and well in England before both Colquhoun's and Peel's respective schemes and ideas were published and partially instigated.

Although Bentham was too young to have personal knowledge of Henry Fielding, he was in his early thirties when Henry's younger half-brother Sir John died and he would certainly have been aware of the efforts of both Henry and Sir John (together with their successors) in creating the Bow Street Police Office, which encompassed a system of both preventive and detective policing that continued until a decade after the creation of Sir Robert Peel's Metropolitan Police.[2] The innovative nature of the Fielding brothers and their creation of the Bow Street policing system have been previously recognized by numerous crime and policing historians and, indeed, as Francis Dodsworth states:

> The debate about crime and its prevention can be said to begin with the work of Henry Fielding. Fielding's *Enquiry into the Causes of the Late Increase of Robbers*, published in January 1751, defined the problematic of the prevention of crime. … Colquhoun himself praised Fielding's 'excellent ideas, and accurate and extensive knowledge upon every subject connected with the police of the metropolis'. (Dodsworth 2006, 441; see also Pringle 1956; Styles 1983)

Both prevention and detection played a significant part in the Bow Street policing system; as John Styles remarks: 'Earlier police reformers, like Sir John Fielding in the third quarter of the eighteenth century, had seen prevention as being a matter both of pro-active surveillance and deterrence through effective detection' (Styles 1987, 17). One of the main weapons in Fielding's armoury was the publication of a number of newspapers advertising details of both offences and offenders throughout the country. A significant part of Quinn's chapter is taken up with Bentham's ideas on the use of a *Police Gazette* – a nationally available publication issued to magistrates and others concerned with the apprehension and sentencing of offenders. While Quinn does acknowledge that the Fieldings were the originators of a series of similar publications (variously titled the *Covent Garden Journal*, the *Public Advertiser*, the *Weekly Pursuit*, the *Quarterly Pursuit*, *Public Hue and Cry or Sir John Fielding's General Preventive Plan* and the *Police Gazette*), he argues that Bentham's idea was an innovative and important extension of Fielding's innovation.[3]

I take issue with this view; Fielding's *Police Gazette* was part of his wider General Preventive Plan (often dated from 1772, but with published antecedents dating back to at least 1758), and I would argue that Bentham was simply arguing for the publication's continuance (and drawing largely upon Fielding's ideas without necessarily acknowledging them). Bentham was not primarily an initiator or innovator with regard to preventive policing; rather, he drew upon the large body of work carried out by the Fielding brothers and their successors in creating the first effective professional preventive and detective police force in England. Sir John Fielding, with his General Preventive Plan, was of course himself building upon the work of his half-brother Henry, who had first addressed the problem of crime and its detection in his *Enquiry into the Cause of the late Increase of Robberies, etc. with some Proposals for Remedying this Growing Evil* of 1751. Patrick Pringle stated that point, as follows: 'From the causes of the increase in crime Fielding turned to what he called the "encouragements"; and this part of his Enquiry was mainly a searching analysis of the defects in the law. He recommended fresh legislation against receivers and for the apprehension of vagabonds' (Pringle 1956, 95).

Sir John comments explicitly on both his and his half-brother's ideas concerning preventive policing as early as 1758. In his *Account of the Origin and Effects of a Police set on Foot by His Grace the Duke of Newcastle in the Year 1753, upon a Plan presented to his Grace by the late Henry Fielding, Esq.*, Sir John states that:

> An Attention to domestic Quiet, especially in a Metropolis, which is the Seat of Government, is, to the last Degree, praiseworthy, as it is productive of the happiest Effects; and when such a Police is brought to due Perfection, it will not only prevent common Acts of Violence between Man and Man, but such a Vigilance will ever defeat any Attempts that Malice, Extravagance or disappointed Ambition, may contrive against the Government itself. (Fielding 1758, iv–v)

He goes on further to specifically comment on the role of the police: 'Artificers, Servants and Labourers compose the Bulk of the People, and keeping them in good Order is the Object of the Police, the Care of the Legislature, and the Duty of the Magistrates, and all other Peace-Officers' (Fielding 1758, vii).

This clearly foreshadows both Bentham's and Colquhoun's arguments concerning the purpose of a police for the metropolis: that such a body must have both a didactic and moralizing influence. Dodsworth perceptively argues that: 'The argument established by Henry Fielding and perpetuated and transformed by his successors up to Patrick Colquhoun is that crime was the consequence of a transformation of manners and habits amongst the common people occasioned by the introduction of trade and commerce' (Dodsworth 2006, 449).

As part of this 'transformation of manners and habits', Sir John was acutely aware of the power and influence of the burgeoning press; in his 1758 tract he gives a detailed description of the functioning of the preventive element of the Bow Street policing system, as well as stating that:

> And what adds much to the Efficacy of this Police, there is a Correspondence settled with many of the active Magistrates in the Country, at all Distances, who constantly give Notice to Mr Fielding, when they have committed any desperate Rogue or suspicious Man, especially, if a Stranger in that Country; by which Means they are often furnished with Materials to bring such Offenders to Justice. (Fielding 1758, 39)

This was clearly the genesis of what from 1772/3 became *Hue and Cry or Sir John Fielding's General Preventive Plan*. John Styles states that: 'It was the integration of these procedures into a national system for collating and circulating the information thus obtained that was the second and truly innovatory element of the 1772 Plan. Fielding proposed to redistribute this information throughout the country in a printed format suitable for public display' (Styles 1987, 136). The newspaper from 1773 carried the strapline 'Sent to the Mayors and Chief Officers of Corporations, the Acting Magistrates in the Counties at large, and the Keepers of every County Gaol throughout England'.

Quinn accepts at face value Mark Neocleous's argument that:

> In this context it is worth noting that Colquhoun's [and by extension, Bentham's] proposed Police Gazette is very different from the earlier and better-known Gazette of John Fielding, for Colquhoun [and Bentham] sees the Gazette as a moralizing force. Not only should the Gazette detail crimes committed, list stolen goods, and provide criminal statistics in the way Fielding had envisaged, but it should also be used to 'excite in the minds of the labouring people a strong sense of moral virtue, loyalty and love of their country'. Short essays, articles, and selections from the more moral sections of statutes should be printed to show the importance of industrious activity and good behaviour. (Neocleous 2000, 716)

Quinn further states that:

In a draft which was omitted from his final text, Bentham was candid about the duplicity involved: [']But the sort of Sermon which might be practised and practised without ceasing in the *Police Gazette*, this *unannounced, and unsuspected Sermon, cautiously, sparingly, and in a manner imperceptibly, though at the same time unremittingly, insinuated into a publication composed principally, and to appearance exclusively,* of that sort of matter which, so long as man is man, can never lose … its hold upon the affections—especially of those otherwise untutored minds, for whose direction it is more especially designed—there would be neither end nor limit to its influence[']. (63)

But I would argue that Fielding's *Hue and Cry* had a similar didactic underpinning; in many of the early issues there are moralizing and sermonizing letters from contributors – for example, on 19 February 1773, a letter from 'Senex' was printed, arguing that profane oaths and perjury under oath should be sermonized against by the clergy on a weekly basis (Quinn 2021). In the same issue is an article about the regulation and pricing of bread, together with an editorial 'puffing' the utility of *Hue and Cry*. Similarly, in the issue dated 17–24 November 1775, 'A Friend to the industrious Poor' published a homily entreating prisoners languishing in jails to:

consider the inconvenience that dishonest men bring upon themselves and their families; and in the next place, the great difficulty of escaping justice; and sure I am, that they would rather work their fingers to the bones to get a bit of honest bread, than run the risk of losing their lives or liberties, and be banished from their country for getting things dishonestly, which, when they have got, they are afraid to use. Most unfortunate prisoners! Read this paragraph with care; let these observations sink deep into your hearts; and if it should please God to spare you this time, repent and reform[.] (*The Public Hue and Cry* 1775, 2)

These are not isolated examples; again, Bentham is echoing Fielding rather than proposing a new and innovative method of policing. Although he has a justified place in penal history and together with Colquhoun certainly had a role to play in the discussion about preventive policing in the late eighteenth and early nineteenth centuries, I would argue that in most cases, the Fieldings had got there first; as

Pringle stated: 'Fielding not only introduced into England the idea of a preventive police, but he also showed England (and the world) that is was possible to have an efficient police force without becoming a police state' (Pringle 1956, 113).

Notes

1   Henry Fielding (1707–1754), Chief Magistrate of Bow Street Public Office 1748–54, and his half-brother, Sir John Fielding (1721–1780), Chief Magistrate of Bow Street Public Office 1754–80. It is significant that the term 'Public Office' was synonymous with that of 'Police Office', thus reinforcing the public order nature of policing at the time.
2   For an account of the administrative functioning of Bow Street Public Office, see Beattie (2012).
3   For a brief account of the complex and numerous iterations of such publications, see Waters (n.d.).

References

Beattie, John M. 2012. *The First English Detectives: The Bow Street Runners and the Policing of London, 1750–1840*. Oxford: Oxford University Press.
Cox, David J. 2012. *'A Certain Share of Low Cunning': A History of the Bow Street Runners, 1792–1839*. Abingdon: Routledge.
Dodsworth, Francis. 2006. 'Police and the Prevention of Crime: Commerce, Temptation, and the Corruption of the Body Politic, from Fielding to Colquhoun', *British Journal of Criminology* 47: 439–54.
Fielding, John. 1758. *Account of the Origin and Effects of a Police set on Foot by His Grace the Duke of Newcastle in the Year 1753, upon a Plan presented to his Grace by the late Henry Fielding, Esq*. London: A Millar.
Neocleous, Mark. 2000. 'Social Police and the Mechanisms of Prevention: Patrick Colquhoun and the Condition of Poverty', *British Journal of Criminology* 40: 710–26.
Pringle, Patrick. 1956. *Hue and Cry: The Birth of the British Police*. London: Museum Press.
The Public Hue and Cry or Sir John Fielding's General Preventive Plan. 1775. London, 17–24 November.
Quinn, Michael. 2021. 'Bentham on Preventive Police: The *Calendar of Delinquency* in Evaluation of Policy, and the *Police Gazette* in Manipulation of Opinion'. In *Jeremy Bentham on Police: The Unknown Story and What It Means for Criminology*, edited by Scott Jacques and Philip Schofield, 35–74. London: UCL Press.
Styles, John. 1983. 'Sir John Fielding and the Problem of Criminal Investigation in Eighteenth-Century England', *Transactions of the Royal Historical Society* 33: 127–49.
Styles, John. 1987. 'The Emergence of the Police – Explaining Police Reform in Eighteenth and Nineteenth Century England', *British Journal of Criminology* 27: 15–22.
Waters, Les. n.d. 'The Police Gazette. Part 2: Issues for 1797–1810, 1828 and 1830–1840 from the State Library of New South Wales'. Online. http://www.ampltd.co.uk/digital_guides/police_gazette_part_2/Publishers-Note.aspx (accessed 22 April 2021).

Bentham's Virtue
Stephen Engelmann

Bentham's work on *Preventive Police* is a welcome addition to the new *Collected Works*. We have reason to be grateful to Quinn, not only for that volume, but also for his chapter in this volume, which ably resituates its subject in the history of police and policing. Quinn (2021) shows us just how much in the way of innovation that is currently attributed to Patrick Colquhoun (1745–1820) might originate with Bentham and how *Preventive Police* gives us further insight into Bentham as a pivotal figure in the institutionalization of capitalist modernity. Bentham emerges from Quinn's treatment as a figure who understands well that 'the free market' relies for its functioning on an extensive governmental apparatus and who also understands elements of this apparatus and the markets themselves as forms of 'indirect legislation', technologies that facilitate the self-policing and mutual policing that supplement the work of state agencies in their pursuit of security and abundance (Engelmann 2003). Licences, for example, make dealers in certain trades known to the state and their conditions induce and enable dealers to surveille themselves and one another. Quinn also demonstrates how this period of Bentham's work shows him at his most politically conservative. In the context of the continuing war with Revolutionary France, the political suspicions of the author of *Preventive Police* are trained on the threat of subversion from the subject many, while the ruling few – soon to be the target of his ire and of his robustly democratic reform proposals – are largely let off the hook. Bentham was on the whole a very consistent thinker not given to self-doubt, but he would come to be embarrassed by some of the more reactionary moments of this work on the police.

Quinn's chapter provides an excellent introduction to Bentham's place in the history of the police and to the police's place in Bentham's work. In this brief comment I merely offer a friendly amendment: I argue that the chapter glosses over an important difference between Bentham and Colquhoun that in my view informs Bentham's work as a whole. Although Quinn is certainly correct that Bentham is concerned in *Preventive Police* with what the period called moral reform, it is important to see what his approach assumes and does not assume about the causes of and remedies for delinquency. Keep in mind that the majority poor – who would before long come to be known as the working class – were then, and are still now, considered to be fundamentally different from those chattering about them. Thus Colquhoun, in his brief *General View of the National Police System*, simply speaks to the prejudices of his audience when he understands crime as rooted in 'the growing corruption of Morals, by which every species of delinquency is generated' (1799, 13). It is 'the morals and habits of the lower ranks in Society' that 'are growing progressively worse and worse' (24). Social problems find their source in 'the unruly passions peculiar to vulgar life' (28) and the function of a modern, well-regulated and scientific police is to 'lead the inferior orders, as it were, insensibly into better Habits, by gentle restraints upon those propensities which terminate in Idleness and Debauchery' (29). To be sure, people's inner depravity does not necessarily have to be transformed: the virtue of a good police is that it can make it such that 'even the idle and the dissolute may possess a resource for subsistence by honest industry, without having any pretended plea of necessity for resorting to Crimes' (29). But it is inner depravity that is at the root of crime, and this depravity – whether delivered by the hand of God or Nature or simply by lack of education or narrow circumstances – is evident in the community of the poor, which is itself properly divided into '*noxious*' and '*blameless* and useful' parts (25).

This perspective is very different from Bentham's. Yes, Bentham – especially prior to his radical turn – was occasionally given to write in terms of fundamental types; his panopticon, he infamously wrote in a 1791 letter, was a 'mill for grinding rogues honest and idle men industrious' (1981, 342). But what is remarkable about the bulk of his writing on the poor, even in his most reactionary period, is his lack of interest in distinguishing them by their inner lives as opposed to their conditions and practices. For Bentham, unrelieved indigence – the condition of not being able to work, for whatever reason – leads directly to crime as a rational result; no one individual is more presumptively dissolute or depraved than another and thus virtue as understood by most contemporaries is not a priority. In the commentary on his 'Table of Cases Calling for Relief' of 1797, Bentham does sort different types of 'hands' and will even classify some as 'habitual depredators', but his solutions to finding them out are stunningly universal: work registries and public avowals of employment, *from the King on down,* will serve both to incentivize lawful occupations and catch those who have been making their living in other ways (2010, 238–40). In his poor law writings, Bentham (2001, 27) ridicules the idea that the withdrawal of relief would enhance virtue among the rich by stimulating charity:

> By the same rule, dangers of all kinds are to be embraced: foreign wars should be kept up for the sake of keeping up courage: civil wars, insurrections and seditions, to keep alive the sacred flame of patriotism: disease propagated for the advancement of medicine. ... By the same rule, gin ought to be made as cheap as possible to promote the habit of sobriety: brothels with apt signs planted at the corner of every street, to afford exercise to continence.

It is not that people are somehow all the same. Bentham's lack of interest, however, in what the English nineteenth century would call 'character' – a previously exterior and reputational but newly interior and natural bundle of qualities – would be noticed and criticized by his protégé John Stuart Mill (1806–1873), in his first published remarks on Bentham following the master's death, as perhaps his greatest failing as a moralist (1985, 7–8). Mill would in turn help to cement an all-too-familiar argument through successive editions of his highly successful *Principles of Political Economy* (1965): the road to social progress lies in working-class uplift, particularly with regard to education that can help them abstain from excessive reproduction.

In *Preventive Police* we find a desire in Bentham's (2018, 49) proposals generally to strengthen in everyone 'the connection between interest and duty', which foreshadows the 'junction-of-interests prescribing principle' (Bentham 1989, 235) that would inform his late constitutional thought. This principle leads with the virtues and vices of institutional *arrangement* rather than with the inner proclivities of institutional actors, who are simply for the most part expected to abuse their offices if such abuse would go undetected and thus unpunished. Bentham (2018, 128) does distinguish throughout the licensing discussions in *Preventive Police* between 'honest' and 'dishonest' dealers, but honesty here seems more a matter of practice than of disposition, as honest dealers are affirmed 'whether the system of control has found

[them] honest or whether it has made them so'. Bentham goes so far as to say, in a passage on fraud related to coinage, that 'The mischiefs that prevail in this department ought not to be imputed to the individual, who is whatever the law makes him or suffers him to be, but to legislation' (145). Much discussion in 'Notes to the Police Bill' of 1799 (e.g. 255, 295, 299) lines up with an abiding preoccupation, in Bentham's extensive work on the penal code, to avoid either over- or under-punishment, i.e. with the importance of calculation and calibration for a utilitarian art of government. Such a preoccupation in his hands leans more on a survey of consequences than it does on the presumptive division of a population into the 'noxious' and everyone else.

Quinn is not wrong to see in Bentham's anxiety about subversion a fear of the 'susceptible and thoughtless multitude' (Bentham 2018, 326) that contrasts strongly with reliance on this same multitude in its capacity as Public Opinion Tribunal in the later constitutional work. But what is remarkable throughout about Bentham's orientation is that he never posits any inherent depravity in either the poor (in his most conservative phase) or in the ruling classes (in his most radical phase). Instead, in contrast to Colquhoun and so many contemporaries and successors from across the political spectrum, for Bentham what we might call the moral equality of individuals seems to be a fundamental and unshakeable premise.

References

Bentham, Jeremy. 1981. *The Correspondence of Jeremy Bentham, Volume 4: October 1788 to December 1793*, edited by Alexander Taylor Milne. London: Athlone Press.
Bentham, Jeremy. 1989. *First Principles Preparatory to Constitutional Code*, edited by Philip Schofield. Oxford: Clarendon Press.
Bentham, Jeremy. 2001. *Writings on the Poor Laws, Volume I*, edited by Michael Quinn. Oxford: Clarendon Press.
Bentham, Jeremy. 2010. *Writings on the Poor Laws, Volume II*, edited by Michael Quinn. Oxford: Clarendon Press.
Bentham, Jeremy. 2018. *Writings on Political Economy, Volume III: Preventive Police*, edited by Michael Quinn. Pre-publication version. Online. http://discovery.ucl.ac.uk/10055084/ (accessed 20 April 2021).
Colquhoun, Patrick. 1799. *A General View of the National Police System, recommended by the Select Committee of Finance to the House of Commons; and the Functions of the Proposed Central Board of Police Revenue: with Observations on the Probable Effects of the General Designs in the Prevention of Crimes, and in Securing the Rights of the Peaceful Subject.* London: H. Baldwin and Son.
Engelmann, Stephen G. 2003. '"Indirect Legislation": Bentham's Liberal Government', *Polity* 35: 369–88.
Mill, John Stuart. 1965. *The Collected Works of John Stuart Mill, Volumes II and III: Principles of Political Economy with Some of Their Applications to Social Philosophy*, edited by John M. Robson and Jack Stillinger. Toronto: University of Toronto Press.

Mill, John Stuart. 1985. *The Collected Works of John Stuart Mill, Volume X: Essays on Ethics, Religion and Society*, edited by John. M. Robson. Toronto: University of Toronto Press.

Quinn, Michael. 2021. 'Bentham on Preventive Police: The *Calendar of Delinquency* in Evaluation of Policy, and the *Police Gazette* in Manipulation of Opinion'. In *Jeremy Bentham on Police: The Unknown Story and What It Means for Criminology*, edited by Scott Jacques and Philip Schofield, 35–74. London: UCL Press.

On Policing Before Bentham: Differences in Degree and Differences in Kind

G. Geltner

In his chapter, Quinn (2021) aptly stresses the ancient pedigree of policing as a largely preventive endeavour meant to protect the public good. Polity, *Polizei* and the French *police* all indeed harken back to the Latin word *politia* and the Greek *polis*, a valued (if culturally contingent) form of civic order.[1] As such, their positive social connotations live on, imbuing for instance the present-day adjective 'polite' and even the noun 'polish'. To Bentham, public order is something to be pursued and, if need be, restored. Yet in treatises and other reflections and policies(!) stretching back millennia, it is above all something to be *maintained* through a combination of surveillance and deterrence, including investigation and punishment. Either way, apparatuses of surveillance and deterrence, as entities explicitly set up to defend the public well-being, were common in earlier societies. And not just in the vague sense that any 'public' institution, such as third-party dispute resolvers, could be construed as benefiting the community; there is abundant evidence for regular, trained, salaried and sometimes even uniformed officials tasked with patrolling cities, monitoring at-risk sites and fining hazardous behaviours for the benefit of all. What is more, the remits of such outfits were commonly and explicitly informed by moral and economic as well as medical considerations. So, to what extent does Bentham usher in a new wave of thinking about policing?

Bentham avers that: 'between Police and Revenue there is happily a sort of natural connection' (Bentham 2018, 132). The insight was certainly shared by earlier policing agents and those who composed their briefs. Across the vast Islamicate world, for instance, evidence dating back to at least the ninth century situates the *muhtasib* or market inspector at the centre of routine policing activities, similarly justified (al-Shayzarī 1999; Chalmeta Gendrón 1967–8; Ghabin 2009; Glick 1971; 1992). This official's duty derived directly from the khalif's paramount duty of 'commanding right and forbidding wrong' (Cook 2010),[2] here interpreted as a responsibility to ensure, among others, just prices, correct weights and measures, the regular provision of healthy food, the certification of physicians and the upkeep of hygienic facilities, including public latrines. To Muslim rulers, then, moral hygiene and a well-functioning marketplace were mutually reinforcing endeavours. Such centralized and all-encompassing officials as the *muhtasib* were rare in western Europe before the nineteenth century, but in countless cities in the British Isles, Scandinavia, the Low Countries and Italy, government organs collectively shared similar burdens, combining moral, physical, economic and political agendas (Coomans 2019; Geltner 2019; Geltner and Roberts forthcoming; Jørgensen 2008; Rawcliffe 2013; Roberts 2019). In doing so, moreover, they adopted an environmental approach to the sites, amenities and even the zones under their care, once again in line with Quinn's assessment (2021, Introduction, 39) that, to Bentham: 'police includes action against calamity as well as against crime' (see Rawcliffe and Weeda 2019).

The similarities between such bodies and the Thames police constables profiled by Bentham are in many respects remarkable. Take his prefatory definition (Bentham 2018, 6) of the proposed corps as essential 'for the preservation of peace and good order in, upon and in the vicinity of the said River and especially for the detection of felonies and misdemeanours, the apprehension of offenders and the preservation of the several Vessels, with their materials, furniture, stores and cargoes'. Before the advent of railways, air freight and the internet, rivers and roads furnished Europe with the main infrastructural hubs linking producers and consumers. Non-luxury goods may certainly have travelled shorter distances before colonialism and imperialism, but monitoring took place in very similar nodal points, following similar routines and serving very similar purposes. Wharves, toll gates, weigh stations, sluices, dams, bridges, drains and warehouses, as well as industrial sites in and along rivers, such as fisheries and mills, were widely considered at-risk sites and treated accordingly by local police agents (Magnusson 2003; Squatriti 2000; Walton 2006). And they did this, furthermore, both in and outside the city walls. Indeed, the recognition of the hinterlands' importance to urban biological and economic well-being had fostered the creation of rural policing officers at least since the first wave of European urbanization starting in the eleventh century. These men specialized in detecting 'matter out of place' in any of its forms, including trespassing, loose animals, blocked ditches and stolen goods, and had to enforce elaborate regulations on the quality and transport of produce into and from cities (Geltner forthcoming).

To be sure, the apparatus of licensing and financing that the Thames constabulary would have relied upon seems to have been far more elaborate than that of, and perhaps even unimaginable to, earlier magistrates. London itself had some 600,000 residents around 1800 (out of some 10.5 million inhabitants in Britain): a far more populous city than any metropolis on the Continent in its pre-plague days, but hardly beyond the pale for Constantinople or Cairo. More germane, perhaps, was the assumption that humble officials and second-hand tradesmen would be sufficiently literate or at least able to use documents, premised in turn on a nationwide education system and the existence of a cheap, paper-based communication technology that could easily be scaled up and be put to use across different regions. On the other hand, certification was the system's back end, an off-site activity meant to buttress a service that essentially would continue to operate through men-monitoring behaviours, product quality, ships' fabric and the nodal points of trade along a commercial route, a policing modality widely attested centuries beforehand.

If a major shift in the notion of policing is harder to detect among the imagined Thames constables, the second bill Bentham helped develop seems to occupy ground across a clearer qualitative divide. At first blush, the landscape looks familiar. The goals of the proposed *Police Gazette* and *Calendar of Delinquency*, for example, were: 'guarding and preserving the public mind from impressions dangerous to the public peace' (Bentham 2018, 136). One could argue that various media in earlier cultures sought to accomplish just that, from liturgical performances to morality plays and sermons, to stained glass windows in churches. And perhaps more to the point, gallows, pillories and 'infamy paintings' of convicted criminals dotted many cities, as did the skulls, cadavers and limbs of their less fortunate colleagues (Geltner 2014; Merback 2001). But the collation of the *Gazette* and *Calendar* was to take part in a mental, scientific and administrative exercise that has never, to my knowledge, been recorded for any European region beforehand.

It is hardly the case, of course, that earlier magistrates rejected 'the use of evidence in the formulation and evaluation of policy' (Introduction, 55) or that such evidence would herald 'rational policy making based on cost–benefit analysis' (Introduction, 56). Experts and eyewitnesses had regularly been taking the stand in legal procedures for millennia by then, and learned *opiniones* were routinely commissioned by civic rulers. Nor, as Quinn rightly states, did Bentham aver that utilitarian calculations are always and everywhere mathematically precise. Conversely, to Bentham the *Gazette* was a 'Sermon which might be practiced … without ceasing' (Introduction, 63). And lest his formulation be dismissed as a mere analogy, he elsewhere stated that: 'In his Bible, man can *not* be made to read the *Police Gazette*: but in the *Police Gazette* he *might* be made to read his Bible' (Introduction, 64). Despite these apparent continuities, however, I would argue that in this particular instance we may well be dealing with a difference in kind, not degree. This is in part because the same nexus of technologies offering support to the Thames constabulary come to play a far more central role. Indeed, for the *Gazette* and *Calendar* the technology *is* the proposed change.

Both bulletins promised the assembly, packaging and organization of critical and reliable information in an accessible medium, one moreover that is affordable, highly transportable and easily lends itself to rational inquiry and robust decision-making. It was a combination that appealed to diverse branches of government, not least the public health sector, whose claims to expertise were calibrated to exploit this early form of 'big data' (Crook 2016). Beyond the census, for which there is evidence locally going back to the *Domesday Book*, there are some precedents to such processes of gathering statistics, especially about death rates and their causes and for shaping pertinent policies, including in Italy and Britain (Carmichael 1998; Cohn 2012; Skelton 2016). Yet, as far as I am aware, there has been no parallel attempt in earlier eras to understand the scope and scale of social deviancy *per se* and the policies seen to influence it.

It would be remiss of me, a social historian of an earlier era, to evaluate Bentham's role in creating a legal basis for capitalism or ushering modernity. Nor am I in a position to extrapolate from these two groups of writings, however rich, about what must have been his evolving thoughts on a complex ('multifarious') topic such as policing. Yet in analysing these two bills, it struck me that a similar ambivalence concerning continuity and change emerges elsewhere in his *oeuvre*. For it is sometimes forgotten that the feted designer of the panopticon, an edifice often seen as embodying the quintessential principles of Enlightened modernity, is the same productive thinker who proposed to construct (from whale bones, as it happens) a flogging machine that would dispense corporal punishment in an equitable manner in a flogging hall (Bentham 1830, 82; Geltner 2014, 68–70). Scaled-up technology thus served in one context to entrench an existing, violent penal practice and in another to traverse new boundaries. No man, certainly not Bentham, lived outside his times.

Notes

1 I have limited the following notes to a selection of English-language publications covering western Europe and the Middle East, which are but the tip of the scholarly iceberg on the topic.
2 See also Bentham's discussion in his essay on 'Indirect Legislation' concerning the intimate relation between preventing evil and producing good; also Quinn (2021).

References

al-Shayzarī, 'Abd al Rahman b. Nasr. 1990. *The Book of the Islamic Market Inspector [Nihāyat al-Rutba fī Talab al Hisba (The Utmost Authority in the Pursuit of Hisba)]*, translated by R. P. Buckley. Oxford: Oxford University Press.
Bentham, Jeremy. 1830. *The Rationale of Punishment*, II, 1, 1. London.
Bentham, Jeremy. 2018. *Writings on Political Economy, Volume III: Preventive Police*, edited by Michael Quinn. Pre-publication version. Online. http://discovery.ucl.ac.uk/10055084/ (accessed 23 April 2021).
Carmichael, Ann G. 1998. 'The Last Past Plague: The Use of Memory in Renaissance Epidemics', *Journal of the History of Medicine and Allied Sciences* 53: 132–60.
Chalmeta Gendrón, Pedro (ed.). 1967–8. 'El 'Kitāb fī Ādāb al-Hisba (Libro del buen gobierno del zoco) de Al-Saqatī', *Al-Andalus* 32: 125–62, 359–97; 1968. 33: 143–95, 367–434.
Cohn, Samuel K., Jr. 2012. *Cultures of Plague: Medical Thinking at the End of the Renaissance*. Oxford: Oxford University Press.
Cook, Michael. 2010. *Commanding Right and Forbidding Wrong in Islamic Thought*. Cambridge: Cambridge University Press.
Coomans, Janna. 2019. 'The King of Dirt: Public Health and Sanitation in Late Medieval Ghent', *Urban History* 46: 82–105.
Crook, Tom. 2016. *Governing Systems: Modernity and the Making of Public Health in England, 1830–1910*. Oakland: University of California Press.
Geltner, G. 2014. *Flogging Others: Corporal Punishment and Cultural Identity from Antiquity to the Present*. Amsterdam: Amsterdam University Press.
Geltner, G. 2019. *Roads to Health: Infrastructure and Urban Wellbeing in Later Medieval Italy*. Philadelphia: University of Pennsylvania Press.
Geltner, G. Forthcoming. 'Rural Policing in the Long *Trecento*: An Urban Project and Its Obstruction'.
Geltner, G. and Gregory Roberts. Forthcoming. 'Social and Environmental Policing in Medieval Cities'. In *Crime and Deviance in the Middle Ages: A Handbook*, edited by Hannah Skoda. Kalamazoo: ARC Humanities.
Ghabin, Ahmad. 2009. *Hisba, Arts and Craft in Islam*. Wiesbaden: Harrassowitz Verlag.
Glick, T. F. 1971. 'Muhtasib and Mustasaf: A Case Study of Institutional Diffusion', *Viator* 2: 59–81.
Glick, T. F. 1992. 'New Perspectives on the Hisba and Its Hispanic Derivatives', *Al-Qantara* 13: 47–89.
Jørgensen, Dolly. 2008. 'Cooperative Sanitation: Managing Streets and Gutters in Late Medieval England and Scandinavia', *Technology and Culture* 49: 547–67.

Magnusson, Roberta J. 2003. *Water Technology in the Middle Ages: Cities, Monasteries and Waterworks after the Roman Empire*. Baltimore: Johns Hopkins University Press.

Merback, Mitchell B. 2001. *The Thief, the Cross and the Wheel: Pain and the Spectacle of Punishment in Medieval and Renaissance Europe*. Chicago: University of Chicago Press.

Quinn, Michael. 2021. 'Bentham on Preventive Police: The *Calendar of Delinquency* in Evaluation of Policy, and the *Police Gazette* in Manipulation of Opinion'. In *Jeremy Bentham on Police: The Unknown Story and What It Means for Criminology*, edited by Scott Jacques and Philip Schofield, 35–74. London: UCL Press.

Rawcliffe, Carole. 2013. *Urban Bodies: Communal Health in Late Medieval English Towns and Cities*. London: Boydell Press.

Rawcliffe, Carole and Claire Weeda (eds.). 2019. *Policing the Urban Environment in Premodern Europe*. Amsterdam: Amsterdam University Press.

Roberts, Gregory. 2019. *Police Power in the Italian Communes, 1228–1326*. Amsterdam: Amsterdam University Press.

Skelton, Leona J. 2016. *Sanitation in Urban Britain, 1560–1700*. London: Routledge.

Squatriti, Paolo (ed.). 2000. *Working with Water in Medieval Europe: Technology and Resource-Use*. Leiden: Brill.

Walton, Steven A. (ed.). 2006. *Wind and Water in the Middle Ages: Fluid Technologies from Antiquity to the Renaissance*. Tempe: ACMRS Press.

Bentham's England and the Longue Durée of Preventive Policing

Joel F. Harrington

Quinn's fascinating description of Bentham's work on behalf of the new Thames Police Office in 1798–9 holds particular interest for the early modernist. While many of Bentham's proposals strike the twenty-first-century reader as unmistakably 'modern', what is less obvious is the evolutionary, rather than revolutionary, origins of this new popular understanding of 'police'. A brief consideration of that long history of crime prevention in Europe, dating back to the thirteenth century, yields a valuable broader context for many of Bentham's 'innovations'.

During most of the Middle Ages, crime in Europe (and here I include the British Isles) was viewed primarily in terms of inter-personal conflicts and damages. The ancient Germanic wergild system of setting compensation values for various corporal injuries is the best-known example of a legal system that in principle and practice aimed not at divine justice but at keeping the peace and forestalling further violence. In that sense, it was both reactive and preventive. Of course, in reality, it did not prevent all retaliations and vendettas, nor did it prevent most thefts or other crimes against property. But what human legal system has? What is most significant for the history of European crime is that before the fifteenth century, political rulers were content to leave such matters to the local level, adjudicated by some mixture of local custom and seigneurial (or royal) law. Initiation of formal procedures accordingly relied overwhelmingly on personal accusation (as opposed to official intervention).

The major exception to this reliance on private initiation was, of course, the inquisitorial procedure of the Catholic Church. Beginning in 1198, the jurist pope Innocent III (c. 1160–1216) instituted a series of legal reforms that culminated in the establishment of a permanent

Inquisition in 1229, charged with combatting the heretical Cathars and Waldensians. Here, too, judges relied on private accusations, but in this instance the complaints could be made in secret and the court was empowered to instigate investigations, depositions and even arrests. Two intertwined influences shaped this and all future inquisitorial institutions, religious or secular. The first was Roman law, already inextricably woven into the Church's canon law and enforced by all of its courts. Active and involved magistrates lay at the heart of the Justinian Code and all of its later imitators. The second key influence was moral, in this case specifically religious (even doctrinal), but always focused on a more expansive notion of justice than that of the surrounding secular courts. Inquisitors did not just react to past words or deeds but sought out the roots of dangerous thinking in an effort to prevent further damage. In that sense, inquisitorial law enforcement, for the time confined to church courts, was always preventive, always concerned about the greater good.

The first secular jurisdictions to share this broader approach to social order were the Italian, Swiss and German city states of the fifteenth century. In humanist-inspired Florence and Venice in particular, the all-encompassing Aristotelian notion of *politeia* resonated especially strongly. As Quinn suggests in his own discussion of the term, 'policy' is perhaps a better translation than 'police' – at least before the institutional changes of the eighteenth century. Accordingly, city councillors on both sides of the Alps attempted for the first time a range of public regulations regarding the registration of travellers, minimal street lighting and some controls over the sale of poisons and weapons. Famously, they also attempted to regulate dress (to maintain the social hierarchy), public dances and attendance at church services. Enforcement, mainly through fines, was exceptionally weak, but significantly, the concept of broader social control had been established. With the arrival of the printing press and later the Protestant Reformation, virtually all jurisdictions extended their preventive measures to rooting out seditious or heretical thought with the establishment of censorship.

About the same time and well into the sixteenth century, the inquisitorial procedures of Roman law gained ever more traction, not just in Mediterranean lands but eventually also in the Holy Roman Empire, most notably in the *Carolina* criminal code of 1532. Even while various German Protestant rulers were seeking to throw off the beliefs and practices of the Roman Church, they and their jurists held tight to both canon and Roman law, both of which better suited the new notions of public order than ancient customs and procedures. Princes and imperial cities bragged about their own maintenance of *gute Polizei* through various top-down statutes and ordinances. As Bentham proposed centuries later, law-enforcement officials attempted to use the printing press to involve the public in investigations, including the widespread use of paid informers and wanted posters offering generous bounties.

Unquestionably, however, the continental authorities' greatest inquisitorial asset was judicial torture, supposedly restricted by the *Carolina* but in fact used almost indiscriminately throughout Europe for a variety of major crimes (including witchcraft, of course). English law supposedly prohibited torture, but it made frequent exceptions for political and religious crimes (not to mention relying on *peine forte et dure* well into the eighteenth century). In fact, politics and religion (often intertwined in questions of regime change) were the two areas where early modern English legal officials did take preventive measures, long before the policing proposals of Colquhoun and Bentham in the late eighteenth century. I think it likely that English authorities also made use of some continental policing methods in more mundane crimes, but I defer to the relevant experts on actual practices.

The fact that most, or even all, of the components of preventive policing had already been attempted on the Continent (and to a lesser degree in the British Isles) does not entirely diminish the significance of Bentham's proposals. Something was clearly changing during the late eighteenth and early nineteenth centuries and I think that it centred around the new understanding (and reality) of 'police' in England and elsewhere that he voices. The desire to reform 'criminals' and prevent crime was not, as Foucault suggests, new. That impulse, as we have seen, dates back to its much earlier religious form in the later Middle Ages and then in the confessionally inspired moral programmes of the sixteenth and seventeenth centuries. Nor can we single out as revolutionary the new prisons, whose rehabilitative function similarly dates back to post-Reformation workhouses. Obviously, these goals and institutions took on a more central significance during the modern era. But these are all components – and here I believe Foucault got it right – of a newly integrated concept and network of institutions we could call 'police'.

What is most striking about Bentham's thinking – and this is why Foucault and others have been attracted to his panopticon as a metaphor – was his holistic approach to criminal deviance. In this sense, his proposed reforms were truer to their inquisitorial roots than any other secular, piecemeal approach. Why did Pope Innocent III's vision take so many centuries to reach fruition? In large part the answer lies in the ruling elite's limited notions of crime and punishment, aimed at preventing future retaliations but not new crimes. The latter goal would have struck them not only as impossible but inconceivable. It took the Protestant and Catholic Reformations of the sixteenth century to instill such preventive and rehabilitative thinking in secular law enforcement, but even then there was no extended and integrated police apparatus.

For Bentham's vision to be realized, European societies (again including Britain) needed to experience the full force of capitalism's expansion, generating fantastic new wealth for a minority and entrenched poverty for the majority of the population. Theft and other crime naturally grew apace with such economic changes, in both the growing cities and the countryside. Without any significant social reform, the default recourse of political rulers was to continue the generations-long struggle to improve law enforcement. What most changed over the course of the early modern period, in other words, was not the nature of intervention but its scope, at both the philanthropic level and the punitive level. Ever larger investments in schools and charities corresponded to ever larger investments in police and prisons. It should not be surprising that the eighteenth century witnessed both increasingly draconian approaches to criminal law enforcement and many remarkable reforms in the same area, including the abolition of judicial torture in most jurisdictions.

In short, what I find most compelling about Bentham on criminal law reform is the philosophical unity of his vision. This is the same vision that attracted another famous philosopher nearly two centuries later, but as an argument against the very modernity project that Bentham embraced. However accurately their shared philosophical schema reflected reality, we must acknowledge that it is merely one stage in the long trajectory of preventive policing that did not deviate significantly in the eighteenth century but rather continues to refine its punitive and rehabilitative methods into our own time.

Bentham on the Complex Role of Police

Jonathan Jacobs

Bentham's writings on police reflect an awareness of many of the most fundamental considerations and chief questions concerning how to understand police in modern broadly liberal nations such as the US and UK. Bentham was an astute observer of social and political conditions and while he was willing to suggest significant and innovative reforms, he also had a studied awareness of their suitability to the political and social culture. He was alert to how various reforms might be received, as well as having very definite ideas about what sorts of aims should be pursued. There is a paternalistic aspect in much of his thought, but this was hardly out of step with theorists and reformers of the age. The present discussion highlights respects in which Bentham's thinking was an early, alert engagement with key issues concerning the modern police, in a form easily recognizable to us.

In the eighteenth and early nineteenth centuries, the conception of police was developing from an understanding of it in terms of a very broad notion of overall public administration to a more specific notion of law enforcement and crime-fighting. As an example of the former, in *The Theory of Moral Sentiments* Adam Smith (1723–1790) wrote:

> The perfection of police, the extension of trade and manufactures, are noble and magnificent objects. The contemplation of them pleases us and we are interested in whatever can tend to advance them. They make part of the great system of government and the wheels of the political machine seem to move with more harmony and ease by means of them. We take pleasure in beholding the perfection of so beautiful and grand a system and we are uneasy till we remove any obstruction that can in the least disturb

or encumber the regularity of its motions. All constitutions of government, however, are valued only in proportion as they tend to promote the happiness of those who live under them. This is their sole use and end. (Smith 1984, IV.i.1.1, 185–6)

In Great Britain at the end of the eighteenth and start of the nineteenth centuries, there was some provision for addressing crime, but not in ways that were adequate to the changing circumstances. Rapid urbanization, growing industrialization and, to a considerable extent, inadequate social provision for the unemployed, those forced off the land, demobilized soldiers and others struggling on account of economic conditions led to increased crime and insecurity of property. To address this, there were magistrates, constables and watchmen. Their efforts, along with the efforts of individual citizens in tracking down criminals and prosecuting them, were among the chief modes of law enforcement. 'In England, with a significant percentage of unenthusiastic magistrates and constables and nothing remotely resembling the *maréchaussée,* arrests and detection often had to be the work of individuals' (Emsley 1984, 125). It would not be quite right to call this a 'criminal justice system' given the high degree of local independence and discretion and the high level of uncompensated involvement by citizens. But it had the sanction of tradition and longevity and there was considerable suspicion regarding the establishment of a trained, dedicated force for law enforcement.

Persons in the offices mentioned were not trained and they did not constitute a systematically organized police force addressing the broad conception of police that Smith indicates, nor were they police in the narrower sense of fighting crime. Police – as a responsibility of a police force in a more recognizably modern sense – began to develop in London in the early nineteenth century before developing in other parts of England. Clive Emsley writes:

Nevertheless, within 15 years of the end of the Napoleonic Wars a significant new and expensive step in policing was taken with the creation of the Metropolitan Police of London. … It was uniformed and hierarchical and much closer to a military organization than the reformers ever envisaged or than subsequent Whig historians have allowed. (Emsley 1984, 82)

Many participants in the debates about the formation of police forces were concerned primarily with: (1) how would they be funded?; (2) what was to be their relation to magistrates, constables and watchmen?;

(3) were the personnel to be armed?; (4) what precisely was the scope of their powers? Also, many in England took considerable pride in what they regarded as their traditional, enduring liberties and they were keen to avoid the acceptance of anything like the French police, which they regarded (to some extent, correctly) as mainly functioning as a state agency of political surveillance rather than primarily protecting citizens from crime.

Bentham gave considerable thought to the social conditions and the sorts of approaches needed to meet the challenges they brought. He distinguished between 'preventive police' and justice:

> As to mischief from internal adversaries, the expedients employed for averting it may be distinguished into such as may be applied *before* the discovery of any mischievous design in particular and such as cannot be employed but in consequence of the discovery of some such design: the former of these are commonly referred to a branch which may be styled the *preventive* branch of the *police*: the latter to that of justice. (Bentham 1982, 198)

He also wrote: 'Other functions, commonly referred to the head of police, may be referred either to that power which occupies itself in promoting in a positive way the increase of national felicity or that which employs itself in the management of the public wealth' (1982, 199n). He recognized that the extant institutions and their practices were not adequate. The overall role of police is in helping maintain the rule of law so that people can exercise their liberties in all manner of contexts, actions and interactions with the expectation of at least some protection against criminality. Bentham's view involved both the larger, overall notion of police as civil administration but also the notion of police as a dedicated force for fighting crime. A trained police force could also help maintain or restore public order if there was a high level of tension or riots and serious public disorder, perhaps obviating the need to deploy soldiers in that role. In nineteenth-century England there were numerous riots and other episodes of serious disorder, sometimes with lethal consequences. Another aspect of civil adminis-tration is that the police could have a role in helping the indigent and homeless find available sorts of support much more effectively than the accustomed and unsystematic enforcement of the Poor Laws. Bentham was piecing all of this together.

He also maintained that it would be important to publish infor-mation about what crimes had been committed, whether offenders had been apprehended and punished and what sorts of punishment had been imposed. This had the two-fold purpose of providing people with useful information and also encouraging certain attitudes and perspectives regarding crime. In his typically encyclopedic manner, Bentham took into account relevant considerations of moral psychology and the impact on people's attitudes and motives and the implications for such behaviour, as well as concerns about public order and the security of property. Regarding Colquhoun's proposed *Police Gazette*, Bentham thought that it had a use:

> though but collateral and not proper to be mentioned in the Bill … still more important perhaps, than even the direct one. … And this is its having the capacity of being employed as an instrument for the propagation and maintenance of social dispositions and affections, and for the preservation of tranquility, harmony and loyalty among the great body of the people. (Bentham 2018, 322)

He added:

> It need not be, nor ought it to be, expressly precluded (and if not expressly, it will not be regarded as virtually precluded) from administering useful instruction and exhortation of the moral and, upon occasion, the political cast, in whatever forms may from time to time present themselves as best adapted to the purpose. (Bentham 2018, 323)

Bentham thought that such news would be of real interest to the 'most numerous classes' and:

> The species of intelligence or news, to the circulation of which it is proposed to be appropriated (consisting of notices of acts of delinquency committed, accompanied with a display of the punishments and perils to which the authors stand exposed) is of itself, in every line of it, a perpetual lesson of morality and of submission to the laws. (Bentham 2018, 322–3)

As noted above, there is a paternalistic aspect to this, but it certainly was no more paternalistic than the prevailing understanding of government in Britain and such a view might have seemed quite plausible given that there was increasing pressure for expanded political participation and state support for social welfare. Britain had a broadly liberal form of political order, but it was not a genuinely liberal-democratic order and there certainly was a ruling class; Bentham saw himself as offering direction to those who shape legislation and policy.

The circumstances in which Bentham was thinking about police gave rise to a number of issues that remain recognizable as important concerns regarding the police. Great Britain had an increasingly commercial and manufacturing economy and the volume and velocity of transactions and trade were growing swiftly. It had an increasingly urban society with the almost inevitable issues concerning poverty, homelessness, the protection of property in homes, shops, warehouses and factories as well as drunken disorder, prostitution and large-scale 'fencing' of stolen goods. It was a period of significant popular political movements and of competing views on how the costs and benefits of an industrializing economy should be distributed. There were new challenges to the project of civil administration, as well as large numbers of soldiers who would soon return from the Napoleonic Wars. Bentham was a combination philosopher, social scientist and crafter of policy and he was thickly informed regarding the intersection of economic, social and political factors, studying them relentlessly and writing about them just as doggedly.

Though committed to a certain theoretical perspective, Bentham was not a brittle ideologue. His conception of police is a good illustration of this. He did not confine police to a narrow notion of crime-fighting (either as crime prevention or the pursuit of offenders). He took into account what he regarded as the much broader interests of society overall.

Bentham's conception had roots in the earlier, very broad notion of police and, in part, this coheres nicely with his overall concern with promoting the public good. But he saw the need for the development of a more professional, more fully trained and dedicated form of police, one that would not function in an almost exclusively reactive way. Bentham did not hesitate to suggest new agencies and policies if he thought they were needed, but he was also attuned to the sorts of changes that were likely to be accepted and how people would react to them. Rapidly changing social and economic conditions subjected overall civil administration to some unaccustomed challenges and Bentham, with his customary thoroughness, brought those into view; he proposed forms of police meant to promote the overall good in ways that could be recognized as doing so and thus win public support. This might require some moral education of the public, for example, by the proposed *Police Gazette*. But that aspect, too, reflects Bentham's awareness that the challenges needed to be met in ways that extended beyond the specific powers and training of personnel engaged in crime-fighting.

References

Bentham, Jeremy. 1982. *An Introduction to the Principles of Morals and Legislation*, edited by J. H. Burns and H. L. A. Hart, reissued in 1996 with a new introduction by F. Rosen. Oxford: Clarendon Press.

Bentham, Jeremy. 2018. *Writings on Political Economy, Volume III: Preventive Police*, edited by Michael Quinn. Pre-publication version. Online. http://discovery.ucl.ac.uk/10055084/ (accessed 23 April 2021).

Emsley, Clive. 1984. *Policing and Its Context 1750–1870*. New York: Schocken Books.

Smith, Adam. 1984. *The Theory of Moral Sentiments*, edited by D. D. Raphael and A. L. MacFie. Indianapolis: Liberty Fund.

Bentham and Historical Criminology

Paul Knepper

Bentham has occupied a comfortable, if limited, place in criminology as a founder of the classical school. Along with Cesare Beccaria (1738–1794), he helped establish the political philosophy behind the administration of criminal law. But he did not realize the importance of scientific understanding as promoted by the positivist school, the great rival of the classical school. Nor did he grasp the importance of social milieu, which would need to be advanced by sociologists. Bentham's outlook was, as Geiss (1972, 61) put it, 'unduly individualistic, intellectualistic and volunteeristic', which, when located on the political spectrum, justified the harsh and severe policies favoured by conservatives.

Foucault (1977) cemented these views. He converted Bentham's proposal for a circular prison into a blueprint of industrial society that brought new and subtle modes of surveillance, supervision and control over workers. The panopticon prison embodied the worst aspects of surveillance society and the characterization of Bentham as 'authoritarian, anti-liberal, behaviourist, reductionist and totalitarian' (Schofield 2013, 59).

There is, however, an effort underway to refresh our view of Bentham (Schofield 2013; O'Malley 2009; Freilich 2015). O'Malley (2009) presents Bentham as a scholar not so much concerned with justice or sanctions as with security. Security can be defined as a social condition in which people know key aspects of their future, particularly expectations concerning life and property. This has a profound contribution to crime prevention, as well as theoretical criminology. Freilich's (2015) work on the theory of situational crime prevention advances this refresh as well. He ties situational crime prevention to the theory of the classical school, particularly Beccaria, but also Bentham. As a theorist of crime prevention, Bentham breaks out of the philosophy of punishment and administrative-legal criminology to join those trying to find practical ways to reduce victimization.

This refresh of Bentham has been enabled by the Bentham Project's release of new work. Like many of the individuals we regard as contributors to theoretical criminology, Bentham wrote much more than the few documents we typically cite. University College London possesses some 60,000 folios and the British Library another 12,500, of Bentham's writing. The Bentham Project seeks to bring versions of these texts to scholars, including many never seen before, in a series of volumes, *The Collected Works of Jeremy Bentham*. Quinn has edited several collections, one of which presents Bentham's work on preventive policing (Bentham 2018).

Quinn's (2021) chapter explores Bentham's contribution to drafting bills for a new Thames Police office and efforts to establish a Central Board of Police. Drawing on his concept of 'indirect legislation', Bentham argued for licensing as a method of public finance needed to expand police services and to circulate information known to the police, which was useful in deterring, detecting and apprehending lawbreakers. Quinn provides a historical analysis of Bentham, situating him in his own time. He examines Bentham's relationship with Patrick Colquhoun. Colquhoun linked the spread of crime to indigence and argued in 1799 for the establishment of a 'pauper police'. Quinn observes that Bentham anticipated him on this topic. During the 1780s, Bentham explained how a 'police of charity' also represented a 'police against offences'.

Quinn's chapter further provides an opportunity for historical criminology through his presentation of Bentham's work on the *Calendar of Delinquency* and *Police Gazette*. By historical criminology, we are not assessing a theory in the context in which it was written, but rather its contribution to ongoing work that we refer to as theoretical criminology (Churchill 2017; Knepper 2014). Bentham did not identify as a criminologist, nor did he use the conceptual language of contemporary criminology. Yet looking back with knowledge of the present, we can see how his views contribute to our own time.

The *Calendar of Delinquency* was Bentham's proposal for an annual register of the incidence of crime. It would have presented a count of offences committed and the legal outcomes. Data would have come from the *Police Gazette*, and from returns by magistrates, police surveyors and jailers. It represented, as Quinn explains: 'a classic Benthamite demand for use of evidence in the formulation and evaluation of policy' (54). It would make rational policymaking based on cost–benefit analysis possible. The *Police Gazette* would have been published regularly and offered for sale at an affordable price. It would have included intelligence as well. By intelligence, Bentham had in mind information about the commission of crimes, including curious cases of the 'true crime' genre; but also factual information to alert the public to new forms of fraud and enable compliance with new legislation. Bentham thought the attractive price, combined with a natural curiosity in issues of security and victimization, would make it a success.

Quinn's discussion of the *Calendar* and the *Gazette* contribute to a wider refresh of Bentham's response to crime, efforts that demonstrate his pursuit of 'transparency, economy and accountability' (Blamires 2008, 2). Blamires digs down into the panopticon by focusing on the French translation of Bentham's work. By emphasizing the usefulness of rational analysis and evaluation of gains and losses, Blamires contends that Bentham advanced a broad-minded theory of good government. The implication is that Foucault misread the panopticon in Bentham's thought. The panopticon plan did not express Bentham's ambition for efficient social control, but served multiple purposes across his wide-ranging thinking. By far the most interesting of these was the 'reverse-panopticon' in which government officials working in the minister's chamber would be exposed to the constant surveillance of the public from galleries on the periphery. The whole point was not totalitarianism, but transparency (Schofield 2013, 60–1).

The more we learn about Bentham, the less sense it makes to assign him his usual place next to Beccaria. At some point, the whole discussion of 'classical' and 'positivist' schools not only becomes pointless because it is artificial, but counterproductive because it limits our thinking on the range of topics important to criminology.

References

Bentham, Jeremy. 2018. *Writings on Political Economy, Volume III: Preventive Police* edited by Michael Quinn. Pre-publication version. Online. http://discovery.ucl.ac.uk/10055084/ (accessed 23 April 2021).

Blamires, Cyprian. 2008. *The French Revolution and the Creation of Benthamism*. New York: Palgrave Macmillan.

Churchill, David. 2017. 'Towards Historical Criminology', *Crime, History and Societies* 21: 379–86.

Foucault, Michel. 1977. *Discipline and Punish: The Birth of the Prison*. London: Allen Lane.

Freilich, Joshua. 2015. 'Beccaria and Situational Crime Prevention', *Criminal Justice Review* 40: 131–50.

Geiss, Gilbert. 1972. 'Jeremy Bentham (1748–1832)'. In *Pioneers in Criminology*, edited by Hermann Mannheim, 159–71. Montclair: Patterson Smith.

Knepper, Paul. 2014. 'Historical Criminology'. In *Encyclopedia of Criminology and Criminal Justice*, edited by Gerben Bruinsma and David Weisburd. New York: Springer. Online. https://link.springer.com/referenceworkentry/10.1007/978-1-4614-5690-2_672 (accessed 16 August 2021).

O'Malley, Pat. 2010. 'Jeremy Bentham'. In *Fifty Key Thinkers in Criminology*, edited by Keith Hayward, Shadd Maruna and Jayne Mooney, 7–11. London: Routledge.

Quinn, Michael. 2021. 'Bentham on Preventive Police: The *Calendar of Delinquency* in Evaluation of Policy, and the *Police Gazette* in Manipulation of Opinion'. In *Jeremy Bentham on Police: The Unknown Story and What It Means for Criminology*, edited by Scott Jacques and Philip Schofield, 35–74. London: UCL Press.

Schofield, Philip. 2013. 'The Legal and Political Legacy of Jeremy Bentham', *Annual Review of Law and Social Science* 9: 51–70.

Van Antwerp, Victoria and Skylar R. Steele. 2014. 'Bentham, Jeremy'. In *Encyclopedia of Criminology and Criminal Justice*, edited by Gerben Bruinsma and David Weisburd. New York: Springer.

Bentham: The First Crime Scientist?

Gloria Laycock

This comment will look at the similarities between some of Bentham's ideas about policing, chiefly regarding crime prevention, and contemporary notions reflected in current approaches to policing and crime control. In particular, it will look at his groundbreaking contribution in establishing a 'calendar of delinquency', his notion that policing may be considered a 'new science' and his emphasis on prevention as an important part of the police function.

Introduction

It is salutary to read the works of Bentham, Colquhoun and others. It mitigates against the self-congratulatory tendency of some academics to feel a certain smugness when ideas that they claimed as their own are revealed as having emerged a few centuries earlier and were somehow lost in the plethora of journals, books, pamphlets, dissertations and theses generated in the intervening period. Is there nothing new under the sun?

As will become clear in the remainder of this essay, some of the ideas of Bentham and his colleagues are reflected in developments in policing that were recently presented as 'new' or 'innovative'. In the next section, three ideas taken from Bentham's writings (or more accurately the presentation of those writings by later scholars) are briefly outlined, while the following section links these ideas to current developments in policing in the UK (although similar trends can be seen in the US, Australia, New Zealand and elsewhere). The final concluding section speculates about the future of the ideas and their relevance to twenty-first-century crime.

Key ideas from Bentham and colleagues

A calendar of delinquency

Bentham's interest and enthusiasm for evidence in the formulation of policy called for data, which in the case of policing, was in the form of the *Calendar of Delinquency*. The calendar was to provide an annual statement showing the extent and nature of offences committed and prosecuted, with the outcome of the subsequent legal proceedings also recorded. It appears to have had a number of purposes beyond informing policy and included providing a monitoring system for yearly comparisons; providing the basis of an assessment of police efficacy; an indication of the cost-effectiveness of various elements of policing; and a means of informing (educating?) the public on the specifics of crime and associated misdemeanours (Quinn 2021). A calendar of delinquency also begs questions on the classification of crimes, another subject on which Bentham had firm views following his observations on the trajectory of the natural sciences (Steintrager 1977).

The science of policing

Bentham was an enthusiastic advocate of science. His observations of what was developing in the natural sciences led him to the view that similar approaches would be beneficial if applied to government policy and in particular to policing. This would require a clear set of statements on what was illegal (the problem), data collection to estimate the scale of the problem and the adoption of scientific method to test the efficacy of any proposed solutions, including their cost-effectiveness. It would result in a police service focused on the detection and prevention of crime.

The importance of prevention

Bentham's ideas in the area of crime prevention are, for me, the most significant and to some extent surprising. He talks of efforts made to combat 'mischief', which well reflects the concerns of the modern-day police with not only crime but disorder and antisocial behaviour more broadly. The surprise is the extent to which Bentham appears to understand that crime prevention is not just about preventive patrol. His notion of indirect legislation was seen as a means of social control without recourse to punishment. So, for example, street lighting, registers of travellers and regulation of weights, measures, poisons etc.

all contributed to the prevention of crime, but establishing these was the responsibility of government, and not under the direct control of the police.

The current manifestation of Bentham's ideas

In 2001, in recognition of the earlier murder of Jill Dando, a hugely popular UK journalist and broadcaster, the Jill Dando Institute of Crime Science was founded at UCL. Crime science was hailed by its advocates as a revolutionary new approach to crime control, placing science and scientific method at the centre and drawing on a wide range of disciplines to address the challenge of bringing crime under greater control and specifically of reducing it – there was to be a concentration on prevention.

In a similar vein, an article published in 2011 by Weisburd and Neyroud calls for a radical reformation of the role of science in policing; they suggested the need for a new paradigm that changes the relationship between science and policing in which the police themselves work as scientists in active collaboration with universities. Despite various 'experiments' in policing such as 'Compstat' (Weisburd et al. 2004) or problem-oriented policing (Goldstein 1979), together with a more constructive relationship with academics than had been seen in earlier decades, they maintained that most police agencies had little interest in applying scientific method to their work and there was little penetration of systematic experimentation.

The ideas of crime science and police science are not themselves far apart: crime science focuses on the crime (including antisocial behaviour, organized crime and terrorism) and police science focuses on the police and their use of science, but neither mentions Bentham in describing any developments. Both call for an increase in the use of scientific method by the police in evaluating their activities against some stated goals. Crime science, in particular, stresses the importance of prevention and the need for the police to act in partnership with other agencies to make changes in the broader environment that would lead to reductions in offending.

This approach is known as situational crime prevention (Clarke 1995) and could be directly compared to Bentham's notion of indirect legislation in that it draws on the fact that behaviour (including criminal behaviour) is heavily determined not just by disposition (which is difficult to change) but by the situation within which one finds oneself.

The easier it is to commit an offence, the more people will offend. Controlling situations reduces crime, but it generally requires action from agencies other than the police and has been called third-party policing (Mazerolle and Ransley 2005).

Bentham's ideas on the importance of data collection are also very evident in modern-day policing. In the UK, for example, we not only have heavily regulated statistics on crimes reported to the police, but also the crime survey for England and Wales, which was started as the British Crime Survey in 1981 and enables (as recommended by Bentham) the comparison of crime trends over time. Interesting as these trends are, relatively little use is actually made of the crime data to inform police activities other than perhaps identifying 'hotspots' of problems at which to direct police attention.

Perhaps astonishingly, many of the manifestly sensible ideas of Bentham and his colleagues are still struggling to gain traction and sustainability, despite the evidence as to their effectiveness. A recent major UK research study of what works in crime reduction, which contributed to the development of the UK College of Policing Crime Reduction Toolkit (n.d.), shows how little attention is paid to investigating the *cost-effectiveness* of the initiatives listed.

Similarly, Goldstein's ideas on problem-oriented policing, which essentially advocate that the police take a scientific approach to the development and assessment of their crime prevention efforts, wax and wane with the enthusiasm of the police chief of the day. It has proved extremely difficult to change police culture as would be required were these ideas to become a stable element of policing (Goldstein 2018).

Conclusions

The ideas on policing as set out by Bentham and his colleagues are reflected in recent policing developments, but it would be wrong to say that they are all well established and flourishing. The collection of crime data is a fundamental element of virtually all police agencies, although carried out with variable degrees of validity and reliability. And other elements have been evaluated, such as problem-oriented policing, and declared effective. But the general application of science, with all that this implies, has proved far more difficult to implement.

Thinkers such as Bentham can and do have great ideas, but the real challenge is their successful implementation. It is only now that some of the suggestions for better policing that were first developed in the eighteenth century are beginning to penetrate to any significant extent. But the future will require less emphasis on detection and greater attention to the preventive approach of which Bentham was such a protagonist. The reason for this can already be seen in the rise of cybercrime driven by the internet. The detection of such crime (indeed the reporting of it to the police) is already proving to be immensely difficult and cries out for better design of the systems themselves. As new technologies continue to be developed, policing will also need to change radically. Implementation failure will not be an option.

References

Clarke, Ronald V. 1995. 'Situational Crime Prevention', *Crime and Justice* 19: 91–150.
College of Policing Crime Reduction Toolkit. n.d. Online. https://whatworks.college.police.uk/toolkit/Pages/Toolkit.aspx (accessed 23 April 2021).
Goldstein, Herman. 1979. 'Improving Policing: A Problem-Oriented Approach', *Crime and Delinquency* 25: 236–58.
Goldstein, Herman. 2018. 'On Problem-Oriented Policing: The Stockholm Lecture', *Crime Science* 7: 13.
Mazerolle, Lorraine and Janet Ransley. 2005. *Third Party Policing*. Cambridge: Cambridge University Press.
Quinn, Michael. 2021. 'Bentham on Preventive Police: The *Calendar of Delinquency* in Evaluation of Policy, and the *Police Gazette* in Manipulation of Opinion'. In *Jeremy Bentham on Police: The Unknown Story and What It Means for Criminology*, edited by Scott Jacques and Philip Schofield, 35–74. London: UCL Press.
Steintrager, James. 1977. *Bentham: Political Thinkers No. 5*. London: George Allen and Unwin.
Weisburd, David, Stephen D. Mastrofski, Rosann Greenspan and James J. Willis. 2004. *The Growth of Compstat in American Policing*. Police Foundation Reports.
Weisburd, David W. and Peter W. Neyroud. 2011. *Police Science: Towards a New Paradigm (New Perspectives in Policing)*. Washington, DC: Department of Justice, National Institute of Justice.

Bentham on Modern Social Control: Prescient, Clairvoyant and More

Gary T. Marx

Students of social ordering and one of its prime components – social control – owe Quinn and his colleagues at the Bentham Project a great debt for publishing the 80 Bentham volumes that will eventually be available. For the non-specialist to offer impressions of even a tiny fraction of Bentham's work goes beyond humility to chutzpah.[1] However, as Henry James said: 'We work in the dark, we do what we can, we give what we have.'

Bentham, writing more than two centuries ago, is prescient bordering on clairvoyant in his anticipation of contemporary social control themes. This speaks to his brilliance, as well as to the enduring characteristics of modern society, which are discoverable through systematic empirical observation of systems from a qualified positivist perspective.

The Bentham excerpts here deal largely with policing and rule violation. These need to be seen within the broader context of the initial meaning of policing as the state's means of social control for order and civic improvement, beyond the specifics of a police organization focused on crime control.

Bentham was perhaps the first modern Anglophone theorist to offer an integrated approach to the intellectual and practical problems of social order as we think of them today. Criminologists rushing from one classroom or crisis to another give insufficient attention to the historical roots of current control regimes. Things have origins, and contrary to George Santayana's oft-quoted observation, even those who can remember the past are too often condemned to repeat it. In the eighteenth-century beginnings of contemporary social control, there was the word and the word was Bentham's.

Quinn's grounded and thoughtful excerpt on preventive policing illustrates Bentham's insight, breadth and honesty and his centrality to the intellectual underpinnings of our contemporary taken-for-granted law-and-government policy worlds.

Social control, whether viewed as a mighty fortress or a dungeon, is a structure with many rooms set within a small area or vast acreage. It involves the creation of norms and processes of discovery, adjudication and sanctioning. It also involves efforts advocated by Bentham: using socialization and social policy, and engineering the physical environment, to prevent or inhibit violations and/or limit the harm caused. Given the often ironic and imperfect nature of prevention, Bentham also emphasized strategic efforts to discover violations and apprehend violators when prevention failed.

The enduring conflicts and challenges Bentham saw in how efforts to do good could bring risks of doing harm, or at least unwanted costs and trade-offs, may be universal. But in the face of so many moral and economic entrepreneurs offering us alternative, selective (or no) facts, the potential of good to do harm must be acknowledged. The pie does not get any larger, and choices and legitimate and illegitimate power differentials are always present, whether explicit or implicit (and with the latter, there are always the unknown unknowns). No righteous contemporary reformer of criminal justice should be granted a licence (let alone licence) without an awareness of Bentham's work on public administration and policing. He is a social theorist and an ironist, if not always explicitly so.

In the passages Quinn discusses, Bentham is acutely aware of the levels of causation and of the interconnectedness of parts of the social order. He adopted a social systems view before Vilfredo Pareto (1848–1923) and Talcott Parsons (1902–1979): while the system(s) are loosely joined, they are joined. He is an empiricist, a scientist (at least of the social variety) and a pragmatist. The interweaving of these elements is central to his programmes. Yet he sees the limits of quantitative measurement for many of the elements that ideally should be measured and the risks of ignoring factors not subject to such assessment.

Impinging upon the semi-closed notion of a system are the temporal and other dynamics that alter the system's components. Bentham's distinction between 'justice', as applied to the judiciary's response to the discovery of 'mischief from internal adversaries', contrasts with 'prevention' by the police before that discovery. Presumably, if successful, such prevention means there will be no need for justice. Yet a reverse linkage not considered in the text is possible.

What if prevention causes a crime, thus triggering the need for justice? Just how do these relate? Under what conditions does prevention lead to crime rather than inhibiting it? This can lead to injustice for those subjected to categorical suspicion without individual cause and those wrongly caught up in stings gone awry (e.g. as a result of entrapment). There may also be harm to those victimized by an offence that would not have occurred absent efforts at prevention, not to mention wasting resources that could be better used elsewhere. Such unintended consequences are at the core of the social and ethical issues around prevention. I saw this clearly in studying the preventive efforts of undercover policing (Marx 1989). The questions take on increased importance in an age of big data sets presumed to offer clues to potential violations (e.g. Brayne 2017) and the rush to apply techno-logical solutions.

Bentham locates much of the motivation for rule-breaking at the level of the presumably rational, calculating individual. Nevertheless, he is also a social determinist in looking at the centrality of the social and physical environment with respect to how communication, opportunity and social control forms condition rule enforcement and violations. These structures critically inform individual decisions, as well as broad crime patterns. For example, Bentham writes: 'the mischiefs that prevail in this department [re coin police] *ought not to be imputed to the individual, who is whatever the law makes or suffers him to be, but to legis-lation*' [emphasis added] (Quinn 2021, 43) and we can add the absence of legislation. Once belief in God was eliminated or greatly reduced from a daily role in human affairs, the reform advocate needed to look elsewhere for causes. Crime reflected the environment and, as for Emile Durkheim (1858–1917), was an offence against society, not the King or God. Intervention is not only possible, but morally demanded.

Bentham's writing on prevention connects to social control at three levels. The first, at the level of culture, communication and socialization, involves the broad ordering of society and the values communicated by government. The second involves institutional social structures of government, law and the economy as these are con-ditioned by policies that are central to life chances. A third level involves the concrete artefacts and social processes at the situational level, seen in the interaction between rule-breakers and rule-enforcers. For Bentham, to have civil peace in the face of the rapid social change then occurring in England, government needed rationality (which can be read as common sense in light of logic and empirical reality). Preventive policies were needed at each of these levels.

Communication and the moral order

Soft control

As democracy with its tilt towards softer controls dawned, Bentham saw a need to craft a better moral order via 'indirect legislation' in the face of the disruptions associated with the emerging urban industrial society. This need was central to Emile Durkheim and other later nineteenth-century theorists. The ruptured moral order needed reparation. For Bentham, communication by the state for moral education was a vital component of this in socializing citizens to lawful behaviour and making them aware of the consequences of acting unlawfully.

In his advocacy of indirect legislation, we see the soft social control themes that have gained ascendancy over the past several centuries as the pragmatic and moral limits of coercive control became more evident (Elias 1978; Leo 1992; Marx 1981; 2006; 2015). As an early advocate of democracy, Bentham was morally repelled by the extremes of physical coercion and opposed the death penalty. Living at the same time as Napoleon, he appreciated the duality in Napoleon's reference to control via the iron fist within the velvet glove.[2] Influencing people via manipulation, deception and the creation of uncertainty and rewards was viewed as morally and strategically superior to relying on direct coercion after the fact. Even when those were ineffective, clear communication about the risks and penalties might bring conformity out of fear of being caught.

Thus, within the panopticon, inmates could never be sure if they were being watched and overheard, thus conformity is seen to be prudent (at least to the extent that potential violators are rational as seen by Bentham). A related process is the uncertainty created by the watchmen who might come around at any moment. Peel's reforms involving a permanent uniformed police presence, rather than the intermittent watchmen, was a similar effort to enhance self-control through the possibility of apprehension. Yet these efforts have their limits (beyond the corruption of authority), since conformity does not depend on believing that the rules are right (legitimate), but on fear of being caught. It is far better to convince people of the legitimacy of the rules and self-discipline, thus avoiding the need for an enforcement response after the fact, with the expenditure of resources and the potential for unintended consequences.

The printing press, moral suasion and propaganda

The rise of the printing press and the spread of mass literacy provide a valuable, new, soft tool to shape hearts and minds, as does the internet today. The propagation of messages of moral and political instruction, which previously were left to the clergy and rulers using scribes, stained-glass windows and proclamations with limited reach, can now be more efficiently delivered and directed by those controlling the printing press. This leads to strategic efforts to propagate a view of the world favouring the status quo and restricting those opposing it. Given inequality, such an effort is contestable, even as it claims to benefit society as a whole ('the greater good') and provide the potential for equalization through the technology.

Bentham's veiled 'indirect legislation', involving the state's early use of the printing press for propaganda purposes is important for the history of mass communications.[3] In such proposals we see seeds of twentieth-century (and current) authoritarian states' messaging via control of the mass media – a control later seen in the fiction of Aldous Huxley (1894–1963) and George Orwell (1903–1950), modern consumer advertising and public relations.

The hope was that the *Police Gazette* would gradually come to be seen as 'an interesting but objective source of information [that] would make possible the undetected transmission of preferences and of will, by exploiting a cognitive gap – an asymmetry in knowledge about the functions of the *Police Gazette* – between government and its readers' (Quinn 2021, 62).

His next sentence is rich grist for the social critics' mill:

> And when, for purposes not exposed to repugnance or suspicion, this sort of channel of communication [the *Police Gazette*] has once been established in the several assemblies and the minds of the members have become familiarized with the use of it, it will be easy, if on any occasion it should become desirable, *to make use of it for the purpose of conveying any impressions which it may be wished to produce with a view to the execution of justice or the preservation of the public peace.* (2018, 322 {UC cl. 575}, emphasis added)

Certainly, there is much to be said on behalf of citizens trained as a result of government publications to value self-reliance, hard work, frugality, sobriety and family responsibility, and to guard against sloth (although I have some doubts about seeing no value in 'lounging in ale houses', at least after a hard day's labour). Who could be against 'indirect legislation' that offers the public literature that features 'virtue represented as amiable, vice in odious, colors: the former rewarded; the latter punished'? (Bentham n.d., UC lxxxvii. 18). But to welcome that, we need a means of agreeing (or at least reaching conclusions) on what is virtue and what is vice.

All democratic governments advance the 'culture of moral sanction', setting aside the issue of whose morals. But with this, particularly if its purpose is hidden, as Bentham seems to advise, there are obvious risks of propaganda posing as truth and the door is opened to censoring ideas that are not seen to be supportive of the current government's brand of moral uplift.

There are of course limits to moral suasion via the mass media. Yet the message need not be believed to have an impact. Those able to detect manipulation and deception or who are otherwise not convinced (taken in?) by moral indoctrination (i.e. socialization) might still be scared into calculating that 'it's not worth it' in learning what fate awaits violators. The ritual reminder and affirmation provided by publicizing punishment for those who stray might strengthen rule abidance.

Whatever its challengeable role as a force for establishment morality, the *Police Gazette* would also offer information about potentially disloyal minorities. Quinn observes that the *Police Gazette* 'would serendipitously, beyond its' publicly stated goal of conveying information about and to the poor, offer information on various groups of non-conformists, permitting 'an exact and constant with the numbers and situations of them will be obtained *without the appearance of being sought* and *the attention of the local Surveyors of the Board will be pointed to the numbers and deportment of the individuals of whom these congregations are respectively composed*' (Bentham 2018, 321–2 {UC cl. 574}, emphasis added). This must be understood against the background of perceived threats from those sympathetic to the French Revolution.

This is an early example of systematizing government intelligence for the control of dissident populations, beyond garden variety street and highway crimes. The expansive net that comes with the bureaucratization of surveillance organizations, and that identifies suspected individuals *before* any violations have occurred, is a key element in authoritarian control. The efforts of the Stasi are an extreme illustration.

Transparency can also control the governors

Bentham's preference for soft, rather than coercive, control can be seen in his favouring transparency as a way to inform the public and hold those with authority accountable. Such visibility contains the seeds of our expectations regarding freedom of information and openness in government. Government had to be closely watched and calibrated to see that things worked according to plan and to guard against abuses of power. Appeal to reason and propagation of the idea of openness could also support the state's legitimacy in the absence of the divine right and wisdom of kings. Bentham sought to subject claims about society to empirical inquiry. He is a parent of the fields of evaluation research and policy studies.

As a not-always-explicit proponent of democracy (at least before 1809), he saw transparency/visibility as central to limiting the crimes of authority. He sought justice for those who, in Howard Becker's (1967) words after Shakespeare were: 'more sinned against than sinning'. For example, in his plan for the panopticon, the two-way-street aspect of vision served to control the prisoners, but also those who ran the prison. His concept of 'sinister interest' in which the vested interests of elites conspire against those of the public fits well with views from the sociology of knowledge and stratification and the rise of critical social science. From these perspectives, the imperial, hegemonic, asymmetric and manipulative potential role of culture and communication tie to power.

Social organization and crime

The effort to engineer a mass media-led improved moral sense in citizens fits seamlessly into the calculative model of utilitarian conformity. But beyond stirring cries to do right via 'indirect legislation' and to view law enforcement as emanating from the community, not something imposed upon it by the king or the state, Bentham advocates tinkering with the social order via legislation and policy in order to effect the potential rule-breaker's incentives, disincentives and capabilities as these connect to their calculations and motivations. Humanism and pragmatism intertwine on behalf of prevention in the call to create social conditions that permit individuals to meet their basic needs.

Merton (1957) in writing about anomie as a cause of crime embodies this view. He suggests that the type of rule-breaking involving the 'innovator' reflects the lack of fit between shared goals and the means to reach them. In Bentham's time, a central goal was basic sustenance. Provision for the well-being of the less fortunate was seen as a crime inhibitor. A fair social order that provided for people's basic economic needs and gave them hope of legitimately meeting their future needs lessened the incentive to steal, particularly if the penalties for violations were understood, clear, proportional and swiftly applied.

With respect to rational calculation, the emphasis is on self-control and the 'economic person'. The risks, gains and punishments for violation must be clearly communicated and specified according to a scale where the more severe the violation, the more severe the penalty. The need for punishment reflects the failure of prevention, although violations may be thwarted during imprisonment and the punished may calculate differently next time. Punishment rituals are also intended to reaffirm conformity for the broader community. Of course, all cultures likely have some version of deterrence and justice via a 'let the punishment fit the crime' ethos, no matter how varied the specifics. However, Bentham is distinctive with respect to how explicit and calculating punishment was to be.

Bentham's view of prevention reflects a social systems perspective involving networks and temporal social processes. For example, the proposal to license various occupations touching property theft, rules for operation (e.g. receipts and record-keeping) and consent to inspections, along with the creation of new offences such as receiving stolen goods extends the law to those within the system who had previously been immune as enablers or facilitators. This is intended to make it harder to dispose of stolen goods. Here, as elsewhere, we see the roots of a neoliberal, self-control approach in creating incentives for the licensed to control themselves for fear of losing their licence or worse.

The rule expansion involving markets for stolen goods is a small strand of the astounding proliferation of rules associated with the rise of modern society. We see the greedy, expansive nature of social control as suggested in 'net widening' (Cohen 1979) and the appearance of 'secondary deviance' (Lemert 1951). With this comes the potential for the unintended consequences that nestle within interconnected social orders. The new violations and punishments resulting from the new rules of course heighten the risks, but can also create new black and regular markets via displacement.

Using data to set policy

The Police Gazette and the *Calendar of Delinquency* had multiple goals. They would offer intelligence for the prevention and discovery of violations and new classes of violation, for warning potential victims 'to be on their guard', and for citizens to report suspicious activities and identify fugitives to the police. Plus, it would be more difficult for criminals to operate in the same location or in the same manner. They would also serve as moral education and a warning even 'to the innocent and well disposed'. However, we are not told how being innocent relates to being well disposed.

Of particular importance was Bentham's argument for the use of observation and measurement in setting policy and law and the effort to approach governance in the most rational manner. Of course, with several centuries of hindsight, it is easy to raise issues about his foresight. Thus, for Parliament to unreflectively use crime statistics to formulate and evaluate policy and for Bentham to assume that with legal improvements reductions in the number of offences of any given type would occur without any subsequent increases in the number of other types of offence is doubtful given what we now know about displacement – whether in terms of the means chosen, offences, locations or victims.

Regarding the victims of crime, he is prescient in discussing 'alarm' and the 'subjective apprehension of danger'. He notes that this can lead to withdrawal and actions not taken. Here he acknowledges 'the imperfections of moral calculation' and the difficulty of measuring the 'imponderable' issue of intensity. He would have appreciated the advances in assessing fear of crime, various tools and scales for determining the strength of feelings and various indirect and unobtrusive measures from which inferences can be drawn.

While Bentham shows a humility too often lacking in those in the world of politics, he does the best he can with what he has. He implicitly argues for the realism required for public policy choices – favouring the least bad alternative involving 'direct object measurement'; as Quinn (2021, 58) observes: 'Utilitarian calculation might be less exact than one would wish, but it remained the only defensible approach for those seeking a rational criterion for the evaluation of rules or institutions'. The effort to bring a *measured* (whether meaning quantification or balance) degree of sanity to the emotionally explosive and politically manipulated issues of crime and control must be welcomed by all persons of good will and rational mind. Sometimes the choices are between the good and the good (or the better), or at least between the bad and the worst (or in Machiavelli's words, viewing 'the least bad as good').

Local contexts: The situational level

In his consideration of several kinds of prevention, Bentham connects to the two main social control traditions noted by Janowitz (1975). One is the broad social ordering of society and the other the inter-actions of rule enforcers and violators at the situational level. The former – culture and communication and the creation of a fair social order with broad opportunities and an emphasis on the welfare of citizens – was discussed above. We next turn to locations directly involving rule enforcement and violation, where we see Bentham's emphasis on using science and technology to condition choices and influence outcomes.

In his focus on the material, physical elements of the immediate situation, Bentham was an early social engineer. He applied the engineer's logic to both physical and social factors. The assembly line relies on the speed of the conveyor belt rather than the will of the worker. In the same fashion, engineering the physical environment for conformity limits or takes away opportunities for violation, bypassing the will of the potential violator.

With the physical engineering of social control, we see a very different kind of prevention beyond calculation or sentiment. Here Bentham's focus is less on the subjectivity of the potential violator and the effort to induce self-control via belief in the legitimacy of the rules or via rational choice and calculation. The will of the subject hardly matters if the offence is made impossible or very difficult to carry out via environmental alterations or if such alterations facilitate the identification of and inhibitions upon potential violators (à la Cesare Lombroso half a century later).

Illustrative of this is the architecture of the circular panopticon, with its visibility for the centrally placed, unseen watcher and its restrictions on the interaction and communication of inmates who are isolated from each other and the outside world. His design of three other panopticons (for paupers, students and leaders) was different given other organizational goals. For the latter, the constitutional-panopticon was to be a 13-sided polygon with the office of prime minister in the centre and communication to be carried out through inspectable communication tubes (Galic et al. 2017). Beyond the architectural design, he identified 25 'crime-preventing expedients' such as street lighting, traveller registers and identification marks for all subjects of the state.

Bentham followed and helped inspire the ever-evolving protective tradition from the inventors and builders of the first locks, safes, moats, walled castles, armour and biological identification systems to the present environmental design (Newman 1972), situational crime prevention (Clarke 1997) and related efforts (Byrne and Marx 2011). Bentham's various examples fit well with a classification framework offered for technology-based engineering of social control efforts (Marx 2015). Such preventive efforts involve target or facility removal, target devaluation, target insulation, offender weakening, incapacitation or exclusion, victim warning and, when those fail, offence/offender target identification.

In helping stuff and unpack the Pandora's box of technology, Bentham introduces a cornucopia of social and ethical issues. Of particular interest are the surprises that appear when poorly understood tools are too unreflectively and hastily introduced into complex, poorly understood systems. Marx and Guzik (2017) note a number of uncertainties involving technical crime control efforts. Of course, a lot can go wrong and, given the fluid nature of social dynamics, while these efforts close off some opportunities, they may open up others as well, such as new markets and material techniques of neutralization. Marx and Guzik identify five sources of *the uncertainty principle* with respect to the not infrequent failure of technical solutions to work as planned, Five prominent factors here are: uncertainties of functioning (e.g. does the tool operate technically as designed?); goals (e.g. will it be used for purposes other than those for which it was designed?); consequences (e.g. will it result in unintended consequences?); context (e.g. how do social contexts shape how the tool is used); and environment (e.g. will it function in adverse weather or cultural conditions?). Since Bentham's panopticon was never built, its failures cannot be analysed. However, PhD theses regarding the reasons for and types of nineteenth-century failed (or partially failed) preventive efforts inspired by Bentham are waiting to be written.

Technical artefacts may fail to work, break or require costly unanticipated inputs and revisions; as they say, 'stuff happens'. There are uncertainties of intended function – most technical artefacts are not limited to their specified function. Thus, Ihde (2008) identifies the 'designer fallacy' and the 'ambiguous multistable possibilities' of artefacts. An aircraft can get you to a desired destination, but it may also be a weapon to destroy buildings. There are uncertainties of consequence – technologies may bite back. (Aspirin can be ameliorative, but taking too many can kill.) Policy and practitioners need to be particularly alert to gradient effects, short and longer time periods and diverse settings and groups.

Additionally, there are uncertainties of context – social actors (individual or organizational) use technological/behavioural extensions in ways that are unpredictable and often 'irrational'. Contexts with varied goals and interests may collide and react differently to the same tool. There are uncertainties of environment – physical environments can also be unpredictable and overwhelm the tool, as with the case of a meteorite hitting the Earth or a monumental earthquake. Surprise outcomes are more likely when the assumptions buried within the celebratory rhetoric of uncritical technology enthusiasts are not examined.[4]

Beyond the empirical failings of social control technologies that can sometimes be seen – for instance, when a security robot took an unprogrammed and unexpected dip in the pool in front of the building it was guarding[5] – there are the unseen ethical consequences. While to his credit, Bentham wanted some visibility as a check on efficiency and accountability, he apparently did not consider the ways in which tools could bootleg in (or better) simply ignore ethical implications. If these are to be considered, they must be acknowledged both when making decisions about whether or not to apply a technique and when evaluating its impact.

A great problem with technology and social control, whether in the eighteenth century or today, is the numbing or hiding of the possibility of awareness. When one is cognizant of what is occurring and data about impacts are available, a reaction may be possible, even if only to negate or withdraw, let alone to try to change a situation. Zygmunt Bauman's concept of adiaphorization in which ethical implications are divorced from an action is helpful here (Bauman and Lyon 2013). This generates a specious sense of neutrality and an unreflective deferral to instrumentality as the pre-eminent value divorced from other values.

The observations of Erich Fromm (1955) apply today and to the early advocates of science and technology in the service of social order such as Bentham and Lombroso:

> The danger of the past was that men became slaves. The danger of the future is that men may become robots. ... Men are increasingly

automatons, who make machines which act like men and produce men who act like machines; their reason deteriorates while their intelligence rises, thus creating the dangerous situation of equipping man with the greatest material power without the wisdom to use it.

I began my recent book, *Windows into the Soul: Surveillance and Society in an Age of High Technology*, with a quote from Kafka's 1919 cautionary story 'In the Penal Colony'. The story is about a new technology described as 'a remarkable piece of apparatus' – a highly acclaimed, state-of-the art machine invented by a corrections officer for punishing inmates. The story ends when the machine malfunctions and kills its operator – an enthusiastic advocate of the benefits and infallibility of the machine. The sky is not now falling, even if that offers only modest grounds for rejoicing, yet there are after all holes in the ozone layer.

Notes

1   I will respond as if the ideas were Bentham's, although they mingle with those of Patrick Colquhoun and others. What is central is to see the contours, assumptions and origins of many current ideas about social control in the fermenting and fertile time period of Bentham, Colquhoun, Edwin Chadwick and Robert Peel. The difficult task of sorting out original ownership of the ideas is best left to the specialists.

2   Bentham viewed punishment as an evil that could be justified only if it served to counter an even greater evil (this is consistent with Tom Paine, who wrote about the same time that government was a necessary evil). Thus, Bentham was not opposed to whipping and torture under certain circumstances presumed to involve 'the greater good'. Nor did he confront the ways in which 'soft' forms such as solitary confinement and a prohibition on speaking, although 'soft', could be terribly cruel forms of punishment. Whatever the moral or pragmatic calculus, the soft surveillance of deception may backfire if the deception becomes known. There is a bit of a hat trick here in socializing citizens to the idea that the rules are neutral in the service of legitimacy. While the other golden rule (those who have the gold make the rules) alerts us to the fact that rules proffered as fair because they are universal may, nonetheless, disproportionately serve the interests of elites that Bentham believed to be more enlightened than others.

3   This is central to whether and when the police can or should be viewed as neutral public servants or as the protectors of an unequal social order. In any complex social system, rules are likely to disproportionately favour the more privileged who will have a disproportionate say in what the rules are and their enforcement. However, that does not negate the fact that many rules (e.g. regarding safety and health) can be said to serve a broad public interest. Neutrality can also be seen in the presence or absence of due process.

4   Marx (2016) identifies five basic categories for organizing techno-fallacies. These are: fallacies of technological determinism and neutrality; of scientific and technical perfection; of questionable legitimation; of logical or empirical analysis; and those involving subjects or targets. Examples of the first category include: (1) the fallacy of autonomous technology and emanative development and use; (2) the fallacy of neutrality.

5   The Verge, 'DC Security Robot Quits Job by Drowning Itself in a Fountain', 17 July 2017. Online. https://www.theverge.com/tldr/2017/7/17/15986042/dc-security-robot-k5-falls-into-water (accessed 21 May 2021).

References

Bauman, Zygmunt and David Lyon. 2013. *Liquid Surveillance: A Conversation*. New York: Polity.

Becker, Howard. 1967. 'Whose Side Are We On?', *Social Problems* 14: 239–47.

Bentham, Jeremy. 2018. *Writings on Political Economy, Volume III: Preventive Police*, edited by Michael Quinn. Pre-publication version. Online. http://discovery.ucl.ac.uk/10055084/ (accessed 23 April 2021).

Brayne, Sarah. 2017. 'Big Data Surveillance: The Case of Policing', *American Sociological Review* 82: 977–1008.

Byrne, James and Gary Marx. 2011. 'Technological Innovations in Crime Prevention and Policing: A Review of the Research on Implementation and Impact', *Journal of Police Studies* 20: 17–40.

Clarke, Ronald V. 1997. *Situational Crime Prevention: Successful Case Studies*. New York: Harrow and Heston.

Cohen, Stan. 1979. 'The Primitive City: Notes on the Dispersal of Social Control', *Contemporary Crises* 3: 339–63.

Elias, Norbert. 1978. *The History of Manners: The Civilizing Process, Volume I*. Oxford: Basil Blackwell.

Fromm, Erich. 1955. *Escape from Freedom*. London: Rinehart and Winston.

Galic, Masa, Tjerk Timan and Bert-Jaap Koops. 2017. 'Bentham, Deleuze and Beyond: An Overview of Surveillance Theories from the Panopticon to Participation', *Philosophy and Technology* 30: 9–37.

Ihde, Don. 2008. *Ironic Technics*. Automatic Press.

Janowitz, Morris. 1975. 'Sociological Theory and Social Control', *American Journal of Sociology* 81: 82–108.

Lemert, Edwin M. 1951 *Social Pathology*. New York: McGraw-Hill.

Leo, Richard A. 1992. 'From Coercion to Deception: The Changing Nature of Police Interrogation in America', *Crime, Law and Social Change* 18: 35–59.

Marx, Gary T. 1981. 'Ironies of Social Control: Authorities as Contributors to Deviance through Escalation, Nonenforcement and Covert Facilitation', *Social Problems* 28: 221–46.

Marx, Gary T. 1989. *Undercover: Police Surveillance in America*. Berkeley: University of California Press.

Marx, Gary T. 2006. 'Soft Surveillance: The Growth of Mandatory Volunteerism in Collecting Personal Information – "Hey Buddy Can You Spare a DNA?"'. In *Surveillance and Security*, edited by Torin Monahan, 37–56. New York: Routledge.

Marx, Gary T. 2015. 'Technology and Social Control: The Search for the Illusive Silver Bullet Continues'. *International Encyclopedia of the Social and Behavioural Sciences*. 2nd ed. New York: Elsevier.

Marx, Gary T. 2016. *Windows into the Soul: Surveillance and Society in an Age of High Technology*. Chicago: University of Chicago Press.

Marx, Gary T. and K. Guzik. 2017. 'The Uncertainty Principle: Qualification, Contingency and Fluidity in Technology and Social Control'. In *The Routledge Handbook of Technology, Crime and Justice*, edited by M. R. McQuire and Thomas Holt, 481–501. New York: Routledge.

Merton, Robert. 1957. *Social Theory and Social Structure*. Glencoe: Free Press.

Newman, Oscar. 1972. *Defensible Space*. New York: Macmillan.

Quinn, Michael. 2021. 'Bentham on Preventive Police: The *Calendar of Delinquency* in Evaluation of Policy, and the *Police Gazette* in Manipulation of Opinion'. In *Jeremy Bentham on Police: The Unknown Story and What It Means for Criminology*, edited by Scott Jacques and Philip Schofield, 35–74. London: UCL Press.

Utilitarianism and Policing in the US
Daniel S. Nagin

Bentham, the father of modern utilitarianism, ranks among the most influential nineteenth-century philosophers. Quinn's (2021) chapter, 'Bentham on Preventive Police', is a reminder that, in addition, Bentham pioneered what we now call 'policy analysis'. In so doing, the Quinn essay illustrates that policy analysis, at its best, can also be path-breaking scholarship.

The Quinn essay is well-timed, too. Public attention to policing is episodic. Policing is again a hot button issue in the United States. The death of Michael Brown at the hands of a Ferguson, Missouri, police officer – followed in quick succession by other instances of police use of deadly force – spawned protests, heated debates, riots and social movements such as Black Lives Matter.

Bentham's (1982) dictum is that the greatest good to the greatest number is morally right. In this comment, I remark about how neglecting this dictum contributes to needless social costs and a regrettable level of distrust of the police in many communities, particularly those composed mostly of disadvantaged minorities.

Utilitarianism requires a balancing of costs and benefits. It is surprising how often this principle is neglected in policy debates about the police, even as utilitarian arguments are otherwise being advanced by supporters of policy alternatives. In an essay with Cynthia Lum, 'Reinventing American Policing: A Seven-Point Blueprint for the 21st Century' (Lum and Nagin 2016), we make the uncontroversial argument that two major goals of policing should be building and maintaining community trust in the police and preventing crime and keeping citizens safe. We then observe that policy often goes through cycles where one of these objectives is emphasized to the neglect of the other. An example is the response to an upsurge in crime in which the focus on prevention results in inattention to the impact on citizen trust. We go on to argue that in a democratic society, neither goal should trump the other.

Concerning the crime prevention goal, Quinn's essay asserts the utilitarian-based principle that 'crimes averted, not arrests made, should be the primary metric for judging police success in meeting their objective of securing public safety' (340). This principle is inspired by the Enlightenment philosopher Cesare Beccaria (1995), whose views presage Bentham. Beccaria (1738–1794) observed: 'It is better to prevent crimes than to punish them' (103). Embodied in this observation is the recognition that punishment is costly to all involved: society at large, which must pay for it; the individual, who must endure it; and the police, whose time is diverted from crime prevention. While arrest plays a role in the crime prevention function of the police, arrest also signifies a failure of prevention; if a crime is prevented in the first place, so too is arrest and all of the ensuing costs of punishment (Nagin 2013; Nagin et al. 2015).

Police interaction with citizens may impose cost even if it does not result in an arrest. A prime example is the New York Police Department's controversial use of 'stop, question and frisk' (SQF) from 2002 to 2013. Only 12 per cent of SQF encounters resulted in an arrest or summons (NYCLU 2014), but that does not mean the remaining 88 per cent were costless. It is hard for any police officer to avoid the indignity suffered by an innocent citizen in being stopped, questioned about their criminal intent, physically searched and only then allowed to continue on their way.

The debate about SQF was not conducted in a way in which I suspect Bentham would have approved. One side argued for the crime prevention effectiveness of SQF with no attention to its cost while the other side argued that SQF was ineffective in preventing crime – and was itself illegal. In an article with Chuck Manski (Manski and Nagin 2017), we attempt a Benthamite approach. The model therein expresses a central tension: increasing the intensity of a confrontational tactic yields more benefit in crime reduction but also a higher cost of intrusiveness. Society's problem is to choose a level of intensity that appropriately recognizes benefit and cost.

Manski and I also point out that a delicate issue of disparate racial impacts may arise if crime rates in the absence of confrontational tactics vary with race. Then a policy that strives to optimize social welfare may be implemented without racial animus, yet, nonetheless, generate disparities in the intensity with which confrontational tactics are directed at innocent persons of different races.

In this response to Quinn's excellent essay, I have attempted to demonstrate how Bentham's revolutionary ideas about social justice remain as important today as they were two centuries ago.

References

Beccaria, Cesare. 1995. *On Crimes and Punishment.* New York: Cambridge University Press.

Bentham, Jeremy. 1982. *An Introduction to the Principles of Morals and Legislation*, edited by J. H. Burns and H. L. A. Hart, reissued in 1996 with a new introduction by F. Rosen. Oxford: Clarendon Press.

Lum, Cynthia and Daniel Nagin. 2016. 'Reinventing American Policing: A Seven-Point Blueprint for the 21st Century', *Crime and Justice* 46: 339–93.

Manski, Charles F. and Daniel Nagin. 2017. 'Assessing Benefits, Costs, and Disparate Racial Impacts of Confrontational Proactive Policing', *Proceedings of the National Academy of Sciences* 114: 9308–13.

Nagin, Daniel. 2013. 'Deterrence in the Twenty-First Century: A Review of the Evidence', *Crime and Justice* 42: 199–263.

Nagin, Daniel, Robert M. Solow and Cynthia Lum. 2015. 'Deterrence, Criminal Opportunities, and Police', *Criminology* 53: 74–100.

New York Civil Liberties Union (NYCLU). 2014. *Stop and Frisk During the Bloomberg Administration, 2002–2013.* Online. https://www.nyclu.org/sites/default/files/publications/stopandfrisk_briefer_2002-2013_final.pdf (accessed 6 September 2020).

Quinn, Michael. 2021. 'Bentham on Preventive Police: The *Calendar of Delinquency* in Evaluation of Policy, and the *Police Gazette* in Manipulation of Opinion'. In *Jeremy Bentham on Police: The Unknown Story and What It Means for Criminology*, edited by Scott Jacques and Philip Schofield, 35–74. London: UCL Press.

Bentham in the Weeds

Graeme R. Newman

In this modern age, trying to think like Bentham seems too confining, limited by his slavish commitment to the pleasure–pain dichotomy. But he was neither the first nor the last to indulge this oversimplification. Freud fused the opposites into each other, lost sight of what they were or might be and was stuck in the end with the death instinct. Is it too far-fetched to say that Bentham was on the right track and that maybe the post-Enlightenment thinkers such as Freud analysed pleasure and pain far too deeply? Maybe Bentham, who was inclined to obsessive-compulsive thinking (a 'superficial' rationality, but exhaustively rational nonetheless), managed after all to unravel the many consistent characteristics of human behaviour, placing emphasis on those behaviours that were visible, countable and describable, rather than the indulgence of Freud and post-Freudian thinkers who speculated upon unobservable unconscious desires and thoughts. And what of the latter-day cognitive psychologists who have tried in vain to convince themselves and others that human beings are overwhelmingly conscious beings? Must we answer such a question in order to, as did Bentham, simply proceed on the assumption that all behaviour follows a rational, linear progression that is observable? I do not think Bentham cared whether behaviour was intended (conscious) or not or whether individuals were driven or not (though he described both in detail). It was enough to observe that individuals' behaviour responded to pleasures and pains in predictable ways. Why dig any deeper? And did not the learning psychologists (primarily behaviourists) of the first half of the twentieth century demonstrate this?

One of the interesting things about Bentham's voluminous writings is that so little of it was ever translated into law or policy in spite of his having on many occasions direct input into legislative writing and a friend or two in Parliament. In regard to criminal law and punishment, his writings led to very little legislative action. He attempted to impress upon the American framers of the US constitution his idea of criminal law (radical even by today's standards) – most definitely not that of William Blackstone (1723–1780), whose writings on this topic he viewed as chaotic and irrational (Newman 2005), causing more evil than it prevented. This was because Blackstone's *Commentaries* reproduced case law, in all its massive and incoherent detail, constructed on what Bentham saw as imaginary or invented psychological concepts, such as intent – which indeed forms the crux of all Western criminal law today. This impossibly abstract idea, attacked by psychologists and psychiatrists early in the twentieth century, led to the strange legal fictions of 'irresistible impulse', 'guilty but insane', 'not guilty on grounds of insanity', 'unfit to stand trial' and many more. Bentham called the gap between law and psychology, 'a dreary waste: trackless. ... I propose to take [it] in hand for cultivation and in so doing to open a communication between them' (Bentham 1982, 26).

Bentham argued that the criminal justice of Blackstone's *Commentaries* led to enormous inefficiencies and that nothing short of a new language was needed to replace the chaotic mechanisms of catching criminals, finding them guilty and punishing them sensibly, and ultimately that the most efficient generator of 'happiness' was to prevent crime from occurring – his idea of indirect legislation. He pleaded with the framers of the American constitution to adopt his radical approach, to throw out the old criminal justice system of Blackstone (Newman and Marongiu 2009) and replace it with his scientific 'novum organum' echoing Francis Bacon (1561–1626), with a scientific way of assessing the maximum happiness of the people and resorting to as little pain as necessary. Unfortunately, the framers chose Beccaria as their Enlightenment guide over Bentham. His incessant writings, teasing out all of the logical consequences of public policies, implementation and their predicted consequences, were simply too much for legislators to comprehend.

Bentham produced mounds and mounds of weeds, making it hard to find the central ideas that guided his thinking. And when he did produce something startling, his design for the panopticon, for example, it was misapplied and misunderstood. Though never built in his own country, versions of the prison were built well after his death and the surveillance aspect of modern prisons probably owes something to his panopticon. The awful image of the panoptic prison served to foster a view of Bentham as some kind of evil person who advocated draconian punishments. Far from it. In typical style, he composed exhaustive lists of the types of punishments – 11 practical types of punishment and 11 properties of punishment – all of which he insisted were 'artificial' because they did not get at the prime causes of mischief that produced crime (Bentham 1982, 125–73), that is, reduce the opportunities for crime (see Ronald Clarke in this volme).

However, his emphasis on total surveillance in prison was taken by twentieth-century pundits out of the prison context, implying that what Bentham wanted was total surveillance of everyone in society. This does, of course, imagine 'society' as a prison, with all of its dastardly consequences. Yet Bentham would surely be the first to rail against the total surveillance of society, unless it were also accompanied by total surveillance of those who govern: as shown in the Quinn chapter, his insistence on accountability, the recording and collection of data concerning policies and their implementation, the observation and recordings of their consequences, the making of lists, easily his favourite tool, to provide the necessary information upon which to form policy, whether concerning finances, public safety or criminal punishment. It is a fair conclusion that Bentham was just as concerned with the surveillance of government as with the governed.

Still, there is a problem with Bentham's advocacy of governmental production of data: he did not take into account that the lists were those constructed by the mechanisms of government, so that these data may well be presented and collected in such a way that they put government in a good light. The production of crime statistics, for example, statistics that reveal the end result of policing behaviour, are a prime example of this problem. The twentieth-century solution to this puzzle has been to invent various 'independent' bodies, police commissions, law commissions, ombudsmen, inspectors general and so on as the overseers. The American Constitution foresaw a government that had self-surveillance built into its structure, based on the idea of checks and balances. But this idea, for all its merits, is slowly being undermined by both the government (a fictitious entity, Bentham would call it) and the governed (who are, after all, in a democratic republic, the government). One is inclined to conclude that humans are ungovernable and for that reason Bentham's belief in rational government is doomed to failure.

Yet in the modern field of criminal justice, we see an increasing shift in modes of social control, from the 'justice model' (crime–guilt–punishment) to the regulatory model (prevention–rules–compliance)

(Freilich and Newman 2018), which reflects Bentham's holistic approach to social control. It is unlikely that this shift is in any way 'caused' by Bentham's writings, though some would argue that it has occurred in other fields such as finance (Bowrey and Smark 2010). It may be more prudent to observe that Bentham was a man before his time, prepared to speculate on what might result from thinking through social and human problems freed from the received 'wisdom' of the past. It has taken more than 200 years for the Western world to catch up with him.

References

Bentham, Jeremy. 1982. *An Introduction to the Principles of Morals and Legislation*, edited by J. H. Burns and H. L. A. Hart, reissued in 1996 with a new introduction by F. Rosen. Oxford: Clarendon Press.

Bowrey, Graham D. and Ciorstan J. Smark. 2010. 'The Influence of Jeremy Bentham on Recent Public Sector Financial Reforms', *Journal of New Business Ideas and Trends* 8: 25–35.

Freilich, Joshua D. and Graeme R. Newman. 2018. 'Regulating Crime: The New Criminology of Crime Control', *Annals of the American Academy of Political and Social Science* 679: 8–18.

Newman, Graeme R. 2005. *The Punishment Response*. 2nd ed. New Brunswick: Transaction Publishers.

Newman, Graeme R. and Pietro Marongiu. 2009. 'Introduction'. In *On Crimes and Punishments*, by Cesare Beccaria. New Brunswick: Transaction Publishers.

Quinn, Michael. 2021. 'Bentham on Preventive Police: The *Calendar of Delinquency* in Evaluation of Policy, and the *Police Gazette* in Manipulation of Opinion'. In *Jeremy Bentham on Police: The Unknown Story and What It Means for Criminology*, edited by Scott Jacques and Philip Schofield, 35–74. London: UCL Press.

A Genealogy of Bentham's Preventive Policing

Pat O'Malley

If Bentham's writings on indirect legislation are viewed as 'a sort of manual of preventive police', we could broadly break down his array of preventive initiatives into three forms. The first is situational crime prevention, broadly conceived as proactive measures such as the installation of street lighting and the provision of information to the public so they can avoid being victims of crime. The second encompasses what is now referred to as 'intelligence-led' policing and 'predictive policing', where police gather and process information to be used in proactive interventions. Third and arguably the most important to Bentham was the deterrent effect of successful reactive policing (i.e. the detection and capture of offenders). Each of these, in turn, Bentham wanted to be subjected to a kind of monetized cost–benefit analysis in order to determine their relative utility, ideally with respect to specific kinds of offence. All three forms of crime prevention were to be informed and assessed by the crime data provided regularly in the *Calendar of Delinquency*. But what legacy was left behind from these writings? How did preventive policing develop over the following two centuries?

Certainly, Robert Peel's (1788–1850) legislation establishing the Metropolitan Police envisioned proactive policing – especially in the form of gathering intelligence from the community. Moreover, Victorian governments developed situational crime prevention in such forms as street lighting and the demolition of criminal 'warrens'. But as Hudson has pointed out, in Britain from 'the mid-nineteenth century to about 1960 the trend in police activity was *away* from organized preventative activity' (Hudson 1974, 293). Instead, reactive policing was overwhelmingly to become the model for the police from the time of Bentham's death until quite recently, and the deterrent effect of successful arrest and prosecution became the vigorously defended police representation of their role in crime prevention.

Since the mid-1970s, however, proactive policing – policing that seeks to intervene before the commission of offences and on the basis of predictive evidence – has been promoted under such banners as 'intelligence-led policing', 'community crime prevention' and more recently 'predictive policing' (Chan and Bennett Moses 2019). This represented a considerable sea change in policing across the Anglophone world and elsewhere. In the view of some influential works, such as Ericson and Haggerty's (1997) *Policing the Risk Society*, by the late twentieth century, the police were being transformed into a risk-based crime-information brokerage, led in considerable measure by the demands of the insurance industry. In place of reactive work, such as pursuit, detection and apprehension, the police were to be redirected into gathering and mobilizing security-based data that enabled the formation of preventive interventions. Indeed, the vision of a shift towards forms of information-led predictive or pre-emptive prevention – under the rubric of 'risk'-based policing – became almost an obsession among criminologists. As this indicates, while the development of reactive policing proceeded much as Bentham might have desired, the development of a *proactive* preventive focus on crime prevention would have to wait until almost a century and a half after his death. Why was this?

Part of the problem was foreseen by Bentham: the existence of a deep suspicion in Britain of anything that smacked of 'continental' practices of spying on the populace. However, this had rather diminished by the time police legislation emerged in the 1840s. Indeed, Peel's successful initiatives included a substantial place for 'embedded' police gathering intelligence from the community – albeit carefully shrouded in directions about detecting and preventing crimes. So perhaps the principal reason for the turn away from proactive prevention lay elsewhere, arguably in much more mundane realities. After 1856, when the Metropolitan Police model became the standard required by the British state, funding was to be made available relative to efficiency. This clearly was something of which Bentham would have approved. However, Hudson (1974), later supported by Emsley (1983), has argued that it was the difficulties of demonstrating the effectiveness of crime prevention that led to the nineteenth-century shift away from prevention. Despite Bentham's rather optimistic assumptions, it proved hard to demonstrate when a crime had been prevented. Instead, the objectively measurable numbers of arrests, convictions and clearance rates – measures of the effectiveness specifically of reactive policing – came to be the accepted criteria of effectiveness. Accordingly, the emphasis on proactive prevention in Peel's project quickly gave ground to reactive measures backed up by a Benthamite faith in general deterrence. It is a framework that remained dominant for many years, still echoed in the 1960s by the influential Chief Constable of the Lancashire Constabulary who claimed (on the basis of no evidence, it should be said) that 'the most effective crime prevention measure yet devised is certainty of detection'.

While this shift away from proactive preventive policing may be attributable to direction from senior police and their political administrators, it was well supported by the police rank and file. Proactive preventive work of the sort outlined by Peel still has a low public profile, is bureaucratic and tedious to perform. In contrast, crime-fighting and reactive detection 'must have looked like a glamorous and more productive alternative to an occupational culture geared primarily to the removal of sources of trouble from the streets' (Gilling 1997, 111). Equally to the point, as the plethora of studies on police 'working culture' reveal, this specific 'cops and robbers' orientation became embedded in the informal organization of policing. So much so that while (masculine) crime fighting appears as 'real' police work, crime prevention and its sibling 'community policing' have not proved popular with rank-and-file police even into the present century (Chan 2001). Certainly, this police working culture is bolstered by the imagery of the masculine-heroic police officer culturally valorized in the mass media. Even recent technologically minded police television shows – such as *CSI* and the mass of forensic police serial dramas – focus overwhelmingly on reactive rather than preventive work. Exceptions, such as the movie *Sixth Sense*, depicting humans who could envisage crimes about to occur, are firmly in the realm of science fiction.

Winds of change

As late as the mid-1960s in Britain, it was still possible for the British Home Office Working Party on Crime Prevention to believe that 'crime prevention was the responsibility of every member of the service and that it would be a retrograde step to set up crime prevention departments'. As the contemporary *Report of the Royal Commission on Police* (1962) stated succinctly, the prevailing view was that 'the uniform man on the beat … provides the most effective deterrent to crime' (quoted in Rawlings 2002, 203). While throughout much of the 1960s crime prevention thus occupied 'a position of relative obscurity and unpopularity' (Gilling 1997, 69), some police forces began to introduce designated crime prevention officers. The development, however, was largely symbolic. Usually one-officer concerns, these crime prevention units were very small in scale and marginal in the organization. As Muir (1962, 190) indicates, prevention was primitive: 'CPOs (crime prevention officers) did little more than fill in forms and provide advice to those who had suffered property loss'.

The story of how and why a preventive (pre-emptive) police eventually emerged after the 1960s is a tangled and disputed one that can be outlined only briefly here (for more details, see O'Malley and Hutchinson 2007). One development certainly involved the concerns of the increasingly influential insurance industry about the rising levels and costs of property offences made possible by the emergence of the consumer society. During the 1960s, while this concern resulted only in largely token change, as noted, insurers began to respond to increasing losses in retail settings by imposing more stringent crime prevention requirements on businesses (Pugh 1976). Under such pressure from insurers, but also driven by their own concerns about losses to theft, businesses joined the demand for crime prevention measures. However, frustrated by the lack of police mobilization in preventive work, industry increasingly turned to private security. This triggered a massive growth in private policing and investment in preventive technologies, while unintentionally taking pressure off the public police. In a sense, reactive public policing was given a lease of life by industry's privatization of prevention.

At least in the view of the insurers ('Companyman' 1977, 2094), this had a roll-on impact, for so effective were commercial crime prevention interventions that insurers pressured householders to take greater precautions (Litton 1982, 129). The consumer revolution had meant that opportunities for high-yield burglary and theft were growing exponentially as households accumulated valuable movable commodities such as televisions, hi-fi sets and cameras. As early as the mid-1960s, the British *Security Gazette* estimated that for the first time crime losses had reached half the level of fire losses and bemoaned the fact that police resistance meant 'the CPO is left to fight a lonely battle'.

Ultimately, increasing pressure from the insurance industry was to find a supportive political environment during the 1970s with the rise of neoliberal governments focused on more economic and enterprise approaches to crime control. The successful preventive model of industrial security, together with the data mobilized in insurance lobbying, now provided evidence in cost–benefit terms for the superiority of crime prevention over reactive policing. In Britain, the police were increasingly directed to develop or become involved in information-based crime prevention programmes – most notably Neighbourhood Watch, the 'Safer Cities' movement and instruments such as Police Community Crime Prevention Committees and audits of consumer satisfaction with policing. Citizens were mobilized not only through such channels, but also through 'empowering' strategies. These included the provision of crime data particular to the area and police-led training in domestic crime prevention techniques that supposedly enabled citizens to be proactive in their own right, but that also made them responsible for their own security. Such features of this emerging period of crime prevention were often seen to link preventive policing changes directly to neoliberal modes of governance with its themes of increasing individual responsibility and decreasing reliance on state apparatuses (O'Malley 1992; O'Malley and Palmer 1995).

By the 1980s, therefore, proactive elements of Bentham's vision of preventive policing were finally being mobilized within a neoliberal framework. In the twenty-first century, advances in preventive policing have focused more on predictive police work. Current predictive work focuses on such matters as crime mapping in order to forecast where crime outbreaks are likely to occur, profiling of high-risk individuals and places and even the use of computer modelling to predict how effective predictive policing strategies will be (Uchida 2014; Perry et al. 2013). As Chan and Bennett Moses (2019, 42–3) argue, a 'new orthodoxy' has emerged 'that technology can make policing smarter and information based rather than subject to human bias and occupational habits'. But the transformation has been far less thoroughgoing than suggested by this new criminological orthodoxy or as predicted by such influential analyses as Ericson and Haggerty's (1997) *Policing the Risk Society*.

As suggested, the deterrent architecture of reactive policing has retained a strong and probably dominant presence, which is at least partly an effect of police conservatism. As Cote-Bouchere (2019, 233) points out: 'analytical tools do not readily modify daily policing which remains very much concerned with providing a rapid reactive response to citizens' calls' (see also Chan 2001; Manning 2008; Sanders et al. 2015). This is partly because the police resist moves they interpret as undermining their on-the-job expertise and exposing them to greater surveillance (Willis 2014). But in addition, as Chan and Bennett

Moses (2019) map out at length, a host of intervening variables have restricted the practical and effective implementation of these new technologies. These include unforeseen technical and communication problems created by the innovations, a lack of fit between the outputs of predictive technologies and the ability of the police to comprehend them, and problems experienced aligning them with daily police work.

Arguably, therefore, the picture of contemporary police reflects something far more consistent with Bentham's plans for a preventive police than with the insurance-driven preventive image provided by Ericson and Haggerty (1997). Reactive policing has not diminished, despite the rise of proactive prevention: and the rise of predictive policing has been less widespread and effective than sensationalist readings suggest.

Nevertheless, it could be argued that these are teething problems and that issues of resistance to the new are to be expected with any large-scale organizational transformation. If so, then we could say that preventive police is gathering momentum. While Bentham's *Calendar of Delinquency* never took off, policing driven by informatics and 'big data' is advancing rapidly today: reactive policing is increasingly being data driven. And while proactive policing remained virtually dormant until the 1970s, clearly by the early twenty-first century both risk-based crime prevention programmes and the development of information-led preventive policing do embody the ideal of proactive policing based on statistical evidence that clearly was at the core of Bentham's vision of preventive police.

Yet perhaps this does after all understate the extent to which Bentham's visions of preventive police have been realized, precisely because it reflects current criminology's narrow vision of what policing consists of in the twenty-first century. While it is rarely recognized as such, the increasingly ubiquitous network of 'safety cameras' monitoring vehicle speed, red-light and priority-lane traffic laws has become the most extensive and voluminous field of contemporary policing (O'Malley 2010). Developed to an extent far greater – and far more rapidly – than other areas of policing, part of the success of this apparatus is that it has been introduced to one side of orthodox policing. Increasingly unmanned and electronically automated, it has been subject to very little police resistance and is not reliant on police cooperation or comprehension at the ground level. And while doubtless it has replaced police in large numbers, its effect has not been to reduce those numbers but instead to release officers to areas traditionally associated with 'real' police work. In operation terms, these safety cameras are preventive in several ways.

First, of course, is the police- and government-generated 'jurisprudence of safety' (O'Malley 2013) that promotes the array of technologies because they are demonstrated to prevent traffic accidents, injuries and death. What is slightly less evident here is that the offences themselves have become risk-based. What is being policed is not – as with assault, robbery or fraud – something that has caused harm. Rather, the focus is on something that carries the risk of harm. Increases in speed are statistically correlated with increases in the risk of death, injury and property damage. Consequently, increases in speed are matched by increases in penalty. Second, while operating preventively through risk reduction, these apparatuses also begin to realize Bentham's dream of perfect prevention through certainty of capture. While they operate proactively to reduce risks, they also work reactively in that they respond to breaches of the law. More to the point, as networks of safety cameras are rolled out, electronic surveillance – which never tires, is technically capable of registering all infractions in its range, and operates 24/7 – begins to increase the certainty of capture and thus (in principle at least) the certainty of deterrence. Bentham's dream of perfect prevention may not, after all, be so far away from being realized.

References

Chan, Janet. 2001. 'The Technological Game: How Information Technology is Transforming Police Practice', *Criminology and Criminal Justice* 1: 139–59.
Chan, Janet and Lyria Bennett Moses. 2019. 'Can Big Data Analytics Predict Policing Practice?'. In *Security and Risk Technologies in Criminal Justice*, edited by Stacy Hannem, Carrie B. Sanders, Christopher J. Schneider, Aaron Doyle and Tony Christensen, 41–85. Toronto: Canadian Scholars Press.
'Companyman'. 1977. 'Spare a Copper, Guvnor?', *Policy Holder Insurance Journal* (November): 2094–6.
Cote-Boucher, Karine. 2019. 'Smart Borders? Customs, Risk Targeting and Internal Politics in a Border Agency'. In *Security and Risk Technologies in Criminal Justice*, edited by Stacy Hannem, Carrie B. Sanders, Christopher J. Schneider, Aaron Doyle and Tony Christensen, 225–52. Toronto: Canadian Scholars Press.
Emsley, Clive. 1983. *Policing and its Context 1750–1870*. London: Macmillan.
Ericson, Richard V. and Kevin D. Haggerty. 1997. *Policing the Risk Society*. Toronto: University of Toronto Press.
Gilling, Daniel. 1997. *Crime Prevention: Theory, Policy and Politics*. London: UCL Press.
Hudson, F. 1974. 'Crime Prevention – Past and Present', *Security Gazette* 1974: 292–5, 332–3.
Litton, R. A. 1982. 'Crime Prevention and Insurance', *The Howard Journal of Penology and Penal Reform* 1982: 6–22.
Manning, Peter. 2008. *The Technology of Policing: Crime Mapping Information Technology and the Rationality of Crime Control*. New York: New York University Press.
Muir, A. 1962. 'Man on the Beat is Essential to Help Specialists', *Security Gazette* 4: 190–9.
O'Malley, Pat. 1992. 'Risk, Power and Crime Prevention', *Economy and Society* 21: 252–75.
O'Malley, Pat. 2010. 'Simulated Justice: Risk, Money, and Telemetric Policing', *British Journal of Criminology* 50: 795–807.

O'Malley, Pat. 2013. 'The Politics of Mass Preventive Justice'. In *Prevention and the Limits of the Criminal Law*, edited by Andrew Ashworth, Lucia Zedner and Patrick Tomlin, 273–95. Oxford: Hart Publishing.

O'Malley, Pat and Steven Hutchinson. 2007. 'Reinventing Prevention: Why Did "Crime Prevention" Develop So Late?', *British Journal of Criminology* 47: 439–54.

O'Malley, Pat and Darren Palmer. 1995. 'Post Keynesian Policing', *Economy and Society* 25: 137–55. ·

Perry, Walter L., Brian McInnes, Carter C. Price, Susan Smith and John S. Hollywood. 2013. *Predictive Policing: The Role of Forecasting in Law Enforcement Operation*. Santa Monica: Rand Corporation.

Pugh, J. 1976. 'Insurance and Crime Prevention'. In *Major Property Crime in the United Kingdom*, edited by P. Young. Edinburgh: University of Edinburgh School of Criminology and Forensic Studies.

Rawlings, Philip. 2002. *Policing: A Short History*. Cullompton: Willan. ·

Report of the Royal Commission on the Police. 1962. (Command Paper No. 1728). *Final Report*. London: Her Majesty's Stationary Office.

Sanders, Carrie B., Crystal Weston and Nicole Schott. 2015. 'Police Innovations, "Secret Squirrels" and Accountability: Empirically Studying Intelligence-Led Policing in Canada', *British Journal of Criminology* 55: 711–19.

Uchida, Craig D. 2014. 'Predictive Policing'. In *Encyclopaedia of Criminology and Criminal Justice*, edited by Gerben Bruinsma and David Weisburd. New York: Springer Verlag. Online. https://link.springer.com/referenceworkentry/10.1007/978-1-4614-5690-2_260 (accessed 16 August 2021).

Willis, James J. 2014. 'A Recent History of the Police'. In *The Oxford Handbook of Police and Policing*, edited by Michael D. Reisig and Robert J. Kane. New York: Oxford University Press. Online. https://www.oxfordhandbooks.com/view/10.1093/oxfordhb/9780199843886. 001.0001/oxfordhb-9780199843886-e-011 (accessed 16 August 2021).

Bentham on Crime Analysis and Evidence-Based Policing

Eric L. Piza

The belief that the police can meaningfully affect crime is considered, by some, to be a fairly new development. An influx of studies on standard methods of policing, such as preventive patrol (Kelling et al. 1974), rapid response to calls for service (Kansas City, Missouri, Police Department 1977; Spelman and Brown 1981) and retroactive investigations (Greenwood et al. 1977; Eck 1983), found these bedrock strategies to be largely ineffective at reducing crime. This body of research provided a foundation for the belief that the police are incapable of ensuring public safety, a belief that persisted over the ensuing decades (Weisburd and Braga 2019). This negative assessment stands in stark contrast to current times, with the police as well as other criminal justice actors seen to be capable of addressing public safety problems across various contexts.

An impetus for this change is Sherman and colleagues' (1997) landmark report to the 104th Congress of the United States, *Preventing Crime: What Works, What Doesn't, What's Promising,* which reviewed the research evidence on approximately 500 crime prevention programmes. The report has had a profound effect since its publication, ushering in an era of evidence-based crime policy, reaffirming the importance of rigorous research designs, providing a readily accessible catalogue of effective (and ineffective) practices and establishing a commitment to readily communicate scientific findings to stakeholders beyond the research community, including policymakers, practitioners and the general public (Welsh and Wexler 2019).

Policing, in particular, benefitted from rigorous evaluation research identifying a number of effective strategies that law-enforcement agencies should include in their crime prevention portfolios, including hotspot policing (Braga et al. 2019), problem-oriented policing (Hinkle et al. 2020) and focused deterrence (Braga et al. 2018). What distinguishes effective policing tactics from the ineffective programmes of the past? The cumulative body of policing research points to three main lessons (Lum and Koper 2017; Weisburd and Eck 2004): the police can be more effective when they are proactive, not reactive; when they focus on places, not just people; and when they tailor their actions to identifiable problems, not employ a 'one-size-fits-all' application of general strategies to all problems that surface.

A closer look at the research evidence, however, shows that the foundation of effective policing may very likely be the systematic analysis of data by crime analysts (Kennedy et al. 2018; Piza 2019). Contemporary policing strategies require quantitative predictions of where and when crime is most likely to occur (Sherman 2011), the social networks containing the persons most at risk of committing or being victimized by crime (McGloin and Kirk 2010), as well as the theoretical understanding of the causal mechanisms underlying crime patterns (Eck 2006; Sampson et al. 2013). Given the need to understand the nature and scope of crime problems, crime analysis is a staple of modern policing (Piza 2019), with its products essential in the design of many evidence-based policing strategies (Santos 2014). Crime analysts also advance evidence-based policing by contributing to the implementation of evidence-based practices and 'translating' research knowledge into practice through constant interactions with police officers and commanders (Lum and Koper 2017).

Bentham's writings on preventive police

Bentham's writings on policing advanced numerous concepts that would become central to the fields of evidence-based policing and crime analysis nearly 200 years later. In conceptualizing the *Calendar of Delinquency*, Bentham envisioned a mechanism to actively track crime trends across disparate areas of the United Kingdom. While the *Calendar of Delinquency* was initially advanced as an annual document, Bentham later argued that a 'series' of such calendars would allow for the constant tracking of crime trends and identification of crime problems in need of rectifying. This mirrors the type of performance measurement that provides the foundation for CompStat, which arguably elevated crime analysis as a core component of policing beginning in the mid-1990s (Bratton and Malinowski 2008).

The *Calendar's* link to crime analysis becomes more pronounced when considered alongside the *Police Gazette,* which Bentham saw as a vehicle of knowledge dissemination that could identify high-risk offenders. This overlaps with the modern concept of criminal intelligence analysis, the identification of offender networks and their overlapping criminal activity (Santos 2013), which plays a central role in many heralded offender-based, problem-oriented policing programmes (Braga 2008). In short, Bentham's conception of the *Calendar* and *Police Gazette* and his view that they should be leveraged by the police speaks to the heart of the crime analysis role: assist the police in understanding why a crime problem exists and identify strategies that offer the best solutions (Ratcliffe 2019, Chapter 4).

The *Calendar of Delinquency* and *Police Gazette* provide a basis for the use of data in policymaking: the bedrock of evidence-based policing. Indeed, Bentham did not advocate the constant measurement of crime merely for measurement's sake, but instead so that such evidence could play a direct role in the 'formulation and evaluation of policy' (Quinn 2021, 55). In *Preventive Policing*, Bentham openly advocated specific strategies to prevent crime, advancing a list of 25 crime-preventing expedients, including street-lighting and regulation of the sale of poisons. While Bentham's advocacy of these strategies lacked mention of the type of case-controlled scientific evidence privileged by evidence-based policing scholars, the classification of specific strategies as more effective than others fits within their paradigm. Crime-prevention scholars will also note the parallels between Bentham's crime-prevention expedients and situational crime prevention, given the emphasis on reducing criminal opportunities and a typology of 25 techniques (Cornish and Clarke 2003).

Bentham further foreshadowed calls made by contemporary scholars to improve upon evidence-based crime prevention by moving beyond an exclusive focus on the outcomes of crime and disorder. In particular, while the crime and justice field now has a deep knowledge base regarding the effect of many strategies, cost–benefit analysis has been used fairly sparsely in the evaluation literature (Weisburd et al. 2017). This issue is exacerbated in policing. Police-led interventions are largely absent in Welsh and colleagues' (2015) review of cost–benefit analyses in crime prevention, which identified only 23 sufficiently rigorous evaluations meeting the inclusion criteria. While some cost–benefit analyses of police-led prevention strategies have been published since (e.g. Piza et al. 2016), still little is known about the cost effectiveness of contemporary policing strategies.

This modern-day issue played a prominent role in Bentham's late eighteenth-century writings. In considering crime prevention policies, Bentham emphasized the importance of measuring whether police services 'afford sufficient payment for the vexation and experience' associated with various crimes (Bentham 2018, 335). In illustrating this point, Quinn (2021) noted that the *Calendar of Delinquency* estimated the annual value of property lost through highway robbery as £20,000, whereas the cost of the *Marechausée*, a hypothetically proposed national watch for guarding roadways, was twice that amount. A cost–benefit analysis based on these monetary figures suggests that 'the pain of taxation necessary to fund the watch easily outweighs the potential benefit' (Quinn 2021, 57). Basing policy decisions on such monetary considerations sits at the core of modern cost–benefit analysis (Cohen 2016; Domínguez and Raphael 2015). Interestingly, while advocating measures of cost-effectiveness in policymaking, Bentham readily noted the inherent limitations of this approach. He recognized that not all aspects of crime or crime prevention policy could be expressed in monetary terms, meaning that the findings of cost–benefit analyses will always be at least a bit imprecise. Bentham's statement echoes the complications inherent in measuring intangible crime costs, such as pain and suffering and the potential issues that could be introduced when including such measures in cost–benefit analyses of crime prevention programmes (Piza et al. 2016; Tonry 2015). This is another example of how Bentham's *Preventive Police* still resonates today.

References

Bentham, Jeremy. 2018. *Writings on Political Economy, Volume III: Preventive Police*, edited by Michael Quinn. Pre-publication version. Online. http://discovery.ucl.ac.uk/10055084/ (accessed 23 April 2021).

Braga, Anthony A. 2008. *Problem-Oriented Policing and Crime Prevention*. 2nd ed. New York: Criminal Justice Press.

Braga, Anthony A., Brandon S. Turchan, Andrew V. Papachristos and David M. Hureau. 2019. 'Hot Spots Policing and Crime Reduction: An Update of an Ongoing Systematic Review and Meta-Analysis', *Journal of Experimental Criminology* 15: 289–311.

Braga, Anthony A., David Weisburd and Brandon S. Turchan. 2018. 'Focused Deterrence Strategies and Crime Control: An Updated Systematic Review and Meta-Analysis of the Empirical Evidence', *Criminology and Public Policy* 17: 205–50.

Bratton, William J. and Sean W. Malinowski. 2008. 'Police Performance Management in Practice: Taking COMPSTAT to the Next Level', *Policing* 2: 259–65.

Cohen, Mark A. 2016. 'The "Cost of Crime" and Benefit-Cost Analysis of Criminal Justice Policy: Understanding and Improving upon the State-of-the-Art'. Online. https://ssrn.com/abstract=2832944 (accessed 16 September 2016).

Cornish, Derek B. and Ronald V. Clarke. 2003. 'Opportunities, Precipitators and Criminal Decisions: A Reply to Wortley's Critique of Situational Crime Prevention', *Crime Prevention Studies* 16: 41–96.

Domínguez, Patricio and Steven Raphael. 2015. 'The Role of the Cost-of-Crime Literature in Bridging the Gap between Social Science Research and Policy Making', *Criminology and Public Policy* 14: 589–632.

Eck, John. 1983. *Solving Crimes: The Investigation of Burglary and Robbery.* Washington, DC: Police Executive Research Forum.

Eck, John. 2006. 'When is a Bologna Sandwich Better than Sex? A Defense of Small-N Case Study Evaluations', *Journal of Experimental Criminology* 2: 345–62.

Greenwood, Peter, Jan Chaiken and Joan Petersilia. 1977. *The Investigation Process.* Lexington, MA: Lexington Books.

Hinkle, Josh, David Weisburd, Cody Telep and Kevin Petersen. 2020. 'Problem-Oriented Policing for Reducing Crime and Disorder: An Updated Systematic Review and Meta-Analysis', *Campbell Systematic Reviews* 16: 1–86.

Kansas City, Missouri, Police Department. 1977. *Response Time Analysis, Volume II Part 1: Crime Analysis.* Washington, DC: United States Department of Justice, Office of Justice Program, National Institute of Justice.

Kelling, George L., Tony Pate, Duane Dieckman and Charles E. Brown. 1974. *The Kansas City Preventative Patrol Experiment.* Washington, DC: The Police Foundation.

Kennedy, Leslie W., Joel M. Caplan and Eric L. Piza. 2018. *Risk-Based Policing: Evidence-Based Crime Prevention with Big Data and Spatial Analytics.* Oakland: University of California Press.

Lum, Cynthia and Christopher S. Koper. 2017. *Evidence-Based Policing: Translating Research into Practice.* Oxford: Oxford University Press.

McGloin, Jean Marie and David S. Kirk. 2010. 'Social Network Analysis'. In *The Handbook of Quantitative Criminology,* edited by Alex Piquero and David Weisburd, 209–23. New York: Springer.

Piza, Eric L. 2019. *Police Technologies for Place-Based Crime Prevention: Integrating Risk Terrain Modeling for Actional Intel (Issues in Spatial Analysis, Volume 1).* Newark: Rutgers Center on Pubic Security.

Piza, Eric L., Andrew M. Gilchrist, Joel M. Caplan, Leslie W. Kennedy and Brian A. O'Hara. 2016. 'The Financial Implications of Merging Proactive CCTV Monitoring and Directed Police Patrol: A Cost-Benefit Analysis', *Journal of Experimental Criminology* 12: 403–29.

Quinn, Michael. 2021. 'Bentham on Preventive Police: The *Calendar of Delinquency* in Evaluation of Policy, and the *Police Gazette* in Manipulation of Opinion'. In *Jeremy Bentham on Police: The Unknown Story and What It Means for Criminology,* edited by Scott Jacques and Philip Schofield, 35–74. London: UCL Press.

Ratcliffe, Jerry. 2019. *Reducing Crime: A Companion for Police Leaders.* New York: Routledge.

Sampson, Robert J., Christopher Winship and Carly Knight. 2013. 'Translating Causal Claims: Principles and Strategies for Policy-Relevant Criminology', *Criminology and Public Policy* 12: 587–616.

Santos, Rachel Boba. 2013. *Crime Analysis with Crime Mapping.* 3rd ed. Los Angeles: Sage Publications.

Santos, Rachel Boba. 2014. 'The Effectiveness of Crime Analysis for Crime Reduction: Cure or Diagnosis?', *Journal of Contemporary Criminal Justice* 30: 147–68.

Sherman, Lawrence W. 2011. 'Police and Crime Control'. In *The Oxford Handbook of Crime and Criminal Justice,* edited by Michael Tonry, 509–36. New York: Oxford University Press.

Sherman, Lawrence W., Denise Gottfredson, Doris MacKenzie, John Eck, Peter Reuter and Shawn Bushway. 1997. *Preventing Crime: What Works, What Doesn't, What's Promising.* A Report to the United States Congress. Prepared for the National Institute of Justice.

Spelman, William and Dale K. Brown. 1981. *Calling the Police: Citizen Reporting of Serious Crime.* Washington, DC: Police Executive Research Forum.

Tonry, Michael. 2015. 'The Fog around Cost-of-Crime Studies May Finally Be Clearing: Prisoners and Their Kids Suffer Too', *Criminology and Public Policy* 14: 653–71.

Weisburd, David and Anthony Braga. 2019. 'Introduction: Understanding Police Innovation'. In *Police Innovation: Contrasting Perspectives,* edited by David Weisburd and Anthony Braga, 1–25. Cambridge: Cambridge University Press.

Weisburd, David and J. E. Eck. 2004. 'What Can Police Do to Reduce Crime, Disorder and Fear?', *Annals of the American Academy of Political and Social Science* 593: 42–65.

Weisburd, David, D. P. Farrington and C. Gill. 2017. 'What Works in Crime Prevention and Rehabilitation: An Assessment of Systematic Reviews', *Criminology and Public Policy* 16: 415–49.

Welsh, Brandon C., David P. Farrington and B. Raffan Gowar. 2015. 'Benefit-Cost Analysis of Crime Prevention Programs', *Crime and Justice* 44: 447–516.

Welsh, Brandon C. and Andrew B. Wexler. 2019. 'Elevating the Scientific and Public Policy Discourse on Crime Prevention: Taking Stock of the "What Works" Report's Influence 20 Years On', *Policing: A Journal of Policy and Practice* 13: 271–85.

Bentham and the Philosophical Nature of Preventive Policing

Kim Rossmo and Lucia Summers

The Thames River Police was established in 1798 by merchant and statistician Patrick Colquhoun (1745–1820), based on a proposal by master mariner John Harriott (1745–1817). The first regular police force in England, the River Police sought to deter theft and other crime in the Pool of London by a continued patrol presence. Its primary function was preventive, differing in purpose from that of the Bow Street Runners, which operated reactively to reports of crime. This important distinction was influenced by the utilitarian philosophy of Bentham, who differentiated preventive police from justice. As Quinn (2021, 37) observes:

> Bentham's lifetime witnessed a revolution in this definition of police and the development of a modern understanding of police as, first, a professionalized, expert and non-political institution and second, an institution whose responsibilities were limited more narrowly to the prevention and investigation of crimes.

Cesare Beccaria (1738–1794) argued in 1764 that 'it is better to prevent crimes than to punish them'. This principle later became a central element of Sir Robert Peel's (1788–1850) *Metropolitan Police Act* of 1829. There are at least two different approaches to preventing crime, however. The Thames River Police patrolled the Port of London and made crime *situationally* risky for thieves. On the other hand, Sir John Fielding (1721–1780), who helped to organize the Bow Street Runners, believed: 'It is much better to prevent even one man from being a rogue than apprehending and bringing forty to justice'. There is a subtle but important difference between preventing a crime from occurring in a given situation and inhibiting someone from becoming a criminal (Weisburd 1997).

Bentham understood the role of poverty in criminality and questioned how effective threats of punishment would be for the indigent: 'once the relevant choice became that between committing crime and starvation, no penalty, however draconian, could deter crime' (Quinn 2021, 49). Thus, Bentham encouraged the use of situational crime prevention measures that would limit the necessary conditions for criminal activity, some of which, such as street lighting, are still in use today. Rather than blindingly advocating such measures, however, he suggested these should be carefully scrutinized through cost–benefit analyses. This emphasis on evidence-based policies, as well as his support for appropriate intelligence channels between the police and the public, placed Bentham ahead of his time. It is only in recent decades that his ideas have resurfaced, embedded in strategies such as intelligence-led and community-based policing (Ratcliffe 2016).

In the two centuries that have passed since Bentham and his contemporaries advocated preventive policing, there have been dramatic changes in society, crime and technology. But the core duties of policing remain essentially the same: order maintenance, patrol, crime prevention, investigations, arrests. The specific manner in which these functions are accomplished, however, has matured considerably, primarily – though not completely – as a result of scientific and technological advances. Information systems, digital records and big data have provided law-enforcement agencies with tremendous analytic power (Groff and La Vigne 2002; McCue 2003). This capability has facilitated the evolution of preventive policing into proactive policing and, more recently, into predictive policing.

By definition, prevention involves a future event. Such efforts therefore fall along a temporal continuum. Few would argue with the need to stop an impending crime. But should the police try to deter criminal offences that may, or may not, happen at some point in the future? Such endeavours are more difficult and more socially and ethically problematic.

Proactivity first requires organizational judgement. But while evidence-based decisions can inform the 'where' and 'when', they are not always helpful in determining the 'what' and 'how'. Debate surrounds the manner in which proactive policing has been implemented in certain cities. For instance, proactive stop and frisk practices by the New York Police Department resulted in allegations of bias against visible minorities. These tactics were also found to be largely ineffective in terms of preventing reported crime (Ferrandino 2018).

Even greater controversy exists over predictive policing. Specialized software is employed to analyse past crime reports and neighbourhood characteristics and determine where future crimes are most likely to occur; this information is then used to optimize the spatial-temporal deployment of patrol resources (Perry et al. 2013). However, the proprietary secrecy of some forecasting algorithms has led to accusations of embedded bias. Complicating matters is a difficulty in establishing exactly what 'fair' means in this context, as competing definitions exist (Berk 2016).

In order to prevent future events, analysis and forecasting is required (Silver 2012). Any attempt to predict, however, invariably involves false positives; the more distant the future event, the greater the potential error rate (Orrell 2007). Judges and parole boards struggle to make decisions on someone's (relatively) short-term future behaviour; long-term predictions of criminality are not much better than guesses. As Kahneman (2011, 221) put it: 'The line that separates the possibly predictable future from the unpredictable distant future is yet to be drawn'.

These technologically enhanced strategies go well beyond what Bentham originally contemplated and therefore require a more comprehensive utility assessment. There are four critical questions that should be considered when evaluating the acceptability of modern preventive policing efforts:

1. How serious is the crime to be prevented?

2. How accurate is the prediction?

3. How effective is the police prevention?

4. How invasive is the police response?

People will put up with more invasive police tactics if they are designed to prevent serious crimes, such as terrorism. But if the predicted dangers fail to materialize or the prevention efforts are ineffective, tolerance for intrusive police actions soon erodes.

Determining the desired trade-offs between competing considerations is a matter of public policy, policy that could be informed by utility maximization. Bentham's philosophy provides a more logical and rational basis for optimal decision-making. Unfortunately, today – as in the late eighteenth century – politics often trump rationality, resulting in illogical responses and policies. The utilitarian calculation of 'the greatest good for the greatest number', grounded in a careful evaluation of the data, has been replaced in American politics with 'the most to the noisiest', based on the most compelling (even if less than truthful) narrative. Modern commentators tell us what to think; Bentham told us how to think.

References

Berk, Richard. 2016. 'A Primer on Fairness in Criminal Justice Risk Assessments', *The Criminologist* 41: 6–9.

Ferrandino, Joseph A. 2018. 'The Effectiveness and Equity of NYPD Stop and Frisk Policy, 2003–2014', *Journal of Crime and Justice* 41: 119–35.

Groff, Elizabeth R. and Nancy G. La Vigne. 2002. 'Forecasting the Future of Predictive Crime Mapping', *Analysis for Crime Prevention: Crime Prevention Studies* 13: 29–57.

Kahneman, Daniel. 2011. *Thinking, Fast and Slow*. New York: Farrar, Straus and Giroux.

McCue, Colleen. 2003. 'Connecting the Dots: Data Mining and Predictive Analysis in Law Enforcement and Intelligence Analysis', *The Police Chief* (October): 115–22.

Orrell, David. 2007. *The Future of Everything: The Science of Prediction*. New York: Thunder's Mouth Press.

Perry, Walter L., Brian McInnis, Carter C. Price, Susan Smith and John S. Hollywood. 2013. *Predictive Policing: The Role of Crime Forecasting in Law Enforcement Operations*. Santa Monica: Rand.

Quinn, Michael. 2021. 'Bentham on Preventive Police: The *Calendar of Delinquency* in Evaluation of Policy, and the *Police Gazette* in Manipulation of Opinion'. In *Jeremy Bentham on Police: The Unknown Story and What It Means for Criminology*, edited by Scott Jacques and Philip Schofield, 35–74. London: UCL Press.

Ratcliffe, Jerry. 2016. *Intelligence-Led Policing*. 2nd ed. London: Routledge.

Silver, N. 2012. *The Signal and the Noise: Why So Many Predictions Fail – But Some Don't*. New York: Penguin Press.

Weisburd, David. 1997. *Reorienting Crime Prevention Research and Policy: From the Causes of Criminality to the Context of Crime* (NCJ 165041). Washington, DC: National Institute of Justice.

Bentham in the Colonies

Dean Wilson

Bentham is most familiar to criminal justice historians through his concept of the panopticon and its inspection principle, a concept now widely known through Michel Foucault's influential study *Discipline and Punish*. The publication of Bentham's writings on police, however, provides a fitting moment to re-examine Bentham's significant influence on the historical development of policing. Bentham's utilitarian conception of the perfectly ordered society was exported to the colonies, where it was engaged in the hope of transforming the periphery into a model example of enlightened metropolitan government. This brief comment takes the example of nineteenth-century Melbourne, then in the colony of Victoria, to explore how Bentham's ideas are evident in the policing of a colonial metropolis and how they were mobilized to produce order at the edges of Empire.

In the early 1850s, Victoria was a gold-rush colony. The colony's largest city, Melbourne, rapidly doubled in size and the colonial authorities earnestly feared that the population influx, often of itinerant men, would presage a descent into social chaos. Fearing social collapse, government administrators placed great faith in public symbols to project and reinforce ideals of stable government authority. The city's key cultural institutions – the University of Melbourne, the public library, mechanics' institutes, botanic gardens and the museum – were established to promote order, respect and deference for the cultural values of the Imperial Centre (Wilson 2012, 164). The colonial authorities held great faith that the transplantation of these institutions from Britain would somehow induce order through their mere presence. Police, too, were enrolled in the task of ordering a society apprehended as being on the brink of collapse. In 1853, at the height of the gold rush, the disparate police forces of the colony were amalgamated into one police force, which subsequently became the colonial administration's most expansive bureaucracy. In the colony's capital, Melbourne, policing was redesigned – slavishly following the example of the London Metropolitan Police – with the purpose of fabricating social order in a colonial metropolis experiencing rapid change.

In the centre of the British Empire, London, police constables acting as symbols of impartially and rationally applied authority were mainly intended to hasten acceptance of the police institution. In the Melbourne of the 1850s, however, the context was more complex. In a gold-rush city, where police forces with various levels of adherence to metropolitan standards had existed for several decades, constables were deployed as civilizing emissaries. Police constables were to function, not merely to prevent crime and apprehend offenders, but also as moral exemplars who might be emulated by those being policed. The police of Melbourne, therefore, echoed both aspects of government outlined by Bentham in his essay on 'Indirect Legislation'. Not only were they intended to combat 'mischief', they were also to be a force for 'promoting good' (Quinn 2021). This ideal assumed material form in the police uniform. In 1853, the police of Melbourne adopted the blue uniform of the London Metropolitan Police – one chosen specifically to avoid the military associations of red and considered to be civilian, neutral and 'quiet' (Wilson 2006, 48). The uniform was intended to deter prospective offenders, while also making constables highly visible to members of the public seeking their aid. As a Superintendent of Detectives noted some decades later in 1882, the purpose of the police uniform was 'so that they [police constables] can be seen at a long distance, like lighthouses, so that when people want a policeman they may be able to distinguish him at a long distance' (Wilson 2006, 48–9).

The dual objectives of combating mischief and promoting good were everywhere evident in the colonial administration's vision of the police constable. The *Police Regulation Act* of 1853 stipulated that constables should be 'of good character, honesty and fidelity'. A more detailed template of the ideal constable was outlined in the *Manual of Police Regulations*, published in 1856, which suggested they should be 'extremely cautious in their demeanor and be sober, orderly and of regular habits'. They were, therefore, to function as both models of virtuous conduct and a deterrent to would-be offenders – an aim reinforced by regulations, rule books, district orders and drill practice that sought to craft individual constables into models of dispassionate rationally applied authority. In the gold-rush city, the blue-uniformed constable represented the civilizing mission of colonial authorities, enlightening the frontier metropolis with the benign rule of British government and order.

As Mark Finnane has noted, Bentham's panopticon prison design was never actually realized in the Australian colonies (Finnane 1997, 54). Nevertheless, Bentham's ideas remained influential, more as underlying concepts than through architectural realization – and they are starkly evident in the spatial design of Melbourne's beat system of policing. This was clearly indebted to Bentham's inspection principle, which proposed that 'ideal perfection' would require every person to be under observation 'at every instant of time' (Bentham 1995, 34). However, Bentham conceded that this utopia of continuous observation was unobtainable and that the 'next best thing' was that the person at 'every instant seeing reason to believe as much and not being able to satisfy himself to the contrary ... should *conceive* himself to be so' (Bentham 1995, 34).

The grid layout of colonial Melbourne provided a suitable template to put Bentham's inspection principle into practice on a grand scale. The Chief Commissioner of Police, Frederick Standish (1824–1883), considered Melbourne ideally suited to the beat system due to its 'straight and regular' streets. The distribution of uniformed constables across this grid would, it was hoped, bring about control and order in public spaces, combining regularized surveillance with the virtuous moral example of individual policemen. Developed in 1854 by a former officer of the London Metropolitan Police, Samuel Freeman, police beats divided the city into discrete units that were to be patrolled around the clock. Freeman devised an intricate system, calculating the precise walking pace necessary to cover each city block. Revised in 1859, the beats included detailed maps of each individual route, which, Freeman asserted: 'relate with minuteness the manner in which they should be worked'. Instructions included regulating the walking pace of the constable, who was to walk his beats with regularity, ensuring his position was well known to the public. The Chief Commissioner of Police claimed in 1859 that beats allowed the policeman to 'command a view of the greater portion of his beat, so that he may be found when required, but may also see where his presence is necessary' (Wilson 2006, 50–1).

Bentham's proposals, sometimes filtered through the writings of his disciple Edwin Chadwick, were mobilized to construct order in an urban centre where the threat of chaos loomed large. Melbourne's beat system of policing was conceived as a gigantic outdoor panopticon, in which individual constables functioned as both inspectors and moral examples. The regularity of patrol and the discipline of constables projected ideals of rational and consistent authority. These ideals, it was hoped, would bring order and tranquillity to a turbulent frontier metropolis.

References

Bentham, Jeremy. 1995. *The Panopticon Writings*. London: Verso.
Finanne, Mark. 1997. *Punishment in Australian Society*. Melbourne: Oxford University Press.
Quinn, Michael. 2021. 'Bentham on Preventive Police: The *Calendar of Delinquency* in Evaluation of Policy, and the *Police Gazette* in Manipulation of Opinion'. In *Jeremy Bentham on Police: The Unknown Story and What It Means for Criminology*, edited by Scott Jacques and Philip Schofield, 35–74. London: UCL Press.
Wilson, Dean. 2006. *The Beat: Policing a Victorian City*. Melbourne: Circa Press.
Wilson, Dean. 2012. '"Well-Set-Up Men": Respectable Masculinity and Police Organizational Culture in Melbourne 1853–1920'. In *A History of Police and Masculinities, 1700–2010*, edited by David G. Barrie and Susan Broomhall, 163–79. London: Routledge.

Index

Cohen, Stan 200
Cohn, Samuel K. 170
Colnbrook 105 & n
Colquhoun, Patrick 6–7, 35–9, 43, 45–6,
    48–51, 53–5, 60–1, 67n, 69–71n, 80n,
    116n, 151–3, 157, 159, 161–2, 164, 175,
    180, 184, 187, 205n, 229
Commons, House of 6
Common Pleas, Court of 109 & n
Constantinople 169
Cook, Michael 168
Coomans, Janna 168
Cornish, Derek B. 225
Cote-Bouchere, K. 219
Cox, David J. 14, 155
Crook, Tom 170
Curry, John 28

Dando, Jill 189
Dinwiddy, J. R. 20
Dodsworth, Francis 36–7, 46, 156–7
Domínguez, P. 226
Dublin, Ireland 28
Dumont, Étienne 42, 69n
Durkheim, Emile 14, 195–6
Durlauf, Steven N. 145

Eck, John 223–4
Edinburgh 19, 96, 130
Elias, Norbert 196
Emsley, Clive 178, 216
Engelmann, Stephen 48, 146–7
England 5, 86, 94, 97, 116 & n, 157, 175,
    178–9, 190, 195, 229
England, Church of 59, 94
Ericson, R. V. 216, 219–20
Euclid 117 & n
Europe 168, 173, 175–6

Farrell, Graham 153
Felson, Marcus 152
Ferguson, Missouri 207
Ferrandino, J. A. 231
Fielding, Henry 155–60, 160n
Fielding, Sir John 58–60, 155–60, 160n,
    229
Finnane, Mark 235
Florence 174
Freilich, Joshua D. 183, 214
Freud, Sigmund 211
Fromm, Erich 204–5
Foucault, Michel 18, 175, 183, 185, 233
France 5, 66, 114 & n, 118n, 167, 179,
    198
Freeman, Samuel 235

Galic, Masa 202
Geiss, G. 183
Geltner, G. 14, 167–70

Gendrón, Chalmeta 168
Germany 18, 173–4
Ghabin, A. 168
Gilbert, Thomas 129 & n
Gilling, D. 217
Glick, T. F. 168
Goldstein, H. 152, 189–90
Great Britain 66, 85–6, 94–6, 118n,
    168–70, 173, 175–6, 178, 180–1,
    215–19, 233
Great North Road 105n
Greece 19, 167
Greenwood, P. 223
Groff, E. R. 230
Grote, George 19
Grote, Harriet 19
Guzik, K. 203

Hackney 80, 105n, 127 & n
Haggerty, K. D. 216, 219–20
Halévy, *Élie* 19
Hanway, Jonas 38, 68n, 129 & n
Harefield 105 & n
Harriott, J. 229
Harrington, J. F. 14
Hart, H. L. A. 17, 31n, 68n
Hayek, Friedrich 20
Hawkins, G. J. 147
Hick's Hall 105n
Hitler, Adolf 18
Holy Roman Empire 174
Honderich, Ted 17
Hooker, Sir Joseph Dalton 19
Hudson, F. 215–16
Hume, David 18
Hume, L. J. 41
Hutchinson, S. 218
Huxley, Aldous 197

Ihde, Don 203
Innocent III, Pope 173, 176
International Society of Utilitarian
    Studies 7
Italy 168, 170, 174

Jacques, S. 10, 15n, 148
James, Henry 193
Janowitz, Morris 202
Jørgensen, D. 168
Justinian 174
Juvenal 118n

Kafka, Franz 205
Kahneman, D. 231
Kansas City, Missouri 223
Kant, Immanuel 18
Kelling, G. L. 223
Kennedy, D. M. 145, 148
Kennedy, L. W. 224

Scotland, Church of 94
Serle Court 109n
Shakespeare, William 199
Sherman, L. W. 223, 224
Shinkle, Sarah 13
Silver, N. 231
Skelton, L. J. 170
Smark, Ciorstan J. 214
Smith, Adam 38, 45, 47–8, 68n, 81 & n,
    177–8
Somerset House 109 & n
South Mims/Mimms 105 & n
Southwark 105n, 106, 123n
Spelman, W. 223
Squatriti, P. 168
Sraffa, Piero 20
Standish, Frederick 235
Steintrager, J. 188
Stephen, Leslie 19
Styles, John 156, 158
Summers, Lucia 13
Sutherland, E. H. 15n

Temple Bar 105
Thames, River 6, 11, 50, 70n, 168–9, 173,
    184, 229
Tilley, Nick 153
Tonry, M. 226
Transcribe Bentham 5–6, 15n, 23–7, 32n,
    67n

Twining, William 17, 31n

Uchida, C. D. 219
United Kingdom 31, 98, 177, 187, 189–90,
    224
University College London 4, 10, 19–20,
    24–5, 31, 35, 68n, 77, 184, 189

Van Dijk, Jan 153
Valencia, Technical University of 26
Victoria, Australia 233

Wales 116n, 190
Walton, S. A. 168
Weeda, C. 168
Weisburd, D. 153, 189, 223–4, 225,
    229–30
Welsh, B. C. 225
West Indies 50
Westminster 28, 96, 106, 109, 110 & n,
    123n, 129n
Westminster, Palace of 109n, 110
Wexler, A. B. 223
Willis, J. J. 219
Wilson, Dean 233–5
Wolff, Jonathan 17, 31n
Wollstonecraft, Mary 17
Wright, Richard 3

Zimring, F. E. 147